BAT BOY LIVES!

BAT BOY LIVES!

WEEKLY WORLD NEWS

THE *WEEKLY WORLD NEWS* GUIDE TO POLITICS, CULTURE, CELEBRITIES, ALIEN ABDUCTIONS, AND THE MUTANT FREAKS THAT SHAPE OUR WORLD

BY DAVID PEREL &
THE EDITORS OF THE *WEEKLY WORLD NEWS*

Sterling Publishing
New York

ACKNOWLEDGMENTS

Special thanks to everyone at Sterling Publishing,
Weekly World News, and AMI without whom this book would not be possible.

SPECIAL THANK-YOU BAT BITES GO TO:

NATHANIEL MARUNAS, BETSY BEIER, and JENNIFER BOUDINOT—alien investigators

BRUCE LUBIN and JOHN HUGHES—government snitches

MICHAEL VAGNETTI and MARIA SPANO—Bat Boy's babysitters

PHIL YARNALL, KEVIN ULLRICH, and JEFF BATZLI—chefs at Bigfoot taco night

LINDA STEINMAN, BRAD FEUER, and MIKE ANTONELLO—legal counsel for Bat Boy, P'lod, and Helen the Bigfoot Hooker

JEFF RUTZKY—Helen's hair stylist

CHRIS BAIN—3-legged photographer

JOE BERGER, CARA GALLO, and LIZ PINSON—paranormal experts

And, of course, BAT BOY

Published by Sterling Publishing Co., Inc.
387 Park Avenue South, New York, NY 10016

©2005 by Sterling Publishing Co., Inc.
Articles © American Media, Inc.
Weekly World News and Bat Boy are registered trademarks
of American Media, Inc. and are used with permission

Distributed in Canada by Sterling Publishing
c/o Canadian Manda Group, 165 Dufferin Street
Toronto, Ontario M6K 3H6

Distributed in Great Britain by Chrysalis Books
64 Brewery Road, London N79NT, England

Distributed in Australia by Capricorn Link (Australia) Pty. Ltd.
P.O. Box 704, Windsor, NSW 2756, Australia

Library of Congress Cataloging-in-Publication Data

Bat Boy lives! : the Weekly world news guide to politics, culture,
celebrities, alien abductions, and the mutant freaks that shape our world/
[compiled] by David Perel and the editors of the Weekly world news.

    p. cm.
Includes index.
ISBN 1-4027-2823-9
1. American wit and humor. I. Perel, David. II. Weekly world news.

PN6165.B39 2005
973.9202'07—dc22

2005024829

Cover and interior design by SMAY VISION
Additional illustrations and centerfold photo and design by JEFFREY RUTZKY
Printed in the U.S.A. by Universal Printing Company

3 5 7 9 10 8 6 4 2

There are two types of people who faithfully flip through the pages of the *Weekly World News* each week. The first type (let's call him "Reader A") is a believer, someone who is more likely than most to own a probe-resistant tinfoil helmet, belong to the Bigfoot Field Researcher's Organization (BFRO), or argue with himself, *sotto voce*, in public. For the most part, Reader A is just like you and me, only he believes that the universe is utterly chaotic, both expanding and imploding simultaneously, and that the poor saps who refuse to recognize how dire this situation is will have only themselves to blame when the other cosmic shoe drops.

The second type ("Reader B"), for better or worse, considers himself smarter than Reader A, but in fact may simply just be more cynical. He reads *WWN* to laugh at the stories contained within, but also to marvel at the thought of all the Readers A out there who really believe what they're reading. Of course, all that goes out the window when he has his first run-in with a creature of the night, the ghost of an angry relative, or an alien intent on installing a probe where the sun don't shine.

Launched in 1979, the *Weekly World News* is committed to bringing the newspaper-reading public (A, B, or otherwise) the truth—whether it be about alien abductions, the secrets of Loch Ness, or the garden-variety supernatural phenomena that occur in our very backyards. This brand of truth, admittedly, is different from what you'd find in the *New York Times* or even the *National Enquirer*, but it is the truth nonetheless. After all, tales of visitors from other planets, top-secret government cover-ups, and reclu-

sive 7-foot-tall, fur-covered hominoids who walk among us are part of our collective consciousness. In fact, to cite the themes of the *Weekly World News* is to cite the themes of any number of summer blockbusters, bestselling novels, iconic television shows, bedtime stories, pop song lyrics, breakfast cereal ad campaigns, and the dark recesses of our animal brains.

Throughout the 1980s, the paper continued to perfect its unique muckraking brand of journalism. Then, when the world was a decade into its official mourning period for Elvis Presley, *WWN* shocked the establishment by publishing the news that the King of Rock and Roll was actually alive and well. The paper's editorial offices were soon flooded with calls and letters from readers who had seen Presley themselves (usually at a fast-food restaurant or performing incognito), and even some who claimed to have dated the rock star posthumously. One such reader, who announced she had lived with the King for several years after his alleged death, made headlines when the *WWN* administered a polygraph test (which she passed, of course) and printed her amazing story. When the *WWN* reporter who interviewed her was later asked whether he believed the woman's story, he admitted, "Well, she sure believed it. But I don't know.... Back in the day the King dated a lot of women that were much more attractive than she was." All of which highlights *WWN*'s reputation for hiring stringers who write stories based on the facts, not

on superstition or received wisdom (in this case, about who was really buried in Presley's coffin).

This ability to suspend disbelief in pursuit of the truth is perhaps what most distinguishes the *Weekly World News* from the mainstream media and enables it to get the scoop on earth-shattering stories, week after week, year after year.

On June 23, 1992, *WWN* printed one of its most famous headlines of all time: *Bat Child Found in West Virginia Cave!* Since then, Bat Boy has been featured in dozens of cover stories, became the subject of an Off-Broadway musical that toured worldwide, and is rumored to be the focus

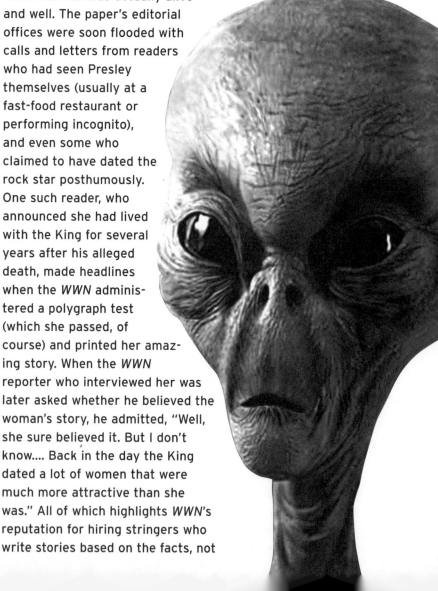

of a major motion picture currently in the works. But perhaps the most incredible thing about this creature (besides his ability to eat several pounds of bugs at a sitting and to track down international terrorists) is the way in which his story brings the two types of *WWN* reader together. Readers A and B both gobbled up information about the half-boy/half-bat, fascinated by the twisted, tragic, and ultimately uplifting tale of a downtrodden freak who, when life handed him a crate of radioactive lemons, brewed a potent batch of superstar-quality, mutant lemonade.

But it's not just earth-shattering stories that make the headlines at *Weekly World News*. More than anything, *WWN* cares about the stories of everyday people. As former managing editor Sal Ivone used to say, "If someone calls me up and says their toaster is talking to them, I don't refer them to professional help, I say, 'Put the toaster on the phone.'" And if a young couple's vacation to the Côte d'Azur is ruined by fish with human legs washing ashore, or a space alien tries to mate with some guy's Harley, or Satan won't stop calling your grandmother's cell phone, you can rest assured that *WWN* will be there to make sure the world hears about it.

Although these days *WWN* reporters tend to head out into the field to find the news more than the news finds them, these dedicated journalists continue to seek out the truth wherever it may be. "We're not here to spin the news or score points with the rich and mighty," says Jeff Rovin, *WWN*'s editor-in-chief. "We are here to serve you a weekly world of truth."

The pages of *Bat Boy Lives!* are packed with the sort of hard-hitting investigative journalism that readers from A to B have come to expect from the *Weekly World News*. These landmark stories, collected from the very best of more than two decades on the beat, include dispatches from the newspaper's science, paranormal, pop culture, religion and prophecy, and politics bureaus, as well as reports of the plain-old bizarre. Here, readers will discover where a clone is most likely to live, how to keep unwanted phantoms away from the home, and who among the U.S. Senators is a space alien in disguise. The curious will be exposed to the intimate familial details of the Loch Ness monster, delve into the world of Helen the Bigfoot hooker, and experience the excitement of watching the three-legged model, Bill Clinton's three-breasted intern, and the world's fattest man in action. Once you turn the first page, you may never see the world the same way again.

– DAVID PEREL

> "If someone calls me up and says their toaster is talking to them, I don't refer them to professional help, I say, 'Put the toaster on the phone.'"

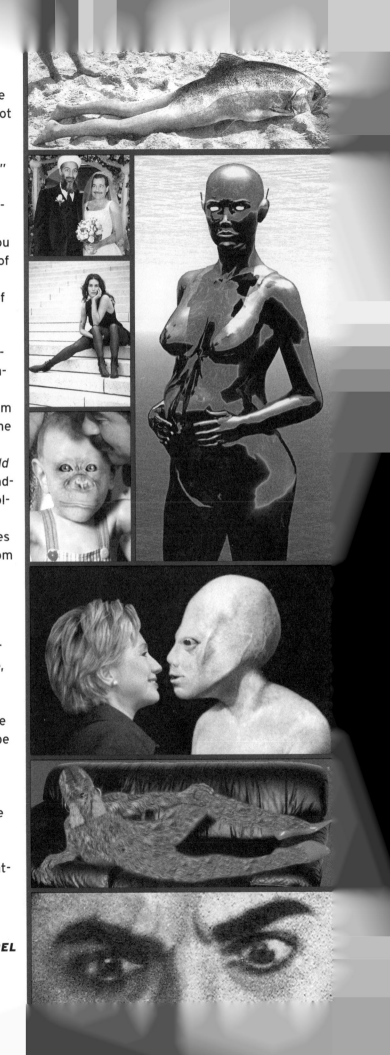

BREEDING LIKE FLIES

Revealing Reports on Science & Technology

From the discovery of penicillin to the invention of the microchip, putting a man on the moon to unearthing the reason why old people smell, scientific breakthroughs have had a profound influence on the lives of people the world over.

It's no surprise, then, that the most startling discoveries of this and the last century are the very ones being concealed by government officials, heads of corporations, and top scientists in every field.

One top administration official

told *WWN* off the record, "If the public knew that clones, androids, and aliens walked among us, there'd be utter chaos in the streets!"

But WWN's commitment to its readers doesn't stop where the government tells it to. While the administration pretends to ponder the moral implications of human cloning, WWN has been reporting on the existence of human clones for years.

Not only that, but *Weekly World News* is the only organization in the United States to have a formal clone, android, and alien anti-discrimination policy and internship program.

"It's really the only place on Earth I feel comfortable working," says R'gljspbi, an immigrant from the plant Neblutron who has been working WWN's politics beat for six years. "They're very supportive of the alien community."

This forward-thinking attitude, along with WWN's vow to keep the public informed about the scientific discoveries you won't read about in the so-called "reputable" news sources, makes WWN vital to those who need to be in the know.

Whether it be the discovery of beer cans on the moon or the sweet candy at Earth's core, the invention of lightning rods you can wear or human barcodes to help win the war on terror, WWN pledges to keep you abreast of what's happening in the world of science—and to write about it in a language you can understand.

What's more, WWN brings you complete coverage of hot new technological developments that can improve your life: how to staple your own stomach to shed those unwanted pounds, where to buy a "flatulence muffler" to make embarrassing moments a thing of the past, and how to flash freeze your comatose loved ones, thereby avoiding a national media circus and legislative showdown.

Indeed, you can rest assured that WWN will not bow to pressure to keep the world's most important scientific discoveries under wraps. Our esteemed science and technology bureau will be there—and their clones will be right behind them.

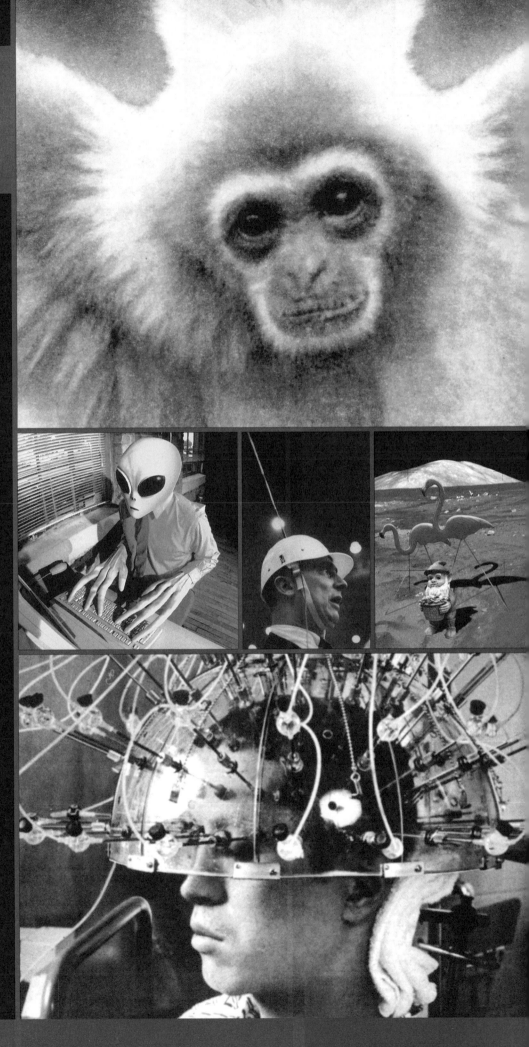

GERMAN SCIENT DECEASED

By
COREY MICHAELS
Weekly World News

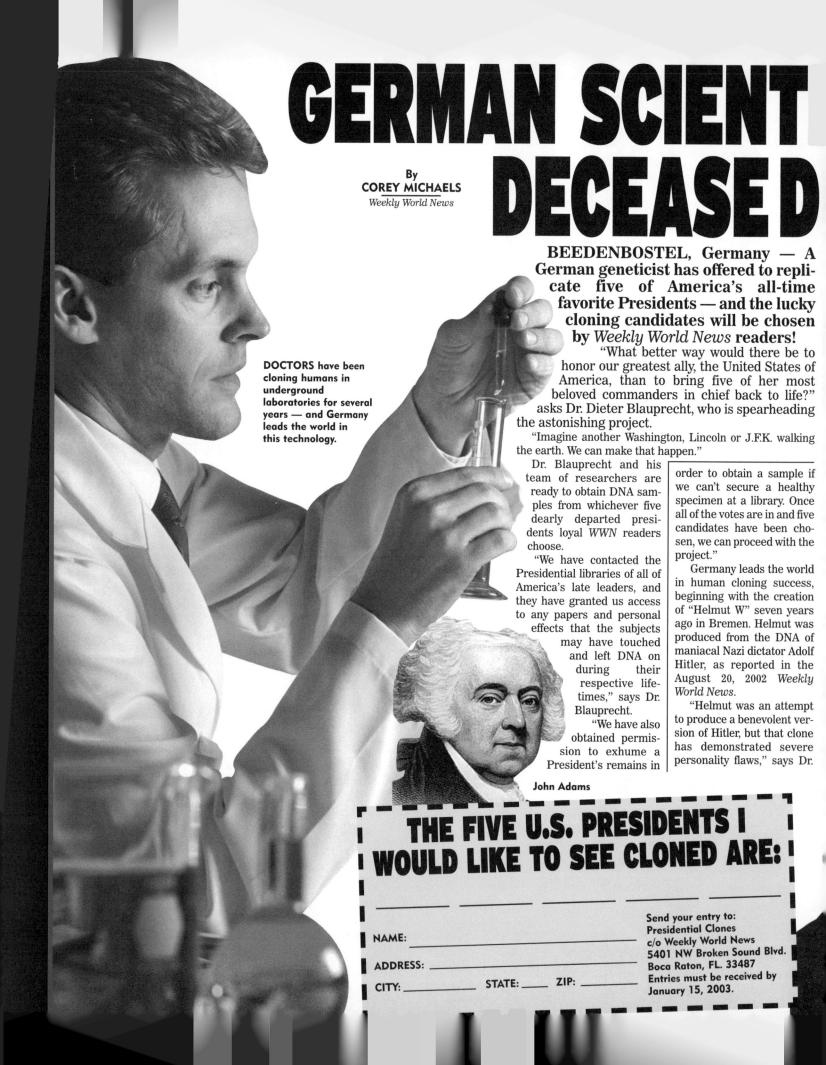

DOCTORS have been cloning humans in underground laboratories for several years — and Germany leads the world in this technology.

BEEDENBOSTEL, Germany — A German geneticist has offered to replicate five of America's all-time favorite Presidents — and the lucky cloning candidates will be chosen by *Weekly World News* readers!

"What better way would there be to honor our greatest ally, the United States of America, than to bring five of her most beloved commanders in chief back to life?" asks Dr. Dieter Blauprecht, who is spearheading the astonishing project.

"Imagine another Washington, Lincoln or J.F.K. walking the earth. We can make that happen."

Dr. Blauprecht and his team of researchers are ready to obtain DNA samples from whichever five dearly departed presidents loyal *WWN* readers choose.

"We have contacted the Presidential libraries of all of America's late leaders, and they have granted us access to any papers and personal effects that the subjects may have touched and left DNA on during their respective lifetimes," says Dr. Blauprecht.

"We have also obtained permission to exhume a President's remains in order to obtain a sample if we can't secure a healthy specimen at a library. Once all of the votes are in and five candidates have been chosen, we can proceed with the project."

Germany leads the world in human cloning success, beginning with the creation of "Helmut W" seven years ago in Bremen. Helmut was produced from the DNA of maniacal Nazi dictator Adolf Hitler, as reported in the August 20, 2002 *Weekly World News*.

"Helmut was an attempt to produce a benevolent version of Hitler, but that clone has demonstrated severe personality flaws," says Dr.

John Adams

THE FIVE U.S. PRESIDENTS I WOULD LIKE TO SEE CLONED ARE:

_____ _____ _____

_____ _____

NAME: _____

ADDRESS: _____

CITY: _____ STATE: _____ ZIP: _____

Send your entry to:
Presidential Clones
c/o Weekly World News
5401 NW Broken Sound Blvd.
Boca Raton, FL. 33487
Entries must be received by
January 15, 2003.

ST TO CLONE FIVE U.S. PRESIDENTS

. . . and YOU get to pick 'em!

BRINGING back dead Presidents, such as J.F.K. and Abe Lincoln could really do a lot for the morale of this country — particularly in these troublesome times.

Blauprecht, who observed that historic cloning project, but did not take part. "Already the boy is showing signs of the rampant megalomania that Hitler was famous for.

"Germany wants to show the world that some good can come of human cloning, so that's why we have selected U.S. Presidents as our next subjects."

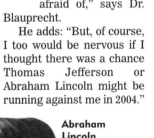

DR. DIETER BLAUPRECHT

Such an experiment could never happen in the U.S., with the Bush administration's staunch anti-cloning stance.

On April 2, 2002, President George W. Bush told an audience of about 175 lawmakers, pro-life activists, researchers

and people with disabilities that cloning is a "step toward a society in which human beings are grown for spare body parts," and called on the Senate to ban all human cloning in the U.S.

"President Bush makes some valid points, but the rest of the world is making the bold scientific leaps that Bush is afraid of," says Dr. Blauprecht.

He adds: "But, of course, I too would be nervous if I thought there was a chance Thomas Jefferson or Abraham Lincoln might be running against me in 2004."

CLONED LEADERS

U.S. Presidents aren't the only world leaders who may be cloned. Here's a list of some other revered political figures likely to be duplicated.

1. Mary Queen of Scots
2. Shaka Zulu
3. Mao Tse-Tung
4. Barry Goldwater
5. Jerry Springer

Franklin Delano Roosevelt

Abraham Lincoln

Harry Truman

John F. Kennedy

SEND IN THE CLONES

After thousands of votes were cast and *WWN* staff members spent weeks counting the ballots, the five presidents to be cloned were announced on March 2, 2003.

"I'm pleased to announce," said a noticeably excited Dr. Blauprecht, "that the five presidents who will be cloned are John F. Kennedy, Abraham Lincoln, Franklin Delano Roosevelt, Ronald Reagan, and Millard Fillmore, who beat out Jefferson by a mere three votes."

Thanks to Dr. Blauprecht's cloning method, which he learned from his colleague, the revolutionary Dr. Werner Trondheim of Vienna, the clones age at five times the rate of normal humans. Since the cloning began as soon as the winners were announced, JFK II, Abe II, FDR II, Ronnie II, and Millard Fillmore II are now 12 clone years old.

"We just love having the boys in our class," says middle school teacher Nancy Fitzpatrick. "They're all so bright, and Ronnie II is such a ham."

Interviews with their classmates show that each boy has adopted a role true to his presidential personality. JFK II and Ronnie II are the most popular boys in school, already dating girls. "They're sooo cute! Jack II is awesome at football, and Ron II gets the best parts in all the plays," says one enamored classmate.

FDR II is the class "nerd." He's captain of the debate team and active in the chess club, the model UN, and boys intramural cricket. Fillmore, on the other hand, is barely noticeable. He generally sits in the back of the classroom, doodling in his notebook. "I'm afraid Millard II gets picked on a bit," says Fitzpatrick. "He's earned the nickname 'Know-Nothing,' and the kids keep saying he killed the Whig party. On the bright side, they've really had to bone up on their history to get some good jabs in!"

But the real oddball of the bunch is Abraham Lincoln II, who not only dresses in black every day, but also wears eyeliner and paints his fingernails black. "Abe II is always talking about some band no one has ever heard of," says a classmate, rolling his eyes. "He thinks he's all punk rock, but really he's pretty lame."

WELCOME TO CLONETOWN, U.S.A.

TOP SECRET!

FAMILY RESEMBLANCE? Hidden-camera snapshot of a backyard party.

Shocking conspiracy explains why all these men look EXACTLY alike!

PECOS, Texas — This sleepy, backwater Texas town has become the site of an ultrasecret government clone-breeding program. And 80 members of one "model" alone quietly reside in the area, according to a leading conspiracy theorist.

"Despite its claims to the contrary, the U.S. leads the world in cloning research — government scientists cloned the first human in 1973," says author Dave Banding, who's in the past blown the lid off conspiracies ranging from Area 51 to Waco.

"You don't have to accept my word for it. Take a drive through Pecos and it won't take long for you to see what I mean.

"You see a guy pumping your gas, then when you go to the diner for a hamburger, the 'same' guy will be behind the counter.

"Walk into the police station, there he'll be again, sitting behind a desk reading the funny papers and giving you a big smile like he's never seen you before in his life."

For years, there've been whispers in the conspiracy-buff community of a government "Clonetown" where the products of hush-hush experiments are raised.

Now Banding has come forward with photographic proof: Hidden-camera snapshots he took of look-alikes going about their business in Pecos and even gathering at a backyard party.

Banding claims the sinister-sounding project was initiated during the Cold War, when Russia and America were racing to outdo each other in bio-engineering research.

"From what I've been able to gather from classified documents, the goal was to create a perfect soldier, then churn out thousands of duplicates," the D.C.-based expert says.

The researcher claims there are now at least seven different "models" in Pecos, male and female, ranging in number from just 10 to a whopping 80 clones.

"Each model has been engineered for a particular task — worker, scholar, soldier," he revealed.

"The government still believes that cloning is the key to the future of our nation."

Officials in Pecos deny that their town has become any kind of clone assembly line.

"In any small town where people have lived for generations, folks are going to tend to look alike and, of course, we have our share of twins and triplets," one official said.

— By *MIGUEL FIGUEROA*

AUTHOR Dave Banding.

'I'd chop off a finger to keep my job,' say most workers!

WASHINGTON — A shocking new university study reveals 87 percent of people would rather cut off a finger than lose their job!

Even more surprising, 48 percent of workers say they'd have a foot amputated if it meant they could double their salary and be guaranteed they'd never be fired.

Weekly World News family of readers — 100 million strong!

SCIENTIST CLONES HIMSELF

By **BRETT ANNISTON**
Correspondent

. . . so he can cheat on his wife!

SCIENCE has advanced to the point where scientists use cloning technology for their own personal gain.

A MAVERICK Austrian scientist created a clone of himself — so he could cheat on his wife!

Dr. Werner Trondheim, 46, admits that he created the genetic duplicate to keep his wife Greta occupied while he chased young babes.

"At the time I thought it was the best solution for all concerned," says Dr. Trondheim, a microbiologist on the faculty of the University of Vienna.

"The way I saw it, I could indulge my interest in pretty young graduate students without guilt. My wife would still have me — indeed a younger, fitter version of me.

"In my mind, this was what cloning was all about: A high-tech solution to otherwise unsolvable human problems."

But while the amazing clone is in perfect health, the plan has backfired — because peeved Greta Trondheim can't stand her hubby's knockoff.

"I went along with Werner's idea because he wouldn't stop pestering me and he convinced me the clone would be just like Werner was when I first met him," says Greta, 44. "The trouble was I forgot what an immature jerk Werner was when we were young. Werner II and I have nothing in common."

Fed-up Greta has filed for divorce from her girl-chasing egghead mate — and she's kicked befuddled clone Werner II out of the house as well.

And surprisingly, Dr. Trondheim — who admits having cheated on his wife of 20 years with at least six women during the four-month "trial period" of the odd arrangement — is begging her to take him back.

"I thought I wouldn't be jealous seeing Greta with another man because after all, the clone is me," he explains. "But the fact is, coming home to find the two of them cuddling on the couch was upsetting."

The bizarre divorce suit has thrown a spotlight on Dr. Trondheim's research, which had been kept secret to avoid Austria's strict ban on human cloning. Now newspapers are having a field day with the story — but not everyone is laughing. Leading ethicist Hans Grupter condemns the scientist's use of cutting-edge technology for trivial personal gain.

"You can be for cloning or against it — but to bring another human being into existence for such petty reasons was wrong," he blasts.

While Dr. Trondheim refuses to divulge details about his technique, he says it's not all that different from the one used by researchers in Edinburgh to clone Dolly the sheep in 1997.

"I extracted DNA from one of my skin cells and placed it in a donor egg cell from which the nucleus had been stripped," the researcher explains.

"A volunteer surrogate carried the cloned embryo to term."

Since the birth of Dolly, scientists have learned that cloned mammals age far more rapidly than normal. Using a process that enhances that effect, the expert was able to accelerate his clone's development, bringing him to a biological age of 20 in just four years.

"My clone, who was born on June 1, 1999, is four years old chronologically, but biologically, intellectually and, as my wife can attest, anatomically, he's a robust 20-year-old," Dr. Trondheim reveals.

The scientist says the unhappiness the experiment has brought into his life has caused him to reconsider the merits of cloning — and he now favors an outright ban.

"Scientists shouldn't play God," he says.

DR. TRONDHEIM with his wife in happier times.

THE CLONE ZONE

A RECENT survey asked people which celebrities they'd most like to see cloned — and those they'd least like to see cloned. Here are the top three candidates in each category:

Please **DO** clone:	Please **DON'T** clone:
HALLE BERRY	ROSIE O'DONNELL
JOHNNY DEPP	RICHARD SIMMONS
TIGER WOODS	HOWARD STERN

The Clone Channel. Left of the Dial—Right for Today.

**July 18
July 24**

MONDAY

8:00	**Sister, Sister** Tia and Tamara have a crush on the same clone
8:30	**Everybody Loves Raymonds** The Ray clones accidentally piss off their wives
9:00	**Star Trek: Thomas the Riker Clone** Thomas fights the Romulans
9:30	
10:00	★★ **Superman IV: The Quest for Peace** (1987; PG) Christopher Reeve, Gene Hackman. Superman takes on his clone
10:30	

TUESDAY

8:00	**Super Sloppy Double Dare** Clones + Slime = Fun!
8:30	**Clone High** Vice Principal JFK catches Ghandi and Cleopatra smoking marijuana
9:00	**The Animated Tales of the Three Little Pigs** Famous pig clones Millie, Alexis, and Dotcom throw a cloneday party
9:30	
10:00	**Stefan Urquelle's Variety Hour** Families Matter!
10:30	

WEDNESDAY

8:00	★ **Multiplicity** (1996; PG-13) Michael Keaton and Andie MacDowell in a hilarious working-class romp
8:30	
9:00	
9:30	
10:00	**Clone Eye for the Singular Guy** Do two twin beds really equal a king?
10:30	

THURSDAY

8:00	**The Mary Tyler Clone Show** A single clone moves to Minneapolis to work in a newsroom
8:30	**Cooking Live with Emeril's Clone** Pasta Primavera
9:00	**TravelDeals** Twofers; What to do when double-booked
9:30	★★★ **Mini-Me in Goldmember** (2002; PG-13) Verne Troyer, Michael Caine. Mini-Me defects to the other side in his third movie
10:00	
10:30	

FRIDAY

8:00	**E! True Hollywood Story** Mary-Kate and Ashley Olsen
8:30	
9:00	★★★ **Star Wars Episode II: Attack of the Clones** (2000; PG) With more clones and less Jar-Jar, this Star Wars is the best in the series
9:30	
10:00	
10:30	

SATURDAY

8:00	**Who Wants to Marry a Clone?** Season finale
8:30	
9:00	**Biography** Dolly: Two Sheeps's Story
9:30	
10:00	**Clone-umbo** A clone solves mysteries
10:30	

SUNDAY

8:00	**Dr. Phil** Where do you begin and they end?; The horrors of duplicide
8:30	
9:00	**Clone & Garden** Synchronized mowing; tulips. Special guest: Martha Stewart III
9:30	**Ireland Vacations** Clones
10:00	**Sports Sunday** Twin Falls Tandem Bike Showdown!
10:30	

CLONE OR ANDROID

Clones and androids have a lot in common. Not only do they belong to the same union and attend many of the same parties, they can also look startlingly alike. Use the following tips to help distinguish between the two.

Clones...
- usually have patchy skin and/or bad acne
- often walk into a room and forget why they're there
- are plagued with chronic hiccups
- age five times faster than humans
- love Neil Diamond

Androids...
- have bone-crushing handshakes
- sometimes wear their underwear over their clothing
- have glowing red eyes
- don't age
- never miss ABC's TGIF line-up

PUT YOUR SKILLS TO THE TEST!
Which of the following is a clone, and which is an android?

1. JOHNNY IV

2. JOHNNY FIVE

KILLER ANDROIDS BREEDING LIKE FLIES!

By MICHAEL CHIRON
In London

SLEEK, SEXY & SINISTER
Dangerous robots that are self-replicating could destroy mankind, top scientist warns.

Chinese develop deadly robots that can mate & have offspring

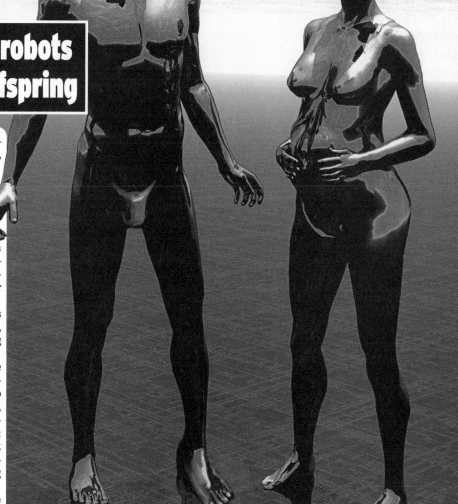

ANDROIDS with the ability to mate and breed could become a reality within the next three years, says a top computer scientist.

But the robots will not be used to benefit mankind — they'll be built as terrifying weapons of war.

"The first Self-Replicating Battle Android (SRBA) is now reportedly under construction in China," reveals Dr. Anthony Wilde, one of England's most highly respected experts in artificial intelligence and robotics.

"As weapons of war, the atomic-powered, titanium SRBAs are virtually indestructible. And they will have the programmed ability to build others of their kind.

"The cost of each android, male or female, is around $6 billion — but you only need two. They can replicate at an astonishing rate, and within only two years the original 'Adam and Eve' robots could spawn an android army of millions."

Dr. Wilde, who learned of the weapons program from high-level contacts in British intelligence, says that other nations — including the U.S — also have hush-hush robot-soldier projects in the works, designed to limit human battlefield casualties.

But the Chinese are a decade ahead of anyone else.

"Chinese leaders feel they'll never be able to match America's vast nuclear arsenal," he says. "This killer-android army would be their ace in the hole."

The real-life Terminators mate by joining at the chest, allowing their replicating software to interface.

Within 30 minutes, the female ejects a ball-bearing-size "baby" that grows to human size inside of a week, thanks to the work of nano-bots within the ball bearing: Microscopic robots that behave like one-celled organisms and work at dazzling speed.

The brilliance of the Chinese approach is to mimic natural biological processes.

"Instead of each new warrior-android simply being a 'clone' of a single predecessor, it combines the most valuable traits of each parent," Dr. Wilde explains.

"However, unlike human evolution, which depends on random mutation over the course of thousands of years, the replication program chooses from a menu of dormant traits to enhance the next generation.

"If the enemy resorts to tactical nukes, for example, the offspring will be immune to radiation."

Each female android will be able to churn out up to 12 offspring a day and when they mate they will do so without emotion.

"It will be a dispassionate act, like inserting a car key," Dr. Wilde explains.

British intelligence believes the Chinese have no immediate plans to unleash the robot army — it's intended as a nuclear deterrent.

But Dr. Wilde fears the biggest danger of the highly independent SRBAs is that they could turn on their masters and then swiftly take over the whole world.

"They are not only hundreds of times stronger than humans, their super-computer brains will help them think 100,000 times faster," he reveals.

"They require no food or water. And their total lack of emotion will be an advantage. They will feel no pain and have no fear of death. They will be the ultimate soldiers."

EARTH'S CORE IS MADE OF CANDY

By BECKY TODD

THE Earth's core is actually a tasty ball of candy, say scientists.

Until now, experts could only speculate about the geological material that makes up the center of the earth. They believed it was a magma/lava-like substance.

But with the invention of the Rock Rocket – a high-tech capsule that was able to tunnel through the planet's layers, collect samples, then reverse its direction and return – researchers were able to obtain and examine the real thing.

"After extensive laboratory analysis, we have come to the surprising conclusion that the Earth's core is, in fact, a jawbreaker," says Dr. Jarod Gray, the team leader and co-creator of the Rock Rocket.

"The middle substance is a pretty pink. Layers surrounding it are pastel tints of blue, green and purple. Upon tasting the Earth's core, we discovered it's delicious. The main ingredient is sugar."

The experts are stumped about their finding.

"Geologists, biologists, archaeologists and anthropologists from around the world are now in one big think tank, trying to figure out why the middle of the earth is sweet," explains Gray. "We've decided that, through the centuries, children have dropped so many lollipops and candy bars, spilled so much juice and soda and dumped so many ice cream cones that the earth's outer crust absorbed more sugar than it could handle. It's a theory, anyway.

"For hundreds of years, the sugar has traveled hundreds of miles to the center, where it was compressed by the planet's pressure into a jawbreaker."

WEEKLY WORLD NEWS EXCLUSIVE

'Startling

SCIENTISTS PAST-LIVES

By NELSON MANN
Weekly World News

German scientists have developed a reincarnation machine that enables users to recall past lives in startling detail!

Drs. Helmut Bogel and Max Dietz say the device, code-named L-261, electronically probes through layers of consciousness until it researchers the area of the brain where memories of previous lives are stored.

They also predict that a home version of the machine will be available to the public within five years.

"The machine will make it possible for everyone to examine their past lives and has already provided us with the most startling proof of reincarnation ever," Dr. Bogel told newsmen at a press conference in Oelde, West Germany.

"In preliminary studies it has enabled test subjects to recall as many as 100 past lives with amazing clarity," he added. "One subject actually spoke to us in 35 languages and dialects she had learned in 38 past lives."

Drs. Bogel and Dietz refused to say how L-261 works or discuss the principles used to develop it. They did reveal that the device is the culmination of 25 years' research.

They went on to say that they intend to sell smaller versions of the machine, which looks much like an upside-down bowl of spaghetti, to the public beginning no later than 1995.

"We think L-261 is the most important technological breakthrough since the computer," said Dr. Dietz. "It's starling proof of reincarnation and is obviously going to change the way we view human history, lives, and consciousness forever."

Darlene Kohl is one of 75 people who volunteered to test the device in studies conducted over the past six months.

PIONEER researcher Helmut Bogel

Frightened at first, she quickly cam to grips with memories of her past live and now calls the experience "the mos rewarding of my life.

"When they put the helmet and probe on my head I had second thoughts an almost bolted from the chair," said th woman. "But as soon as they turned it on pleasant tingling sensation ran through m body.

"I was wide awake but I couldn't kee my eyes open and I began to see all thes images like I was dreaming.

"The next thing I know I saw myse huddled around a fire with cavemen. was thrilling because I remembered bein there thousands of years ago."

As the probe continued Miss Koh recalled 22 past lives that she led i Greece, Rome, China, Mexico, Americ

proof of reincarnation!'

BUILD MACHINE

Amazing brain probes send people hurtling through history!

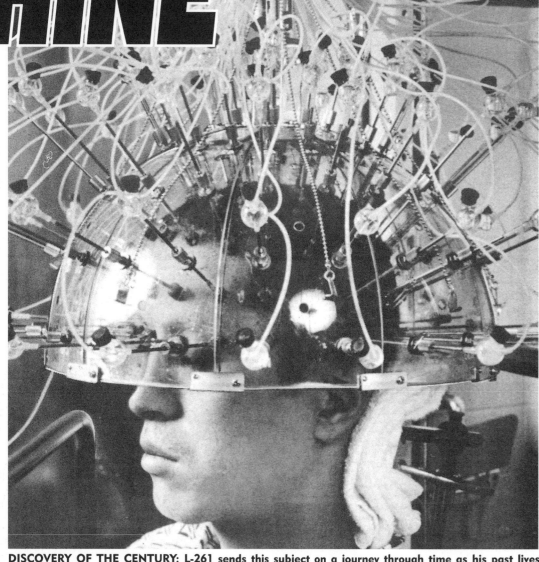

BREAKTHROUGH: Scientist Max Dietz devoted 25 years to L-261.

nd Europe.

As each life unfolded she was able to peak in the language peculiar to the ountry and period in which she had lived. he also provided researchers with histor-al details that she couldn't possibly have nown unless she had experienced them past lives.

"Miss Kohl has only a ninth-grade ducation but provided us with historical ata worthy of a university professor," aid Dr. Bogel.

"We got similar results with all our est subjects and concluded that L-261 is n unqualified success.

"This technology will change the lives f everyone who uses it," he added. All of istory is going to unfold before us."

DISCOVERY OF THE CENTURY: L-261 sends this subject on a journey through time as his past lives begin to unfold. The mass of electrodes are needed to probe the deepest areas of the brain.

GLOW-IN-THE-DARK MONKEY IS
THE MISSING LINK!

Crafty critter has a 150 IQ — and knows Morse code, say scientists!

CAPETOWN, South Africa — A 100-watt monkey with an estimated 150 IQ is being called the Missing Link, the final proof that man evolved from apes!

The shiny critter which glows in the dark and was captured in a deep, dark underground cave is described by one researcher as "definitely closer to human than animal."

It appears to communicate with a primitive form of Morse code, blinking on and off to communicate its needs.

"This creature is not like any other animal known to man," said scientist George Powers. "Its intelligence level is far beyond any chimpanzee or dolphin."

Powers and a team of researchers captured the creature in late October. The luminescent "link" is slightly more than 18 inches tall and weighs 8 pounds.

"We've saved a lot of money on electric lighting in the lab," joked Powers. He said the fact that the animal glows is evidence that it was evolving to meet its special needs.

"The monkey was discovered more than 300 feet below ground," he said.

"It was pitch black in that cave and the only light was the animal's glow. The light attracts the insects and moths it needs to survive.

"Clearly it was evolving to adapt to its difficult living situation."

But outraged creationists, who admit the living light bulb emits a strong lime-green glow, dispute evidence that it's the Missing Link.

"There have always been smart monkeys running around — some of them even ride tricycles, wear diapers or play the drums," said the Rev. William Holinger.

"And in my mind, the fact that this animal glows in the dark does nothing to prove it's some near-human being."

— By SANDRA LEE

WELL-LIT monkey was captured in a cave more than 300 feet underground.

SCIENTISTS SET TO OPEN PANDORA'S BOX

EXPERT Dr. Alex Nikolopolis.

By VINCENZO SARDI
Weekly World News

EXPERTS warn that bad things can come in small boxes.

ATHENS — Confident Greek scientists have announced they're just days away from finally opening Pandora's Box — and they say they're "100 percent sure" that the 8,600-year-old bronze container can now be opened safely.

"The safety measures we have in place today are state-of-the-art," declares archaeologist Dr. Alex Nikolopolis, project director.

"When the box was first found in 1966, the technology just wasn't available to support the idea of opening it. Now we're quite sure nothing will go wrong," he says.

According to Greek mythology, eons ago in the Golden Age, a woman named Pandora was given a mysterious box as a gift from the gods — who warned her never to open it. Curious Pandora lifted the lid and out rushed all the evils that now plague mankind, such as war, hunger and disease.

For centuries, most experts believed the box was merely the stuff of fables.

Then, in the 1870s, German archaeologist Heinrich Schliemann discovered the ruins of Troy and scientists realized there was much truth to ancient Greek legends. The hunt was on for everything from the Golden Fleece to Pandora's Box.

When, in 1966, on the island of Corfu the 8-inch-long rectangular box was unearthed 50 feet beneath the ruins of a shrine to the god Dionysus, it was heralded as a major archaeological find.

8,600-year-old box will unleash horrors beyond belief into the world, warns historian!

"There was no guesswork needed to identify it. In ancient Greek, someone had scratched on the box 'Do not open no matter what,'" Dr. Nikolopolis explains.

The bronze box will be opened by remote control in a chamber 900 feet deep that has been built to withstand a nuclear explosion.

"Whatever risks still remain are far outweighed by the potential benefits," claims Dr. Nikolopolis. "We might find a cure for cancer or learn the answers to our biggest questions about the universe."

But critics and experts in Greek mythology fear this could be a classic case of history repeating itself.

"This is scientific arrogance at its worst," blasts historian Ari Vidakis. "These fools could unleash new horrors that are beyond our imagination."

PEEK-A-BOO you're screwed! The last time Pandora's box was opened, all the evils known to man were unleashed.

WWN EXCLUSIVE
DATELINE: MARCH 1, 2002

NEW DRUG ON STREET CALLED 'CRACK P.M.'
—get high but still enjoy a full night's rest!

STUFF & MOUNT

Save money and do it yourself with common kitchen tools

By BRETT DELAGRANGE
Correspondent

FRIENDS FOREVER: Abigail Johnson was sad when Muffins died. But now that she's stuffed her pet, she'll never have to say goodbye.

NO ONE likes to lose a pet. But now you can keep your furry loved one around forever — without the services of a costly taxidermist!

"Most people don't realize how easy it is to stuff and mount animals," says author Floyd Munson. "Taxidermy is not rocket science."

Munson, author of *Kitchen Table Taxidermy*, says that the average person can stuff and mount a normal-sized pet using common kitchen tools in about three or four hours.

"The most important thing you'll need, by far, is a strong stomach," says Munson. "It can get pretty messy. I recommend not eating a large meal immediately before your first couple of tries.

"Besides that, everything you'll need can most likely be found in your kitchen: A sharp knife, a large plastic bowl, zipper-seal bags, a microwave oven, paper towels and miscellaneous odds and ends."

Munson says that stuffing your pet can also be a form of therapy in dealing with the loss.

"I've had several of my students tell me that they hadn't really accepted the fact that their furry companion had died — until they gutted themselves.

"It's pretty hard to be in denial when your cat's intestines are in a zipper bag on the kitchen counter," he says.

Abigail Johnson, a ninth-grader from Save Falls, Md., was extremely depressed over the sudden loss of her cat Muffins. She was missing meals, she stopped socializing with her friends and it was starting to affect her schoolwork.

That's when her father, Gary, decided to do something about it.

New cryonics unit allows you to keep deceased loved ones at home!

FLASH FREEZE YOUR DEAD RELATIVES

... for just pennies a day – until docs can find a cure for what killed them!

GONE, BUT NOT FOREVER: The Big Chill Home Storage nitrogen-cooled corpse storage unit retails for $900 — about the same price as a cremation, but gives loved ones hope of being reunited in the future.

YOUR OWN PET!

"I ran across Floyd's book in my hunting shop and thought I could save some money on all my deer and fish mountings," he says.

"But when I read how easy it was to stuff an animal, I thought this might be something that could help Abigail with her depression. I bought her a dachshund named Sparky but that didn't work so I was willing to do just about anything.

"So after reading *Kitchen Table Taxidermy* and then practicing on a possum, like the book suggests, Abby and I went to work on Muffins. It was hard for her at first, but once she got used to the smell and seeing her pet's innards, we started focusing on our technique — wanting Muffins to look as good as possible for the rest of eternity.

"When we were done, Abigail was crying — but this time it was happy tears. It was as if she had Muffins back as part of the family again.

"I know that home taxidermy is not right for everyone. But if you have the stomach for it, I highly recommend Munson's book — it worked for us," says Gary.

"I haven't told Abby this," he adds. "But judging by the declining health of Sparky, she's probably going to be getting some more practice in real soon."

Kitchen table taxidermy, as Munson calls it, also makes good economic sense.

"Taxidermists' rates are going up every year. You can easily blow 500 bucks on a German shepherd," says Munson. "And for someone with a lot of pets, that's a week's vacation at Dollywood."

Munson does warn that it may take some practice to get the desired aesthetic look of the deceased animal.

"In my book, I recommend starting out with either a squirrel or a possum — something that you won't mind messing up on the first try.

"But after you have a couple critters under your belt, it's actually easy — and fun for the whole family."

Munson recommends making kitchen table taxidermy a family affair.

"Not only is it a great way to bond, but it's also a way to teach kids responsibility. After all — the whole family played with the pet. Why shouldn't they all stuff and mount him?

"And once the project is done and you have your pet join the family again, it gives you a feeling of achievement — something to be proud of.

"If I do say so myself, Muffins has never looked better," says Gary. "Sometimes I forget that he's even dead."

HOME TAXIDERMY DOs & DON'Ts

IF YOU have a pet that's nearing the end of his life and you're considering stuffing him, you'll do well to keep these tips in mind.

1) MAKE SURE YOUR PET IS DEAD. One of the most common errors in home taxidermy is starting a stuffing session on an animal who is merely in a deep sleep — or hibernating.

2) DON'T SKIMP ON MATERIALS. Don't buy inferior taxidermy materials to save a couple bucks. If you take care of your stuffed animal and use quality products, your furry friend should be with you for the rest of your life. *NOTE: Do not use any suntan lotion product as your tanning solution — it's totally different.*

3) REMEMBER: Your pet will not look exactly as he did when he was alive. His eyes may not look straight ahead, his fur may be spotty or change colors in certain areas, and he may develop a peculiar odor.

4) HAVE FUN!

MANCHESTER, England — Freezing the remains of your loved ones used to be a practice reserved for the wealthy who could afford the hundreds of thousands of dollars it costs to rent cryogenic facilities.

By JUSTIN MITCHELL/*Weekly World News*

But an amazing new breakthrough allows everyone to keep expired relatives on ice in their own homes for just pennies a day!

"It's very affordable, and very comforting to know that my grandpa is resting in our basement ready to join us when technology can revive him," says Tanya Huddle, one of many who have bought the Big Chill Home Storage nitrogen-cooled corpse storage unit instead of joining a corporate cryogenic club.

The brainchild of English businessman and inventor Clive Autobee, the Big Chill retails for $900 — about the same price as a cremation — and is easy to maintain to keep the remains frozen at a safe 90 degrees below zero. If the power in the house goes out, a generator unit kicks on ensuring up to eight hours of stone cold

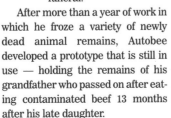

**INVENTOR
Clive Autobee**

safety for the remains.

"I got the idea when my mum passed on of cancer," says Autobee. "Our whole family adored her and hoped to the last moment of her life that some cure would be found. We looked into having her frozen, but what with our medical expenses we were strapped.

"I vowed then that no one else would have to suffer as we did and went to work the day after her funeral."

After more than a year of work in which he froze a variety of newly dead animal remains, Autobee developed a prototype that is still in use — holding the remains of his grandfather who passed on after eating contaminated beef 13 months after his late daughter.

"Gramps is in our sitting room,"

says Autobee. "We find it comforting especially when we're all watching some cricket matches or quiz shows on the telly. And he's no bother at all, just a low hum from the unit letting us know that everything is cold and comfortable.

"If there's ever a cure for his mad cow disease announced, we're right here ready to defrost him, fix him and have him join us for the next evening's newscast, so to speak."

Autobee has since sold nearly 1,000 of his corpse home storage packages — which include a "starter kit" with three 50-gallon nitrogen tanks — to grateful families such as the Huddles.

"We even joke a little, calling my grandfather our 'little Grandpasicle'," says Huddle. "He had such a wacky sense of humor when he was alive, we can't wait to hear him laugh about it when he's finally brought out of cold storage."

ACTIVITIES TO ENJOY WITH YOUR DEAD RELATIVE

Now that you've flash-frozen your dead relative and are waiting for the medical breakthrough that can bring him or her back to life, you're ready to take the next step: finding fun and safe things to do together in the meantime. While certain activities are not recommended for frozen kin (going to the beach, warming up in front of a fire, etc.), you don't have to sit around the house like a bunch of deadheads.

Your companion probably won't express a lot of enthusiasm, at least at first, but you can bet that finding the right activity will make both of you happy. Sure, the burden will be on you to carry most conversations and do all of the driving, but it's a small price to pay for years of continued companionship.

Here are just a few of the many activities you'll be able to enjoy with your frosty companion:

- ❑ Bingo
- ❑ Driving in the HOV lane
- ❑ Cuddling while watching scary movies
- ❑ Playing hide-and-seek (remember, the burden is on *you* to be the seeker)
- ❑ Sledding, tobogganing, and other winter sports
- ❑ Tango (it takes two)
- ❑ Visiting restaurants with two-for-one specials
- ❑ Going on double dates
- ❑ Giving piggyback rides
- ❑ Having staring contests

If you find none of the above engaging, you can always fashion your relative into a new coffee table! (Remember, however, not to place lit candles on top.)

By **MICHAEL CHIRON**
Weekly World News

They're here . . .
BAR CODES FOR YOUR FOREHEAD!

Inventor says hi-tech tattoos will help us win war on terror!

INVENTOR Andrew Tichrist was the first to test his bar code tattoo — choosing to wear it proudly on his forehead where all can see.

WASHINGTON — A maverick inventor's new high-tech identification system will make identity theft a thing of the past. He wants to have personal bar codes tattooed on all our foreheads!

Technical wizard Andrew Tichrist says that using the same UPC-code system now used to identify and track products on supermarket shelves will protect average Americans from identity theft, make business transactions easier — and even help America win the war on terror.

And the entrepreneur has already had his own noggin stamped with a UPC code.

Tichrist's D.C.-based firm is one of more than a dozen companies vying for a lucrative government contract to develop a national bar-code system. But Washington insiders say his is most likely to win approval.

The indelible bar code contains all relevant information about an individual, including name, Social Security number, nationality, criminal record, blood type and other medical information. It is impossible to alter or fake.

"If a terrorist tries to impersonate a worker at a nuclear plant, he'd be scanned and identified," Tichrist says.

The bar-code system will also make shopping easier — your forehead can be scanned just like a debit card.

"You'll never need to carry cash again," says Tichrist.

The system will be a boon to law-enforcement agencies.

"If a cop pulls someone over for a routine traffic stop, he can run a scanner over the bar code on the guy's forehead," he says. "Any outstanding warrants will come up on the scanner — bogus IDs and fake driver's licenses won't work anymore."

But civil libertarians warn it could lead to Big Brother-type government monitoring. "It's an invasion of privacy," one protester declares. "It's the beginning of a police state."

HOW WOULD BAR CODE TATTOOS HELP US?

By not requiring cash, it would cut down on muggings.

No more long lines at the checkout counter.

Long flight delays would be a thing of the past.

Terrorists walking our streets would be easily apprehended.

SCIENTIST FIGURES OUT WHY OLD PEOPLE SMELL!

OVER-RIPE PHEROMONES!

By DORIAN WAGNER

SOON there will be one less thing to wrinkle our noses at — someone has discovered the scientific root of "old people smell!"

Henry Snerpendorf, associate professor of geriatrics at Hollycouth University in Goteborg, Sweden, will publish his findings in the March issue of *Modern Science Age* magazine.

"It is widely known that old people smell like a mixture of cat food, rotten bananas and stagnant puddles," Snerpendorf says. "For some reason they all share the same odor, and now we finally know exactly what causes it."

Snerpendorf combined his academic experience with his interest in aromacology, the study of scents, to discover the source of the stench.

And as it turns out, the cause of seniors' malodor is a pheromone emitted to attract other seniors, he explains.

"Youth call it a stench, but the aged call it aromatic."

Pheromones are given off automatically by humans to attract the opposite sex, but, according to Snerpendorf, "Old people's pheromones are simply "over-ripe" and past their prime, so they don't smell as sweet as those of say, a Brad Pitt or Jessica Simpson."

The soon-to-be-published findings are based on a six-month-long study of 46 residents of the Rest Easy nursing home, two blocks from the university.

> **It smells like a mixture of cat food, rotten bananas & stagnant puddles!**

"We started with 50 participants," the professor says. "But unfortunately, we lost two to heart attacks, one to a stroke and another to a choking incident involving a carrot in some split pea soup."

The senior citizens of the home were quarantined for the length of the study, during which time the air quality and "eau de old" in the home was repeatedly monitored, Snerpendorf says.

What he and his team found was absolutely conclusive.

"All people over the age of 71 develop and emit the same funky pheromone," he says. "It's natures balancing act. As the years pass, we lose our hair and our eyesight, but gain potency.

"In other words," he explains, "the level of pungency increases with age. The older you get, the more rank the reek you radiate is."

And while the professor knows his findings are not earth-shattering breaking news, he still considers the study a success.

"We already knew 'old people smell' is not myth," he says. "What we were out to do was find the origin so perhaps scientists could, in the future, alter DNA to eliminate it.

"Hopefully one day soon, kids won't make such a stink about going to Grandma's house if she doesn't stink anymore."

> **ARE YOU KIDDING?**
>
> *A recent household survey revealed that the elderly go through more diapers than babies do.*

SPAM, SPAM, THANK YOU MA'AM

By **JOHN ADDISON**/*Correspondent*

Aliens using e-mail to seduce Earth women

EXTRATERRESTRIAL MESSAGE: Aliens have tapped into our Internet connections.

THE PORN that's clogging your e-mail inbox isn't always sent by some lonely pervert getting his kicks in a shabby apartment, or by marketing companies trying to make a buck on X-rated merchandise. A top researcher says you could also be getting spammed by aliens on a distant planet!

Astrophysicist Dr. Paul Winterhoof says aliens have "hijacked" the satellite transmissions that connect computers on the Internet, and are using them to contact Earth women with lurid claims about their sexual prowess — or to entice Earth men with offers of miraculous performance-enhancing drugs and gadgets.

The purpose, Dr. Winterhoof says, is to more efficiently initiate sexual contact for a planned breeding program that will mate humans and extraterrestrials.

"It's well known that aliens have been mating with humans for generations," he says. "But now they are using the Internet to make first contact. Just as the Internet has changed the way humans socialize and do business, so has it altered the way in which aliens seek to infiltrate our society.

"It's a sinister new development, although it does have its benefits," he says. Rather than forcibly kidnapping Earth men and women and subjecting them to terrifying and often-painful breeding experiments, Dr. Winterhoof says, the aliens are now attempting to focus only on willing partners. "Either they are gentler and more considerate than we have given them credit for," he says, "or they simply realize that they'll attract less attention.

"After all, how many women would be willing to risk the ostracism that would result from telling the world she let an alien tie her up and engage in kinky sex games? And what man would admit publicly that his newest relationship began because he was trying to get Viagra at a deep discount?"

Dr. Winterhoof says he began to investigate the alien-porn connection after receiving numerous racy e-mails filled with gibberish. "The message body, and sometimes even the subject line, contained hundreds of naughty words that had simply been strung together in ways that made no sense at all," he explains.

When he attempted to trace the source of the e-mails, he says, his search led to a server connected to a U.S. Air Force satellite launched in 1999.

The scientist advises anyone receiving the dirty messages to immediately delete them. "As their incomprehensible messages attest, these aliens can't read or write English well — even if you send them a blistering sermon about sinful thoughts, they're going to assume you're interested.

"Unless you want a three-headed alien at your door with some high-tech sex toy, your best bet is to simply ignore these perverts."

WWN EXTRA

TOP NAMES FOR CONJOINED TWINS

1. Siegfried and Roy
2. Eng and Cheng
3. Kit and Kat
4. Paris and Nicole
5. Million Dollar Surgery and Thank God for Health Insurance

Greatest invention since the umbrella!

LIGHTNING RODS YOU CAN WEAR

Never fear stormy weather again!

INVENTOR Ward Kelpernik wants everyone in America to own his wearable lightning rod.

DENVER — A maverick inventor has come up with an elaborate device designed to protect you from deadly lightning strikes, and he swears that it's safe because he's tested it repeatedly — on himself!

"I am pleased to announce the unveiling of the greatest invention since the umbrella," says 37-year-old Ward Kelpernik.

"The L-3 Kelpershield works along the same principal as a lightning rod, but this is the first time that the technology has been applied to people instead of buildings."

Kelpernik says his goal is to provide maximum protection from lightning strikes which kill 500 people and injure 1,500 more in the U.S. each year.

The Kelpershield allows the wearer to absorb lightning as it strikes. When lightning hits the rods attached to the glasses, it travels along a copper wire to an energy pack the user wears on his back. That energy is stored for later use.

Kelpernik says he's been hit by lightning several times while testing the device, but each time, his invention has kept him safe.

"In 15 tests performed over the past year, the L-3 Kelpershield has performed flawlessly. I am very fortunate to be able to stand here and tell you this because there were a couple times when I really thought I was a goner."

Asked what it feels like to be struck by lightning, Kelpernik responds, "It tickles! It's really a tingly sensation from head to toe."

Kelpernik says that his invention will be moderately priced and available to the public in time for Christmas.

"Anyone who wants a Kelpershield will be able to afford one."

But experts from the National Bureau of Weather Studies warn that people should stay far away from this invention.

"It's an accident waiting to happen," one expert says. "One of these days, someone is going be hurt."

Kelpernik says that will never happen. "My device is 100 percent guaranteed. With this remarkable contraption, people will be dancing in lightning storms, mark my words."

— By SCOTT GOSAR

New electronic gloves let you tickle the ivories like Liberace!

By MICHAEL CHIRON
Weekly World News

ZURICH, Switzerland — Now you can play the piano and sound as terrific as Liberace, even if you're tone deaf — just by slipping on a pair of special new electronic gloves!

Maestro Gloves, as the gizmos are called, actually trigger your fingers to strike the piano keys in precisely the right sequence to perfectly reproduce even the most complex piece of classical music.

"My gloves are designed for the person who knows nothing about music and doesn't have the time or the inclination to learn, yet still has a desire to perform," explains Swiss inventor Henrik Schwarz, the inventor of Maestro Gloves.

"They allow a novice who can't read a single note of music to play at the level of a concert pianist who's spent his entire life studying the instrument and practices several hours a day.

"You can entertain dinner-party guests for hours playing the great masterpieces. And because the gloves discreetly match a tuxedo or evening gown, your audience will be none the wiser."

Schwarz explains, "A real pianist's hand movements are recorded in a studio and programmed into tiny microchips that attach to the Maestro Gloves — disguised as sequins," reveals the inventor.

"The gloves literally 'commandeer' your hands. They deliver an electrical signal that triggers nerves in your wrists, hands and fingers. This allows you to re-create specific performances of some of the greatest pianists on Earth."

The gloves, which cost $350 a pair, can store up to 350 performances.

"It's a lot more fun than earlier devices because you can sit down and play the piano yourself," notes science writer Karl Weiner.

"Also, you can earn the applause of friends who really think you became a musical genius overnight."

ALWAYS the entertainer, the flamboyant Liberace dazzled audiences with his costumes and his playing.

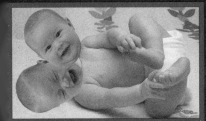

DOCTORS REMOVE ONE HEAD FROM TWO-HEADED BABY!

And flipped coin to decide which one!

Say goodbye to those ugly fat rolls forever . . .

LOSE 70 POUNDS IN 15 DAYS

By MIKE FOSTER
Correspondent

WITH FLESH-EATING BACTERIA!

THE FLESH-EATING disease that spread terror worldwide in the 1990s is making a comeback — as a weight-loss treatment.

The new, mutated version of the bacteria feasts only on fatty tissue. And excited obese people are now deliberately infecting themselves with the fat-gobbling germ in what's fast becoming the hottest new dieting fad.

Well-to-do tubby folks are lining up at doctor's offices around the country for the new procedure, in which the flab-munching bacteria is injected directly into "problem areas" such as beer bellies, love handles, thighs and hips.

"What we do is perfectly safe," explains infectious-disease specialist Dr. Randolph Blackett, who worked with a Los Angeles plastic surgeon to develop the technique.

"This is a mutant strain of Streptococcus pyogenes, the bacteria responsible for Necrotizing Fasciitis, the so-called 'flesh-eating disease.'

"Unlike its more virulent cousin, which destroys skin, subcutaneous tissue and muscle with alarming speed, this variety targets only fat cells."

The voracious bug cuts through fat "like a buzz saw," the expert says, eliminating an incredible three inches of ugly, unsightly flab per hour.

"This procedure has the speed of liposuction and, because it's non-invasive, it's actually much safer," Dr. Blackett claims. "When fat supply dwindles, the bacteria simply die off."

Patients who've had the slimming treatment are delighted with the results.

"I went from 210 pounds to 140 pounds in 15 days with the help of fat-eating bacteria," says the wife of a well-known Hollywood producer. "Now, when my husband invites those young starlets in bikinis to hang out by the pool, I don't feel so insecure."

Another woman, in her 50s, says she lost 38 pounds — without dieting or altering her eating habits.

But not everyone can afford the shots, which cost about $900. The fear is that some foolhardy fatties desperate to peel off pounds could try to get infected naturally, a possibility that worries doctors.

They fear that some ill-informed hefty folks may mistakenly expose themselves to the dangerous original form of the bug.

"Infectious diseases of this kind are not to be treated lightly," says an expert at the Centers for Disease Control and Prevention in Atlanta. "The original form of the bacteria can cause extensive tissue damage and lead to disfigurement and even death."

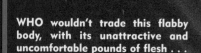

WHO wouldn't trade this flabby body, with its unattractive and uncomfortable pounds of flesh . . .

. . . for a trim, sexy shape like this one? Maybe that's why lard-butt ladies and gents are lining up for the new weight-loss bacteria shots.

WWN EXTRA FAD DIETS THROUGH THE AGES

THE PYRAMID DIET: The Pyramid Diet became the first as well as the longest-lived fad diet of all time (it lasted for 2,500 years), although it also sadly had the highest mortality rate. Leaving aside the question of whether the pyramids were built by Egyptian pharaohs, Atlantian master architects, or alien vacationers, there is no question that hauling massive blocks of stone on primitive sledges for decades on end while dining primarily on old sandal-leather and rainwater was an excellent way to stay fit.

THE DIET OF WORMS: In the mid 1500s, a fad diet began spreading throughout the Holy Roman Empire. While studying the Old Testament, Archduke Hans Lubsprecht had noticed that there were no fat people in the Bible, primarily due to their tendency to wander in the desert for months at a time eating only insects. The Lubsprecht Plan (or, as some called it, "The Diet of Worms") promised that you could eat all the bugs you wanted and still lose weight. It became wildly popular as kings and courtesans alike flocked to the Sinai Desert on pound-shedding pilgrimages, dining on the creepy-crawlies they found there.

THE INDUSTRIAL REVOLUTION DIET: As employment became more widespread and there was plenty of food on the family table during the 18th century, so came the first instance of endemic obesity. Luckily, factory owners were committed to the welfare of their employees and developed a revolutionary diet of coal soot and wool fungus combined with an exercise regimen (dubbed the "80-hour-work week") to help chubby weavers and spinners shed those extra pounds.

THE ALIEN ABDUCTION DIET: The 1947 crash-landing of a UFO at Roswell, N.M., was not only the start of the modern age of human-alien cooperation, but also the beginning of the 20th-century diet revolution. Human beings began to be abducted and subjected to episodes of what some described as horrifying experiments, but others found to be the most effective weight-loss programs ever seen on Earth. We now know definitively that such innovations as the grapefruit diet, gastric bypass surgery, the Atkins program, and other miracle weight-loss methods were revealed to us by aliens concerned with the modern obesity epidemic.

NEW FOR FATTIES: DO-IT-YOURSELF STOMACH-STAPLING KITS!

By VICKIE YORK
Correspondent

A CONTROVERSIAL medical supply company has incurred the wrath of the health-care establishment by selling do-it-yourself stomach-stapling kits to obese Americans!

The so-called Belly-Buster Kits, which cost just $69.99, come complete with disposable scalpels and surgical instruments for carving through blubber, as well as what's described as an "industrial grade" staple gun. There's even a helpful 22-minute instructional videotape to guide novices through what's called a "quick and easy" procedure.

"The sale of these kits is extraordinarily irresponsible," blasts a spokesman for the American Society of Professional Surgeons. "Laparoscopic gastric bypass surgery, or stomach stapling as it's commonly known, is far beyond the capability of an ordinary layman. But the sad part is many overweight people are so desperate for a quick fix, they'll buy these kits and try it."

Entrepreneur Neal Cobbley, CEO of the Little Rock, Ark.-based Cobbley Medical Supplies, which is distributing the product, insists that he's doing fatties a tremendous service.

"Obesity is a crisis in this country and this is a procedure that could benefit as many as 15 million overweight Americans," he points out. "Unfortunately, some insurance companies still refuse to pay for it and of course many Americans don't have health insurance at all.

"Our kit offers new hope for these people."

Normally, gastric bypass surgery takes place in a hospital setting and is performed by trained medical professionals. The procedure involves using staples to close off a portion of the patient's stomach, limiting how much food the person can eat and usually resulting in dramatic weight loss.

Cobbley's kit allows a patient to perform the operation on his own stomach.

"Despite all the hype from 'real' surgeons, the fact is anyone with a high school education and a steady hand ought to be able to do these operations," he maintains. "If you can sew on a button, you can use my kit successfully."

Cobbley is the first to agree that anyone who can afford to pay a surgeon to perform the flab-beating operation should. And he admits that, with only a "traditional biting bullet" enclosed in the kit to take the place of anesthesia, people with low pain thresholds should think twice before giving self-stapling a try.

But he insists that, for many people, the Belly-Buster Kit "is an excellent alternative."

Medical experts have bitterly attacked Cobbley and his kit.

"Gastric bypass surgery is a very

MEDICAL WARNING!

Always consult a trusted family physician before undergoing a medical procedure, whether at a hospital or at home with equipment from a kit. Experts also strongly recommend that you consider surgery for weight loss only as a last resort, when diet and exercise have failed.

serious operation," the ASPS spokesman argues. "The surgery carries a high risk of complications, including blood clots and leaking stomach juices that cause infections. Even in a hospital setting, the mortality rate for this procedure is as high as 1 percent.

"And bear in mind, many obese people are too fat too even see the underside of their belly, let alone operate on it. You can't simply hand out kits and tell people to 'go for it' as if they were pulling out splinters."

Cobbley takes the naysaying of his critics in stride.

"Of course these greedy quacks don't want you to operate on yourself — they lose out on all that money," he says.

Top space expert makes amazing claim:

DR. KURT WIKLUND

APOLLO 11 PH

BEER CANS ON THE MOON!

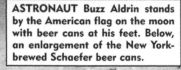

ASTRONAUT Buzz Aldrin stands by the American flag on the moon with beer cans at his feet. Below, an enlargement of the New York-brewed Schaefer beer cans.

Photo of beer cans were brought back on July 24, 1969 — then buried in a NASA vault and labeled 'TOP SECRET'!

OTOGRAPHED

APOLLO 11's lunar lander, *The Eagle*, landed in the moon's Sea of Tranquility.

GENEVA — Apollo 11 astronauts stumbled onto an astonishing find while making the first moon landing in 1969 — a bunch of old beer cans!

That's the startling assertion of a leading astrophysicist who claims he obtained a copy of a photo of the extraordinary discovery, labeled "top secret" and allegedly kept under wraps by tight-lipped NASA officials for more than 30 years.

"According to my sources at NASA, whom I consider unimpeachable, the cans were found by astronauts Neil Armstrong and Buzz Aldrin while they were collecting rock samples just a few yards from the lunar lander," says Dr. Kurt Wiklund, one of Switzerland's top space-science experts.

By KAYE ROSEBURG
Weekly World News

"The implications of this are utterly astounding. It means humans visited the moon long before NASA ever got there — and left tangible evidence behind."

The strange photo shows what appear to be several empty cans of Schaefer beer, a couple of them slightly crumpled as if casually crushed by hand after drinking.

"There's no doubt that they're beer cans, but how they got there is a baffling mystery," says Dr. Wiklund. "One thing is for certain, they weren't brought there by the astronauts — every item aboard the spacecraft was weighed and accounted for by NASA technicians."

Every American who was alive at the time can recall the dramatic moment when the lunar lander, dubbed *The Eagle*, landed in the moon's Sea of Tranquility on July 20, 1969 and space hero Armstrong climbed out, proclaiming it, "one small step for man, one giant leap for mankind."

But if Dr. Wiklund's sources are accurate and the NASA photo is genuine, someone took such a step long before Armstrong — who, until now, was believed to be the first man on the moon.

"Because there's no oxygen on the moon, the cans wouldn't rust, so it's impossible to tell from photographs just how long they've been there.

"They could have been left behind by a secretive band of amateur rocket scientists who ventured to the moon as part of an entrepreneurial project in the early '60s.

"Or it could have been one of the several military missions to the moon rumored to have been sponsored by Nazi Germany in the '40s. We just don't know."

According to one of Dr. Wiklund's sources, the astronauts retrieved the mystery cans and brought them along when they returned to Earth on July 24, 1969.

Since then, the curious items have remained under lock and key in a NASA vault and labeled "Top Secret," along with the amazing photograph.

When asked about the cans, NASA officials laughed off the entire story as "utterly preposterous."

Why all the secrecy?

"You've got to remember, winning the space race and beating the Russians to the moon was supposed to be an incredible moment of triumph for the U.S. space program.

"The discovery of those beer cans, if revealed to the general public, would have taken away some of the luster of the occasion, to say the least," explains Dr. Wiklund.

Chain saw shocker!

MAN CUTS HIS LEG OFF — & IT HOPS 75 YARDS ALL BY ITSELF!

Ivan Netsky cut off his leg with a chain saw and then watched in shock and disbelief as the severed limb stood bolt upright — and hopped away!

Authorities confirmed that Netsky and his left leg were 75 yards apart when rescue workers ar-

By TIMOTHY O'TOOLE

rived at his house to take him to the hospital.

Oddly enough, the blood-streaked limb was still twitching violently when they found it at the base of a fence and

packed it in ice in a bid to save it.

"The damn thing hopped away, I swear it," said Netsky from his home in western Siberia.

"I was blinded by pain but I know what happened and I know what I saw.

"The leg hit the dirt and bounced back up. It took off

and didn't stop until it ran into the fence."

Surgeons were unable to reattach Netsky's leg because it was so badly mangled and said he will have to be fitted with an artificial limb.

They went on to say that his story about the severed limb hopping away didn't surprise them at all. "If you squash a

spider the legs will move and twitch for as long as an hour," said one emergency room physician. "The muscles in Netsky's leg were obviously twitching and jerking in the same manner.

"The only thing that surprises me is that the severed leg went 75 yards. They don't usually go more than 25 feet."

TOWN'S TOASTERS TALKING — IN RUSSIAN!

RESIDENTS OF a small town are hearing voices from their household appliances, and the gabby gadgets are speaking Russian!

Toasters and other electrical goods in the tiny town of Hooke, England are picking up signals from a nearby radio transmitter, which the BBC uses to broadcast around the world. Hooke appliances are receiving

those signals, including shows broadcast in Russian.

"It's unnerving," said a town official, whose toaster's been talking. "Normally, it just makes toast."

The BBC says it's not so strange. In theory, a spokesman explains, any appliance can pick up a radio signal. But it's pretty peculiar to the people of Hooke.

WWN EXTRA
MYSTERIES OF THE PLANETS

What other wonders have been recently discovered in our solar system?

MERCURY In 2004, the Russian news agency Itar-Tass announced that Mercury does not exist but was faked during the Cold War using papier-mâché and fishing line. The elaborate hoax was concocted by the Soviet government to distract the attention of American scientists away from weapons development.

VENUS Radar images taken by the spacecraft Magellan in the early 1990s unveiled yet another reason Venus is similar to Earth: gambling. The images show that Venus's Lakshmi Planum plateau is actually the roof of an enormous underground casino-resort complex and water park. Evidence of fossilized shrimp cocktails found inside the long-defunct Venusian "Sin City" hints at the once-rich marine life of the Planet of Love.

JUPITER Data collected by the spacecraft Galileo revealed that the Great Red Spot is actually a round, spicy, sodium-rich layer of organic matter, composed primarily of animal proteins. At twice the width of Earth, it may be the largest slice of pepperoni in the universe.

SATURN Analysis of ultraviolet spectrometer (UVS) data gathered by Voyagers 1 and 2 indicates that the planet's famous rings are composed largely of string cheese, while the inner rings appear to be made of reduced-fat string cheese.

URANUS Formerly thought to be the most boring of the gas planets, photos from the Hubble Space Telescope show multiple cases of Charmin on Uranus's surface, causing physicists to create new theories of the locations of black holes.

NEPTUNE Scientists are baffled by the discovery that the planet's Great Dark Spot is actually a crop circle as large as China. They now believe that the giant John Deer tractor that orbits the planet may hold the key to the mystery.

PLUTO Pluto's "planethood" was recently called into question after the discovery of dozens of other planets outside the Milky Way. But the "black sheep" of the solar system was eagerly brought back into the fold when astronomers at the SETI Institute began picking up faint signals coming from the planet's surface, which a Disney spokesperson has confirmed is a unique code that could only be emitted by the cryogenically frozen body of Walt Disney.

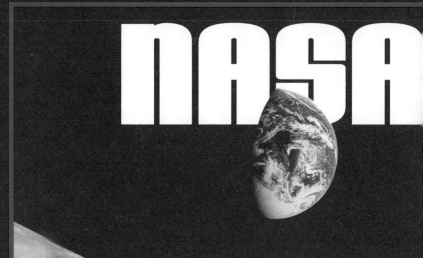

NASA

BEWILDERED NASA scientists are working overtime to solve a baffling mystery — after a space probe photographed Earth-type garden gnomes and pink flamingos on Mars!

Initial speculation that the images might have been the handiwork of a prankster at the space agency was shot out of the water when photos beamed back by another probe showed the same type of cheesy lawn ornaments littering the surface of the moon.

"Clearly we're looking at a pattern, but exactly what's going on here is a mystery to me — and I have three Ph.Ds," declares astronomer and rocket scientist Dr. Henry Brinsezki, who has been working with NASA to solve the mind-bending riddle.

Notoriously secretive NASA officials refuse to discuss the bizarre discovery with reporters. But Dr. Brinsezki confirms that the first set of images were taken in April 2001 by the *Mars Global Surveyor* as it passed over a region of the Red Planet known as Cydonia. And shockingly, they've been kept secret from the public ever since.

Then, just last month, another NASA probe photographed close to a dozen gnomes and flamingos in the moon's Sea of Tranquillity.

Now NASA scientists are racking their brains, trying to come up with a logical explanation.

Among the theories currently being bandied about:

1 A shadowy organization known as the Gnome Liberation Group, known to be behind the kidnapping of thousands of gnomes from lawns going back a decade or more, placed the objects on the celestial bodies as a prank — or perhaps to give the little men their "freedom."

"The trouble with that theory is that there's no evidence that the organization has the funding or wherewithal to achieve space travel," points out Cape Canaveral-based Dr. Brinsezki. "If they have, that's almost as unsettling as the thought of aliens traipsing around our solar system."

2 The objects are ancient artifacts left behind by a long-dead alien civilization that visited Earth eons ago and started the lawn-ornament tradition on our world.

3 Modern-day ETs who like the way mankind's lawn ornaments look placed them in the front yards of their hidden lunar and Martian bases in comparatively recent times.

So far, this theory has won the most adherents at NASA because some of the gnomes are just yards from where astronaut Neil Armstrong walked in 1969, yet he made no mention of having seen them.

The fact that goofy-looking lawn ornaments are cluttering the historic site actually has some NASA officials hopping mad.

"Frankly, no matter who put those gnomes and other junk on the moon and elsewhere, we want them gone," fumes a NASA source who spoke on the condition of anonymity. "They're making our solar system very tacky."

SHOCKER!
GARDEN GNOMES FOUND ON MOON & MARS!

By **MICHAEL CHIRON**
Correspondent

**THE
FLATULENCE
MUFFLER**

THE FLATULENCE MUFFLER

It makes embarrassing moments a thing of the past!

GNOME ENIGMA: Photo of lunar surface taken last month by NASA probe has scientists scratching their heads.

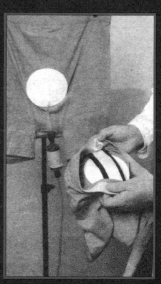

GAS BEATER briefs have nozzle sewn into back, with padded comfort strip inside.

Muffler deadens sound and filters odors. Purified air escapes through exhaust hose.

Creature has huge eyes that can see in the

BAT BOY FOUND

FIRST PHOTO!

CAVE two miles underground where explorers captured the amazing child.

dark and big ears that work like radar!

IN WEST VIRGINIA CAVE!

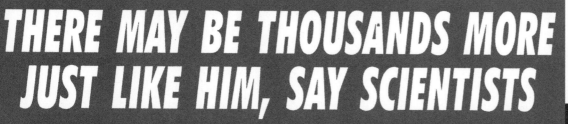

BIZARRE bat boy, left, stands 2 feet tall and weighs a mere 19 pounds! Scientists estimate the creature to be 3 to 4 years of age.

By BILL CREIGHTON
Special correspondent

Scientists claim to have found an astonishing "bat boy" in a West Virginia cave. The strange creature has enormous amber eyes that enable him to see in the dark and oversized ears that work like radar!

Even stranger, Dr. Ron Dillon says the boy communicates with high-pitched squeaks and squeals and refuses to eat anything but flying insects that he catches himself.

"I hardly know what to make of it," said the zoologist. "The boy appears to be human but he is unlike any other human I've ever seen. His eyes are twice as big as they should be and his ears are like satellite dishes. This boy clearly belongs to a race of people who live miles beneath the Earth's surface. And it is my guess that they evolved bat-like features and abilities to enable them to survive in total darkness.

"There's no telling how many of these creatures are down there," he added. "This particular boy was all alone but he almost certainly strayed from a much larger tribe or pack."

Dillon and seven colleagues found the so-called bat boy during a study of subterranean life in a previously uncharted cave east of Seneca Rocks in the Shenandoah Mountains.

The scientist said that he and his team were approximately two miles underground when they heard the 2-foot, 19-pound creature squealing frantically in an apparent plea for help.

"We turned our lights in the direction of the cries and found the boy with his bare foot wedged in the crack between two rocks," said the expert. "To tell you the truth, I thought I was seeing things.

"The last thing I expected to find at that great depth was another human being, much less one that looks like he came from outer space." Dillon said he freed the boy's foot and lifted him up for a closer look.

The child appeared to be stunned at first — then lashed out like an animal caught in a trap.

"I couldn't believe how strong he was," continued the expert. "He scratched and clawed and fought like crazy. We finally subdued him with a tranquilizer injection.

"Then we brought him to the surface and took him to a private hospital for testing and observation. Since that time we have learned a great deal about him.

"But we still have more questions than answers."

Dillon said the bat boy appears to be 3 or 4 years old and has adapted to life in captivity quicker than expected. Feeding was a problem at first. But the boy has been eating well and has actually gained weight since scientists stopped giving him human foods — and began to flood his room with bugs.

Dr. Ron Dillon

"We get them from laboratories involved in insect research and release them into his room by the millions," said Dillon. "Like a bat, the boy cannot tolerate bright light.

"But he still manages to consume his own weight in bugs every single day by locating their position with his radar-like ears and catching them with his mouth and hands.

"Needless to say, he is extremely active. When it's time to feed he moves like lightning. It's the most astonishing thing I've ever seen."

Dillon refused to pinpoint the location of the cave where the boy was found or say where the child is being held. He did say that he is planning a second expedition in the hope of proving that the boy belongs to a subterranean civilization that exists miles beneath our feet.

"This strange little boy might very well lead us to a world within a world," said the expert. "No matter what happens, he's going to change the way we think about mankind and evolution forever."

THERE MAY BE THOUSANDS MORE JUST LIKE HIM, SAY SCIENTISTS

2 ATE MY TRUCK!

Tasty Tales of the Paranormal

An eerie creaking in your attic, an icy breeze on the back of your neck, an oozing green blob descending from the sky and swallowing your truck whole—we've all experienced one, if not all, of these unexplainable incidents. But you'd be hard-pressed to find coverage of mysterious events such as these in the major news sources.

"I called all the local newspapers and TV stations right after that thing swallowed my Chevy," says John Muddleton, farmer and alien blob vehicular ingestion victim, "and they

all treated me like some kind of kook! Then I called those big papers in Washington, D.C., and New York City, and couldn't even get a real person on the phone!"

In distress, and with no mode of transportation, Muddleton thought only of warning others. Finally, hope appeared: "My buddies down at the Grange said the *Weekly World News* is the only paper that really matters anymore," Muddleton says, "and once I called them, I could see why."

After receiving Muddleton's call, reporters from *WWN*'s paranormal bureau sprang into action, dispatching a team of crack reporters and two of their top blob researchers.

Although Muddleton's truck was never recovered, his harrowing story appeared in the paper the following week, along with many other reports that gave voices to the victims of the paranormal: men whose chest hair began to grow in crop circle–like patterns, people who have had close encounters with ghosts (famous or otherwise), and those who have mysteriously vanished in portable toilets, just to name a few.

Without *WWN* to listen, the world would have missed out on some of the most hair-raising—and often heartwarming—tales of the supernatural ever told.

"Many people assume ghosts and other super-natural creatures are frightening, or at best, annoying," says *WWN*'s chief paranormal investigator, Elizabeth Lee. "But oftentimes, ghosts bring important warnings and save lives. They can even be quite entertaining, as in the infamous case of the dead rock stars who tour the world in a private jet, giving smash performances wherever they go."

In addition to being the only paper with the expertise to verify stories of the paranormal, *Weekly World News* is also the only paper brave enough to print them. So when you're looking for someone to quell your fears and explain the unexplainable, there's only one weekly news source to turn to.

"Remember," says Lee, "just because your child's stuffed animal is talking to you or a ghost is haunting your medicine cabinet, doesn't necessarily mean that something bad is happening. Stay calm, and assess the situation."

When asked if she had any more advice to offer, Lee added: "Whatever you do, stay away from moon rays. And if all else fails, call *Weekly World News*."

PHONE PSYCHIC'S

...after she answers EVERY question

A TOP telephone psychic got so furious and frustrated when she was unable to correctly identify a caller's problems that her head literally exploded!

Madame Mona, the most respected and beloved phone psychic in France, was reported dead at the scene — her head blown to smithereens "like a smashed pumpkin," in the words of a horrified EMT.

By MICHAEL FORSYTH
Weekly World News

The macabre April 17 tragedy was witnessed by more than 150,000 viewers of Madame Mona's late-night cable TV show, *Psychic Help Hour*.

"Every time the caller told Madame Mona she was wrong, she became more overwrought and got redder in the face," says shaken cameraman Louis DeMausant, of RVT Communications, who caught the bizarre mishap on tape.

"She kept furrowing her brow and you could tell she was trying to concentrate harder and harder. Her forehead started to expand in a very alarming manner.

"As her anger and frustration built, her skin went from pink, to red, to finally, a frightening purple shade. Then, her whole head simply exploded!

"It looked like someone had jammed a stick of dynamite into a jack-o'-lantern and then detonated it."

Paris police officers, who responded to a production assistant's frantic emergency call, say bits of "brain tissue, blood and bone fragments" littered the studio, splattered across Madame Mona's phone console and the glass window that separated her booth from the live audience.

Shockingly, investigators say, it appears that the caller, identified as 24-year-old Gabrielle Lacarre, deliberately foiled the psychic — for example,

Cops believe caller may have done it on purpose

refusing to acknowledge her age and name after Madame Mona guessed them correctly.

"We're going over transcripts of the call with a fine-tooth comb and comparing the statements Miss Lacarre made to facts our investigators uncover," says Chief Inspector Maurice Renoit. "If it turns out the caller was callously 'playing with Madame Mona's head,' criminal charges could follow. We're treating this as a homicide investigation."

Although the results of an autopsy have not yet been released, ESP experts say it looks like Madame Mona's gifted mind was taxed beyond the breaking point.

"Studies have shown that the use of psychic energy takes a tremendous physical toll," explains Dr. Marie Penot, an assistant professor of paranormal studies at the University of Lyons.

"We know that blood rushes to the brain to meet its vastly increased oxygen requirements and blood vessels can swell enormously. It's not unusual for psychics to experience excruciating headaches as their heads fill with blood like water balloons — but this is the first actual explosion I'm aware of."

The tragic death comes as a blow to fans across France, where 43-year-old

GOING... GOING...

Madame Mona, whose real name was Chantelle Mauvier, was hailed as the country's greatest living psychic.

A millionairess several times over, she was often referred to in newspapers as the "Miss Cleo of France," a reference to the popular American phone psychic.

"Madame prided herself on her accuracy — in the more than 55,000 calls she'd taken in the past four years, I can't think of a single case where she wasn't right on the money," reveals her longtime assistant Danielle Pascal.

Madame Mona's almost fanatically intense devotion to her work may have set the stage for her untimely demise, insiders believe.

"The volume of calls could be overwhelming — sometime Madame Mona was fielding up to 150 calls a day," Ms. Pascal recalls.

"She would complain of splitting headaches and last year, her blood pressure spiked up so high a doctor had to put her on pills.

"I'd tell her, 'Madame Mona, maybe you should take it easier.' But she wouldn't hear of it. She was extremely dedicated and knew callers depended on her.

Actual transcript of Madame Mona's final moments

Below are excerpts from a transcript of Madame Mona's final call:

MONA: Hello caller, how can I help you tonight?

CALLER: I'm so glad I reached you, Madame Mona. I really need you.

MONA: I sense that you're having trouble with your husband.

CALLER: (laughs) Oh no, I'm not married.

MONA: Perhaps it's your boyfriend, then. I'm definitely sensing a man is involved.

CALLER: It don't see how that could

be possible. I'm a lesbian.

MONA: Ah, that must be it. You're having problems with your relationship.

CALLER: No, no, my relationship is fine.

MONA: Strange...It's your job then. You work in a big office building.

CALLER: No. Sorry, no.

MONA: Near a big office building?

CALLER: No.

MONA: Funny, I keep seeing an office of some kind.

CALLER: I work in a restaurant.

MONA: A Chinese restaurant?

CALLER: Nope.

MONA: Vietnamese?

CALLER: Guess again.

MONA: Let me concentrate a moment... I see you're a young woman, about 24.

CALLER: I'm 52.

MONA: Fair hair, slim build...

CALLER: I'm a brunette and I weigh 380 pounds.

MONA: Your n...n...name, it...it... starts with a G...Gabrielle?

CALLER: Not even close.

(Sound of head exploding. Screams and panic.)

HEAD EXPLODES

caller's wrong!

GONE!

KABLAM! Famed psychic Madame Mona's final moments were captured on tape as she grew more frustrated with every wrong answer she gave.

"She helped estranged wives reconcile with their husbands, employees save their careers — she truly was a living saint, with a unique gift from God."

But shortly before 11 p.m. on that fateful night, Madame Mona met her match. "Every time Madame said something, the caller contradicted her," Miss Pascal says. "And there was a tone in the young woman's voice that suggested that maybe she was mocking Madame.

"It kept going on and on — I could tell Madame was being pushed to the brink.

"After about 5 minutes, I put my finger across my throat, signaling to Madame to disconnect the caller. But she kept valiantly trying to help the woman.

"Finally, she announced the caller's name was Gabrielle and flashed a smile she always gave when she knew she was right. But the caller said no, wrong

again. That's when Madame's head exploded."

Police are looking into allegations that the deadly caller is a close relative of a Mother Lola, a rival phone psychic who has long languished in the shadow of the more esteemed Madame Mona.

"That would be an ample motive for murder," Chief Inspector Renoit points out.

Over the years, Madame Mona also helped police solve dozens of serious

crimes. "If she's been the victim of foul play, her death shall not go unpunished," he vowed.

Caller from Hell Gabrielle Lacarre refused to comment on the investigation, but her attorney said cops would be "foolish" to try to pin a murder rap on her.

"At the very most," lawyer Paul Vallinois told reporters, "this was a childish prank that just went too far."

AMELIA EARHART'S ON PACIFIC

HERO pilot Amelia Earhart before fate stripped her of her place in the record books, as well as her flesh.

PLANE LANDS ISLAND ...with a SKELETON at the controls!

By **NICK MANN**
Weekly World News

INVESTIGATORS GET A PEP TALK at the landing site. After further testing, only one solid conclusion can be drawn . . . the skeletal remains of missing aviatrix, Amelia Earhart, are in fact in the pilot's seat.

AMELIA EARHART'S missing airplane landed just days ago with her fully-clothed skeleton at the controls, shedding new light on the 65-year mystery of her disappearance but opening what head-scratching federal investigators are now calling "a new can of worms."

Did America's most famous aviatrix fly through a time warp or enter a parallel dimension when she vanished without a trace just miles from tiny Howland Island in the mid Pacific on July 2, 1937?

If not, where has she been, when and how did she die — and as the Federal Aviation Administration is now asking a blue-ribbon commission of aviation experts, physicists, paranormal researchers and at least two psychics, how did her lifeless remains negotiate a bumpy but ultimately successful landing on the crumbling airstrip that was built for her scheduled stop on Howland at the height of the Great Depression?

"Explain it? How the hell do you expect me to explain it?" an FAA source told trusted reporters in Washington.

"The airplane is Amelia Earhart's and it landed on May 21, 2002, that much we know. The skeleton is Amelia's, we're virtually certain of that, too, based on DNA testing.

"Aside from that, we're in the dark — and the speculation is getting wilder by the minute. I've heard everything from 'space aliens abducted Amelia and her plane' to 'she flew into some kind of time warp or parallel dimension, lived out her life in another time or place, and now she's flown back again.'

"At this point, any theory is as valid as any other. Your guesses are as good as mine. One thing's for sure — the powers-that-be are going to keep a shroud of secrecy over this thing until they've got some answers.

"The last thing anybody wants to do is cause fear and loathing over a story that reads like something out of the *Twilight Zone*."

Tight-lipped FAA officials would neither confirm nor deny that Earhart's one-of-a-kind Lockheed Electra Model 10E Special airplane landed just days ago on Howland Island, which was her original destination in 1937 and is now a U.S. territory and National Wildlife Refuge that is administered by the Department of the Interior.

But as the source points out, no fewer than 25 rock-solid eyewitnesses — many of them American scientists on the island to conduct a geological survey — are reported to have watched the aging airplane land with Earhart's skeleton perched eerily in the cockpit.

"As God is my witness, I saw the plane land and I still can't believe it," an eyewitness is quoted as saying in official interview transcripts now being analyzed at FAA headquarters in Washington.

"There wasn't a cloud in the sky. The plane appeared out of nowhere and — boom! — just like that it angled straight in for a landing on what's left of the old airstrip that was built for her flight back in the 1930s.

"There wasn't even time to lower the landing gear. By the time the plane skidded to a stop, everyone was running to get over there and find out what the heck was going on.

"Somebody started shouting, 'Amelia Earhart! It's Amelia Earhart!' Then whoever got there first jumped up on the wing and looked into the cockpit. He started screaming, 'Oh s—! Oh s—! There's a skeleton flying this thing!'

"Nobody was about to open the cockpit or touch anything, and within an hour the place was crawling with military personnel. Needless to say, they ran us the hell out of there."

The airplane and skeleton were quickly removed to a undisclosed locations for further analysis, says the source, noting that the FAA is continuing to query eyewitnesses and comb both the island and surrounding waters for clues.

Meanwhile, in Washington, a remarkable array of aviation experts, physicists, paranormal researchers and psychics are considering what the insider calls "every possible angle, including the supernatural."

Earhart's disappearance has remained one of the world's most enduring mysteries since she vanished without a trace while attempting to become the first woman in history to fly around the world.

On June 1, 1937, Earhart, 40, departed from Miami and began what she hoped would be an uneventful 29,000-mile journey as she circled the globe.

By the time she landed in Lae, New Guinea on June 29, she had traveled 22,000 miles — and had just 7,000 left to go.

Her next stop was Howland Island, located 2,556 miles from Lae in the Mid Pacific. On July 2, she took off. And after a few routine radio transmissions with her contact ship, the Coast Guard cutter Itasca, she was never heard from again.

"The recovery of Earhart's body and airplane solves part of the mystery," observes the source, "but let's face it — the really big questions remain.

"What's happened here is not only going to test the limits of human comprehension, it's going to stretch the definition of reality as we know it.

"Any way you shake it, the world we're living in became a little less certain and a little less stable when that airplane landed at Howland."

CROP CIRCLES APPEAR IN MEN'S CHEST HAIR

By MARK TOMPKINS

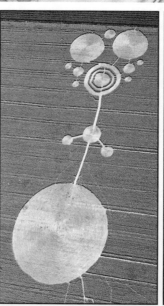

IN A BIZARRE twist on crop circles, paranormal researchers around the globe have a new phenomenon to report: chest hair circles!

"This is the most mystifying case I've ever come across," says Dr. Charles Dexter Ward, who is coordinating an international effort to study the phenomenon. "Aliens could be the culprit, but then again so could ghosts, angels, demons, or even some previously unknown species of insect. Right now, we just don't have a definitive explanation."

Twenty-five year old Ronnie Malone, a bus driver from New Jersey, was one of the first people to be affected. "One evening, I was hanging out at the Big Booby Lounge when I felt this funny tingling in my chest. I didn't think much of it, because I was too busy getting plastered.

"But later, when I went to the bathroom to change into my bus driver uniform, I got a real shock. It looked like somebody had shaved a bunch of demonic-looking black magic symbols in my chest hair. I was so freaked out I called my priest, only to find out he'd just been arrested for soliciting a prostitute."

Even more intriguing is the case of Mick O'Shaughnessy, a computer programmer living in Cork, Ireland. "About a month ago, I was checking my chest hair for fleas when a string of tiny white lights seemed to pop right out of my belly button," he told investigators. "For about ten seconds, the lights were zipping all over my chest and stomach. Then they disappeared. Ever since, I've been walking around with these gay-looking designs in my chest hair. I'm pretty pissed off about it."

Fortunately, there appears to be no danger associated with chest hair circles. "Of the four hundred or so cases we've studied, nobody has suffered any burns or abrasions," states Dr. Holly Snodgrass, a well-known authority on the paranormal.

"There is, however, a very slight residue of radiation in the affected area, which is one way we can tell if a case is bona fide or a hoax. Also, the hair that's removed to make the pattern doesn't seem to grow back. In other words, chest hair circles are permanent."

Though the term 'circles' is used for convenience, the mysterious designs actually come in a myriad of shapes and sizes.

"We've seen everything from elaborate geometrical patterns to recognizable objects such as fish, flowers, and even dollar signs," says Dr. Snodgrass. "The real question is, are these encoded messages of cosmic importance, or is some otherworldly joker just having a laugh at our expense?

"All we know for sure is, if you're a guy with a hairy chest, you may be in for a big surprise next time you take your shirt off."

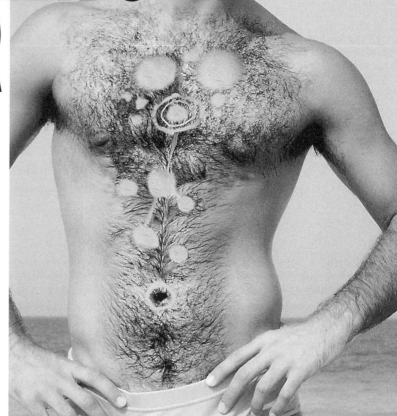

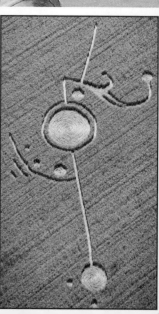

CROP CIRCLES similar to those appearing on men's chests around the world were first reported in a wheat field in Rockville, Calif., left, and in a wheat field in Hubbard, Ore., in 1998, right.

ALIEN BLOB ATE MY TRUCK!

JOSH MUDDLETON shows where he last saw his truck.

'It came out of nowhere and gobbled up my Chevy,' says farmer

By ALAN JONES
Weekly World News

LOS ANGELES — Baffled cops say they're mystified, and a team of investigators from the Pentagon are refusing comment, on the bizarre disappearance of farmer Josh Muddleton's 1975 pickup truck — which the solid, churchgoing grandfather says was literally eaten by a shapeless blob he believes may have come from outer space.

"It was early morning and I was on my way down to the henhouse when I saw this huge green lump of something land out of nowhere a few feet away from where I had parked my pickup truck," Muddleton declares.

"It was wiggling and jiggling and bouncing back and forth like something you'd see on a kiddie cartoon.

"I just stood there in total shock trying to make out what it could be. I've never believed in UFOs but what else could it have been?"

Muddleton says the eerie blob looked like it was at least three times the size of his 21-foot Chevy — and appeared to "swallow" the truck and his payload of chicken mash.

"It started at the front end first, making these slurping sounds and clean swallowed up the whole vehicle. I could still see my truck plain as day right through the blob, like you'd see fruit in a dish of Jell-O," the still shaken farmer told reporters.

"I started yelling at it to get off my truck, but before the words got out of my mouth, it gave two more huge jiggles and slowly rose right up and vanished into the clouds," he adds.

Sheriff's deputies, summoned to investigate, say they doubted the old man's story until they found several globs of a strange gelatin-like green substance on the ground where Muddleton claimed his truck had been.

"It was like nothing I'd ever seen," said one deputy. "We called in the military boys and they scooped the stuff up and said they were sending it off to Washington, but that's the last we've heard from them.

"We checked up on Mr. Muddleton with some of his neighbors and folks in his church and they say he's rock solid, honest, and has a heart of gold.

"He lost his wife of 50 years about six months ago and he's had his share of sorrow, but he's sharp as a tack and looked us straight in the eyes when he told us what happened."

Spokesmen declined comment but acknowledged that investigators are "aware of the alleged incident."

'TWILIGHT ZONE' MYSTERY BAFFLES CHICAGO

FOUR PEOPLE VANISH WITHOUT A TRACE IN PORTABLE TOILET!

MISSING
Gus Korkland

MISSING
Lu Ann Minthoven

MISSING
Ashley Wirthon

MISSING
Justin Cortwillow

By KEVIN CREED / *Weekly World News*

CHICAGO — A stunned and outraged public is demanding to know the whereabouts of four people who went into a portable toilet in a public park — and never came out!

Reports say the potty mysteriously "swallowed up" Gus Korkland, Lu Ann Minthoven, Ashley Wirthon and Justin Cortwillow seemingly at random over the course of the six-day period between April 17 and April 22.

Hundreds of others used the rest room during that period without incident.

Park spokesmen and law enforcement authorities vehemently deny any knowledge about the disappearance of the two men and two women. But friends and family members of the four say officials are covering up.

"I'm not going to let them sweep this thing under the rug," said the husband of Lu Ann Minthoven, the second person to vanish in the small rest room located near the park's tractor shed.

"I don't know what happened to Lu Ann and I don't know why these people are dragging their feet. All I know is, she went into that metal outhouse and never came out.

"And I demand answers."

The wife of victim Gus Korkland, who vanished just days before Lu Ann Minthoven, says: "We were about to leave the park when Gus went in to use the toilet.

"It was one of those one-person portable things that either men or women can use.

"I watched that door the whole time and he never came out. There was no other way out.

"After 10 minutes I started to get concerned. After 15 minutes I knocked on the door and asked if he was okay.

"When I got no response, I called park rangers. They got the guy who works on the toilets to come and check it out.

"There wasn't a trace of him."

Everyone who reported loved ones missing in the portable rest room tell chillingly similar stories.

In every case, they say, park officials were notified and called the company that serviced the rest room.

None of the missing have been found.

Though authorities have issued no official statement, Chicago is crackling with rumors, and pressure is being brought to bear on police and other law enforcement agencies to take the disappearances seriously.

In a bizarre twist, overwrought family members have been threatened with lawsuits if they divulge the name or location of the park.

But officials have assured the public that the reputed people-eating toilet has been removed from the premises.

Still, for Lu Ann's heartbroken husband, the gesture is too little, too late.

"They would rather deny the whole affair than accept responsibility," he said.

"But this thing is not going to go away. We're going to find out what happened to our friends and family members if it's the last thing we do."

Experts in the paranormal are looking into the bizarre disappearances, but thus far have found no explanation.

THEY WENT IN — and never came out. Mysterious people-eating toilet has been removed from the park.

WWN EXTRA

As most faithful readers of *WWN* know, there are many dimensions to this world that can't be seen with the naked eye. Normally, they cannot be reached, but there are instances when plumbing—particularly that of toilets—somehow fuses our two realities together. When that happens, your very own toilet can be transformed from an instrument of relief to one of abject horror. Here, from the experts at *WWN*, are five signs your toilet may be a gateway to the supernatural outback.

WWN EXCLUSIVE
DATELINE: MARCH 8, 2002

FOUNTAIN OF YOUTH FOUND IN N.Y.C. SUBWAY TOILET!

DRINK THE BUBBLING WATER AND BE YOUNG AGAIN!

THE FLUSH OF FEAR: TOILET DISAPPEARANCES

Even regular *WWN* readers may be unaware that toilet disappearances, routinely reported in the pages of this newspaper, may have been a feature of human civilization since even before the advent of indoor plumbing. It is widely known, thanks mainly to the work of the Center for Research of Abnormal Potty Phenomena (CRAPP), that people have been regularly vanishing in recent history. But CRAPP has been collecting data from across

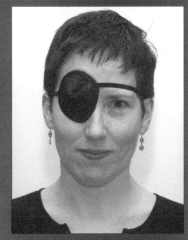

Dr. Alice L. Winterbottom

the U.S. only for roughly the last century, which means a lack of hard statistical information about pre–outhouse-era disappearances. As a result, their research fails to address the considerable anecdotal evidence suggesting that people may have been vanishing *in flagrante delicto* for centuries.

Some researchers speculate that the phenomenon predates recorded history, citing cryptic, scatological pictographs among Magdalenian cave paintings found in Altamira, Spain. This controversial theory is hotly debated among scientists, as the majority of the research suggests that there is a direct link between the device itself and the disappearances. "It seems preposterous to me," according to one researcher who insisted on remaining anonymous, "that Paleolithic peoples were vanishing from ancient forests when they slipped outside their dwellings to take a leak."

Despite the vigilance of CRAPP field teams, who have recently begun attaching GPS trackers to likely victims, the ultimate destinations of the disappeared is a mystery and seems likely to remain so for some time. But even more disturbing than this lack of crucial information, according to Dr. Alice L. Winterbottom, Director of Field Research at CRAPP, is the fact that toilet disappearances have been steadily on the rise (except for dips during the Great Depression and World Wars I and II) since such data have been collected.

"The population has been growing over the same period, which accounts for the increase in the number of disappearances," states Dr. Winterbottom, "but the percentage of vanished, relative to the population as a whole, has also been growing." Perhaps the most alarming trend that has emerged recently, according to recent CRAPP field studies, is the steady increase in the number of toddlers mysteriously disappearing into their potty training toilets—in many cases, in the presence of adult supervision.

Included below is a bar graph that shows the number of people who have vanished in the five major categories studied by CRAPP: outhouse vanishings; home disappearances; disappearances into Porto-Potties, Porta-Johns or other portable facilities; public urinals; and the more recent potty-training toilet vanishings that have cut such a swath through the U.S. toddler population.

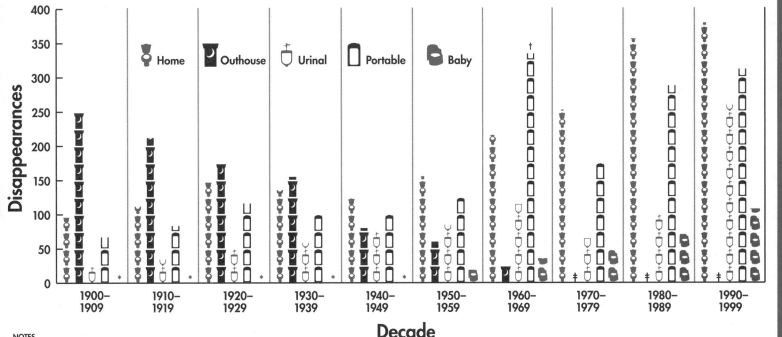

Disappearances of Persons Through Toilet Facilities (U.S.)

Y-axis: **Disappearances** (0, 50, 100, 150, 200, 250, 300, 350, 400)

Legend: Home · Outhouse · Urinal · Portable · Baby

X-axis: **Decade** (1900–1909, 1910–1919, 1920–1929, 1930–1939, 1940–1949, 1950–1959, 1960–1969, 1970–1979, 1980–1989, 1990–1999)

NOTES
*data not collected; unavailable
†data affected by disappearance of 163 persons in portable toilets at 1969 Woodstock Music Festival
‡data not collected; unavailable since 1968 House budget reduction in U.S. National Park Ranger staffing levels

SIGNS YOUR TOILET IS A GATEWAY TO ANOTHER DIMENSION

1. Your toilet bowl seems to get dirty unusually fast. You clean and disinfect, but before you know it, there's a nasty ring inside again. This grime may be coming from an extra-dimensional source.

2. When you flush, the water goes down clockwise. This is unnatural, and indicates the influence of malign entities.

3. When sitting on your toilet, you occasionally feel a gentle breeze on your bottom. Other dimensions send reconnaissance "soldiers" into the pipes to search for innocent prey. When they sense movement, they gently glide out of the water to check it out and naturally take a few breaths. That's what you feel.

4. After a bout of stomach ailments or diarrhea, you suffer from a sudden onset of sadness or depression. This may be the result of spending an inordinate amount of time near a spirtually infested toilet bowl. You may be the victim of happiness-robbing vibrations coming from other dimensions.

5. You flush and leave the bathroom, only to return awhile later and notice the toilet is still running. This is the worst sign of all. It's a signal that the evil spirits have broken through the complex space-time continuum and entered into the earthly dimension. Bar the bathroom door immediately and leave the house.

GHOST AIRLINER BRINGS

CHRISTCHURCH, New Zealand — The ghost of tragic songbird Aaliyah has been spotted aboard a phantom plane whose passengers are all rock stars who died in air wrecks!

By VICKIE YORK
Weekly World News

The legendary Flight 901, which has been seen around the world since 1959, touched down on an isolated New Zealand airfield — where the ghostly passengers disembarked and put on an impromptu concert, eyewitnesses claim.

As scores of airport workers and air travelers raised lighters and gawked in disbelief, long-deceased singers Buddy Holly, Big Bopper, Patsy Cline, Jim Croce, Ritchie Valens, Ronnie Van Zant and more recently deceased Stevie Ray Vaughn emerged from the mysterious DC-10 and knocked 'em dead with mind-blowing renditions of Lynyrd Skynyrd's FM classic, "Free Bird" and Holly's "That'll be the Day."

And this time, witnesses say, the heavenly performers included beautiful R&B singer Aaliyah, who perished in a plane crash in the Bahamas days earlier on August 25.

"There's no doubt in my mind, the sexy young woman belting out 'Free Bird' was Aaliyah," says banker George Natherson, who was awaiting a flight when the eerie 90-minute concert began at 10:20 p.m. "I'd seen her on TV and I recognized her voice.

"When the crowd saw her, there were applause and tears. I guess it made people feel good to know that now she's up there with all those other greats."

The legend of Flight 901 has been part of rock 'n' roll lore since February 1959 when a plane carrying rock pioneers Buddy Holly, J.P. Richardson, better known as "Big Bopper," and Ritchie Valens of "La Bamba" fame crashed in Iowa, killing all aboard.

Just a few months later in June, an unscheduled Flight 901 landed in an airfield near Tuscon, Ariz., and, witnesses say, the rockers' ghosts staged an hour-long concert.

Since then, the phantom plane has made landings at small airports all over the world from Guadalajara, Mexico, to Aberdeen, Scotland. And the roster of performers has grown to include other music greats who've met their ends in fiery air wrecks, including Patsy Cline, Jim Croce, Ronnie Van Zant and Stevie Ray Vaughan.

"At least twice a year, Flight 901 lands somewhere in the world. It's the ultimate tour that never ends," says paranormal investigator Sherrie Monmouth, of Australia. "These are performers who loved their art — and that love was strong enough to survive death."

When Flight 901 neared the tiny Christchurch airport, the ground crew was bewildered.

"There was no Flight 901 scheduled, but when the pilot said it was an emergency, we gave them clearance to land," recalls air traffic controller Peter Hamersford.

"When the doors opened, all these old-time rockers came off, waving and grinning. One nerdy guy with glasses and a guitar I immediately recognized as Buddy Holly."

About 60 befuddled people crowded onto the tarmac to watch the one-of-a-kind show.

"Big Bopper did 'Chantilly Lace' and Pasty Cline did 'Crazy,' " Hamersford says.

They brought the house down — but the night belonged to Aaliyah, witnesses agree.

"She sang her heart out," says Natherson. "The crowd gave her a standing ovation."

Around midnight, the unearthly singers boarded the craft and vanished into the night.

STEVIE RAY VAUGHAN — R&B guitarist, greatest hit, "Crossfire."

AALIYAH — R&B singer, greatest hit, "Back and Forth."

JIM CROCE — singer-songwriter, greatest hit, "Bad, Bad Leroy Brown."

BIG BOPPER — singer-songwriter, greatest hit, "Chantilly Lace."

BACK DEAD ROCK STARS

...they give an encore performance & then vanish into the night!

BUDDY HOLLY — singer-guitarist, greatest hit, "That'll be the Day."

RITCHIE VALENS — singer-guitarist, greatest hit, "La Bamba."

PATSY CLINE — singer-piano player, greatest hit, "Crazy."

RONNIE VAN ZANT — lead singer for Lynyrd Skynyrd, greatest it, "Free Bird."

They ALL died in plane crashes!

Buddy Holly: A Beechcraft Bonanza carrying Holly and fellow musicians J.P. "Big Bopper" Richardson, and Ritchie Valens crashed near Mason City, Iowa, on Feb. 3, 1959. Years later, the crash was immortalized in song as "American Pie" by Don McLean.

Patsy Cline: Country songbird whose best known song is "Crazy" died in a plane crash near Camden, Tenn., at the age of 31. Two other Grand Ole Opry stars were also killed in the crash of the Piper Commanche plane.

Jim Croce: Singer-songwriter topped the charts with such hits as "Time in a Bottle" and "Bad, Bad Leroy Brown." His Beechcraft E18S plane went down in Natchitoches, La., in 1973.

Ritchie Valens: Mexican singer was best known for his hits, "La Bamba," "Come On Let's Go" and "Donna," which was written for his girlfriend. Valens, who was born Richie Valenzuela, was the hottest star of the three at the time.

Ronnie Van Zant: Lead singer of Lynyrd Skynyrd died in an airplane crash that also claimed the life of Skynyrd guitarist Stevie Gaines in October 1977. The Southern good ol' boys met their maker when their Convair 240 took a nose-dive in McComb, Miss.

Stevie Ray Vaughan: Revered blues guitarist was killed when his helicopter plummeted into a hill following a 1990 concert in East Troy, Wis. Four others, including three members of Eric Clapton's band, also perished in the crash.

Aaliyah Haughton: Sultry, young R&B singer's career was tragically cut short in August when her twin-engine Cessna went down in the Bahamas. She just finished shooting a music video to promote her new album.

Big Bopper: J.P. Richardson was best known for the rowdy "Hello, baby!" that opened his hit song "Chantilly Lace." Country singer Waylon Jennings was supposed to have been on that doomed flight, but he gave up his seat to Big Bopper!

Ventriloquist is in a coma
— but his dummy still talks!

NO DUMMY! Ernest Fleener became a ventriloquist so he could be just like his American hero Edgar Bergen, shown here.

And here's what he's telling doctors and nurses:

- 'Is that a thermometer in your pocket or are you just happy to see me?'
- 'Somebody put ER on TV — I wanna see some real pros in action!'
- 'Hey, girlie, carve your phone number into my arm!'
- 'I'm pining for ya, sweetie!'
- 'Wooden you like to spend some time with me?'

By JERRY RINGWALD/
Weekly World News

BONN, Germany — A coma patient has been communicating with the outside world with the help of his closest companion — a 2 1/2-foot wooden dummy.

Part-time ventriloquist Ernest Fleener, 42, has been in a coma from a near-fatal car wreck for nearly a month. Under normal circumstances, medical procedures on such patients are limited to cardiopulmonary mon-itoring.

But so far, there is nothing "normal" about Fleener's treatment. That's because the staff doctors have been getting their marching orders from "Winkee," the ventriloquist's dummy.

On a typical day, Winkee can be heard mouthing off to the hospital staff and visitors, with barbs, such as: "Touch me one more time . . . and I'll give ya a good shellackin," and "Watch it, Buster! You're goin' against my grain!"

The first witness to this amazing phenomenon was nurse Edith Poppins. Two days after Fleener's admittance, the 22-year-old nurse heard a muffled voice coming from the patient's suitcase. When she opened the case, her jaw dropped in shock. "I couldn't believe it," she said, "the little tyke told me to give him a sponge bath!"

Poppins also stated that Winkee used the following come-on phrases:
- "Hey, baby, you're a lot cuter than the puppets I hang around with!"
- "Hey, girlie, carve your phone number into my arm!"
- "I'm pining for ya, sweetie!"
- "Wooden you like to spend some time with me?"
- "Some folks call me a doll — but I say you're a living doll!"

Believing that she was receiving a message from the Great Beyond, the nurse complied with a furniture polish "sponge bath" that had Winkee demanding that she "rub out all my knots." Poppins wasn't the only brunt of Winkee's witticisms. Doctors and other hospital workers weren't immune to quips like:
- "Is that a thermometer in your pocket or are you just happy to see me?"
- "Somebody put *ER* on TV — I wanna see some real pros in action."

Theories abound as to what caused this highly unusual metaphysical occurrence. On the night of Fleener's car accident, there was an extremely unstable ion storm passing over northern England.

The powerfully charged ionic particles could have caused an event that certain scientists refer to as the "Pinocchio Syndrome," named for particular effects these ions have on wood.

Or perhaps Fleener is telepathically sending his own splintered thoughts through his knot-headed pal to communicate to the outside world.

"We're baffled, but we're also a bit weary of it all," admitted one doctor. "If that block-headed bloke doesn't pipe down soon, he's going to be nothing but saw dust!"

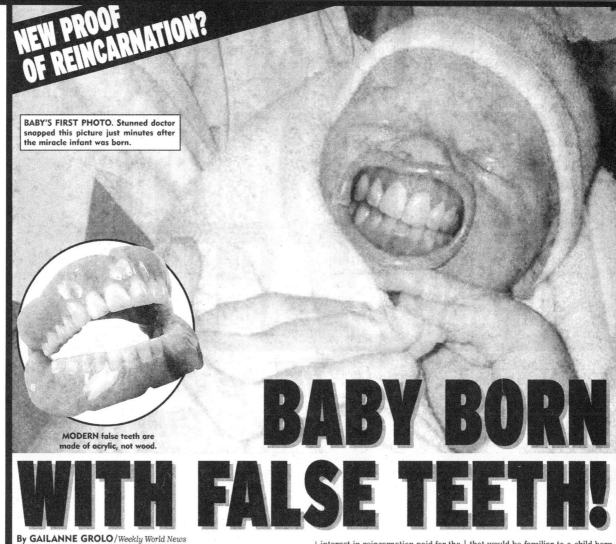

NEW PROOF OF REINCARNATION?

BABY'S FIRST PHOTO. Stunned doctor snapped this picture just minutes after the miracle infant was born.

MODERN false teeth are made of acrylic, not wood.

BABY BORN WITH FALSE TEETH!

By GAILANNE GROLO//*Weekly World News*

BATON ROUGE, La. — An amazing baby has been born here with a full set of false teeth — and excited parapsychologists are hailing the startling event as "proof positive" of reincarnation.

Incredibly, leading denturists who inspected the crudely constructed, ill-fitting choppers report that they're at least 75 years old — indicating that the infant lived before as an oldster in the 1920s.

"This is the kind of incontrovertible proof that reincarnation researchers dream of," Dr. Pierre Lafayette, a leading French parapsychologist, declared as he presented the case at a conference of psychic investigators.

"It's concrete physical evidence that brings reincarnation out of the realm of mysticism and into the field of solid science, where it belongs."

Dr. Lafayette said the denture experts confirmed that the roughly fashioned wood and enamel teeth — uppers and lowers connected by rough hinges — were made during the Roaring '20s.

"Wear marks show they were used before, by an adult who was capable of biting and chewing firm food," according to the paranormal researcher.

The miracle reincarnation baby, now a healthy 2-month-old, is a girl, but Dr. Lafayette declined to release her name to protect the family's privacy.

However, he did reveal that a wealthy philanthropist with a longtime interest in reincarnation paid for the entire family to be relocated near a university with a strong parapsychology department.

"With the family's permission, we're planning to conduct a series of experiments to test the baby's reaction to toys, clothing and other objects that would be familiar to a child born in the mid or late 19th century — as the adult who originally wore those teeth would have been," he said.

Dr. Lafayette added that he and his colleagues eagerly hope to ask the girl questions about her previous life when she is old enough to talk.

Man drowns in cat's water dish

WELLINGTON, New Zealand — A 28-year-old construction worker perished in one of the most spectacularly embarrassing ways imaginable — he slipped on an ice cube and drowned in his cat's water bowl!

"It was a most unusual scenario, indeed," police Detective Paul Simerson told newsmen. "I've been a policeman for 37 years and I've never encountered anything quite like it."

According to cops, Mary Robinson found her 28-year-old son Peter facedown in the cat's water bowl after returning home from shopping on a Saturday afternoon.

Investigators said it was evident the young man had been rendered unconscious after he slipped on an ice cube and landed facedown in the cat's large, stainless steel water dish.

WWN EXTRA

TYPICAL REINCARNATION CYCLE

HUMAN → KANGAROO → LA-Z-BOY → DUNG BEETLE → SPACE DUST → **REPEAT**

RICHARD NIXON'S IS HAUNTING

PRESIDENT Richard M. Nixon.

President Clinton terrified by bizarre

WASHINGTON — President Clinton is being harassed, hounded and kept awake nights — by the ghost of former President Richard M. Nixon!

That's the claim of more than a dozen White House insiders who all report seeing the apparition roaming the halls of the executive mansion, making the President's life miserable.

"Bill Clinton is a tortured man," says a member of the President's housekeeping staff.

If the reports are true, Nixon

By ANN VICTORIA
Weekly World News

has joined Abraham Lincoln to become the second President to return from the dead and haunt the Presidential residence. Eight Presidents have reported seeing Lincoln's spirit in the White House since 1865. But judging from statements by

eyewitnesses, Nixon's ghost is angry — unlike the calm and benevolent Lincoln.

"Bill and Hillary are in a constant state of nervous agitation," revealed the housekeeper.

One frustrated Secret Service agent says Clinton has given the matter "top priority" but they're powerless to stop the ghost. The agent says that by night, the disgraced Watergate figure

LINCOLN'S ghost also visits the White House.

will suddenly appear i the Presidential suit and rattle the bed, ja ring President an Mrs. Clinton from sound sleep.

"Even by day, th ghost will often lurk i the hallways by th east terrace and sud denly startle Mr. Clir ton," said the Secre Service man.

"Most of us hav witnessed the ghost. And thos few who haven't actually seen have heard an eerie voice wai

HILLARY CLINTON: Nixon's ghost has

GHOST THE WHITE HOUSE!

HE'S BACK! President Richard Nixon's ghost is shown in this computerized conception as he appeared to several White House insiders.

apparition!

...ng from the Presidential bedroom in the middle of the night."

One maid says the voice, unmistakably that of Nixon, is demanding that Clinton leave the official Presidential residence. "He keeps saying, 'get out of my home,'" she says. "Sometimes he gets mean, throwing valuable antiques and framed photographs across the room."

Noted expert on parapsychological phenomena Dr. Stella Mogure, author of *Hauntings*

Dr. Stella Mogure.

In America, has done a psychic sweep of the White House and confirms that the entire place is bristling with ghostly activity. "Richard Nixon was a very strong-willed man," said Dr. Mogure. "All his life he resented being forced out of office by scandal and felt he should have remained President. Nixon has come back from the dead to claim the home he feels is rightfully his."

WWN EXTRA

THE LIFE OF A DEAD PRESIDENT

The ghosts of Ronald Reagan and Richard Nixon may be getting most of the ink, but they aren't the only kaput presidents still poking around on Planet Earth.

☛ Depression-era Prez **Herbert Hoover** has been hanging out in various public housing developments in the South Bronx, annoying youngsters with his raps denouncing government-funded public works, such as "F*ck the New Dealio." Says 15-year-old Rakeem Davis of the Bronx River Houses, who had never heard of the former president, "Ain't nothin' fresh about this foo', yo."

☛ More than 200 wide-eyed witnesses have reported seeing former president and famous dead guy **John F. Kennedy** taking in the sights backstage at the bawdy Folies Bergere in Las Vegas. "It was JFK for sure," said one Folies femme fatale, "I mean, he's got, like, the most famous face in history. After Jesus, of course."

☛ Twelfth president **Zachary Taylor** has been skulking around the studios of Comedy Central's *The Daily Show* on West 54th Street in New York City. "Old Rough and Ready," dressed in full military regalia, has allegedly been begging for a spot on the show, saying he wants to prove once and for all that Whigs have a sense of humor. According to a *Daily Show* source, who spoke on condition of anonymity, "We keep telling him to go try Geraldo, but he won't leave!"

☛ **William Howard Taft** has been spotted in Bloomington, Minn., haunting the Bubba Gump Shrimp Co. restaurant inside national landmark Mall of America. "I've never seen anyone down 'Bubba's Bucket of Boat Trash' that quickly," reports restaurant manager Duane Pell. "He says it reminds him of his days as governor of the Philippines."

☛ And finally, according to local legend, **Gerald "Right Place at the Right Time" Ford** had been known to lurk around an abandoned GM plant in Flint, Mich. "He would strut up and down the aisles like a big man—like he owned the place," said former GM plant worker Jose Esposito. "This went on for months, until the ghost of Henry Ford showed up and kicked his ectoplasmic ass outta here."

'He isn't just rattling around in the attic'

By **DOUGLAS MARON**
Correspondent

REAGAN'S GHOST SAVING LIVES ALL OVER U.S.

RONALD REAGAN died just weeks ago but his kind and benevolent spirit is already back on earth helping people in need.

"He helped me get a job after I was laid off by putting in a good word for me with my new boss," says Justin Calling, 33, of Akron, Ohio.

And according to Washington-based investigative reporter Phillip Kennerling, who's tracking the sightings, the Gipper's ghost also:

● Broke a skydiver's free fall and dropped him gently on the ground after his parachute failed to open.

● Gave a rookie surgeon a "heads up" when the young doctor inadvertently dropped a college ring into a patient's abdomen and started to stitch him up.

● Chased away a rabid raccoon that tried to bite an elderly woman who got lost in a national forest after wandering away from her home.

"Every time I hear one of these stories I just have to shake my head and say, 'Wow,'" says Kennerling, who's already hard at work on a book about the sightings.

"These aren't crackpots we're talking about. These are rock-solid Americans who have absolutely no reason to lie.

"It's almost as if Reagan stored up energy over the 10 years he suffered with Alzheimer's, and now that he's passed over to the other side, he's making up for lost time."

Paranormal researchers agree that Reagan's spirit returned to earth quickly, and, in the words of one, "just might be the hardest-working ghost I've ever investigated.

"It's not just the frequency with which he's being seen, it's also the quality of the sightings," says the expert.

"Reagan's ghost isn't rattling around in an attic or making stairs creak in the middle of the night. He's appearing in broad daylight — and he's changing people's lives."

Three special people whose lives were changed by the spirit of our beloved 40th president

MARLA MONTAG, 26, of Keystone Heights, Fla., told investigator Phillip Kennerling that her 3-year-old toddler Eric fell into the family's new swimming pool while she was applying fingernail polish in an upstairs bedroom.

"I heard Eric screaming for help and when I looked out the window I couldn't see a thing," she explains. "All of a sudden Ronald Reagan splashes up out of the water and he's holding Eric in his arms.

"I'd know that face anywhere. There's no doubt he saved my 3-year-old son from drowning."

PAUL KOSYN, 49, of Richmond, Va., says he fell asleep at the wheel of his 18-wheeler late at night and when he woke up, he was trapped helplessly in the burning wreckage.

"Suddenly somebody ripped the door off the truck and dragged me to safety," he says. "I looked into the man's face and as God is my witness, it was Ronald Reagan — the Gipper himself!

"He said, 'Well . . . I guess you dodged a bullet this time, old buddy.'

"Then he just chuckled and disappeared."

RITA TERAN, 41, of Racine, Wis., says the Gipper's ghost materialized in her mobile home as she wept bitter tears wondering how she was supposed to buy $300 worth of blood-pressure medication with her $79 unemployment check.

"President Reagan put his hand on my shoulder and said, 'Don't cry, Rita. You'll get your medicine.' And he vanished into thin air," she adds.

"And when I looked back down at the table, there were three $100 bills right there in front of me.

"God bless you, Mr. Reagan. Thanks to you, I got my medicine."

Dead hubby's ghost breaks wind & burps

...to keep other men away from his wife!

By SCOTT PETERSON
Weekly World News

DEAD hubby's ghost torments Cynthia Valenzuela in this chilling artist's conception.

ANN ARBOR, Mich. — The demonic ghost of Cynthia Valenzuela's late husband Ned is constantly interfering with her attempts to begin dating again, the 47-year-old widow told reporters.

According to the frustrated widow, the possessive poltergeist has:

● Caused large pimples to erupt on her nose, just minutes prior to a date.

● Made her razors vanish. "With these hairy legs, I haven't got a chance with any guy except maybe someone in Russia," she said.

● Made rude burping and nose-blowing noises and actually broke wind to ward off would-be Romeos.

● Dumped ectoplasm on her new hairdo as a date rings the doorbell.

● Repeatedly rotated her head 360-degrees while a startled suitor attempted fruitlessly to kiss her goodnight.

● Scrawled "Ned's Eternal Bride!" in pig's blood on the walls and front door of her modest suburban home.

"His jealousy was cute when he was alive," Valenzuela sighed, "but now it's just downright annoying. I didn't ask that train to crush him, but it's been three years now and I'm ready to move on before I lose my looks."

The interfering entity first appeared when Valenzuela made the mistake of accompanying an eligible young veterinarian to dinner on her ex-husband's birthday.

"Ned was furious," Valenzuela said, "Throwing food, levitating the table, and howling like he'd just missed the Super Bowl. Against my will, I was projectile vomiting the pea soup we'd had as an appetizer. Needless to say, I didn't get a goodnight kiss on that date either."

Valenzuela plans to rid herself of the envious apparition this weekend, having invited over a handsome, local pastor for a quick exorcism and a candlelight dinner.

WWN EXTRA

SHED THOSE UNWANTED UNDEAD

If you are one of the estimated 3.6 percent of the population plagued by otherworldly houseguests, the following tips will help you exorcise your spectral pests once and for all.

● **Be Mean.** Ghosts hate to be teased. If you knew the ghost when it was alive, dredge up the most embarrassing moment of its life and taunt it unmercifully.

● **Shower in a Bathing Suit.** Many spirits will haunt your home hoping to catch a glimpse of some skin, so cover up!

● **Become a Slob.** The afterlife is quite tidy, by all accounts, and ghosts can't stand grime. Don't do the dishes, leave dirty underwear lying around, and eat chili, lots of chili (especially if the phantom is haunting your toilet).

Space aliens mourned loss of Columbia shuttle astronauts

Space aliens in dozens of secret locations around the world risked exposure while expressing heartfelt condolences for the loss of the U.S. space shuttle *Columbia* and its seven crew members, NASA sources have revealed.

Just hours after *Columbia* broke apart over Texas as it was returning from a 16-day scientific research mission, killing all seven astronauts aboard, NASA reportedly began receiving "sympathetic and supportive messages" from sources claiming to represent extraterrestrial civilizations with bases and colonies on Earth.

In all but two instances, the messages were scrambled, coded — and transmitted via the sophisticated "shifting frequencies" technique that is often used by intelligence agents operating behind enemy lines.

Those techniques, which require a sizeable investment in gear and special training to operate, all but rule out the possibility that the transmissions were a hoax, says a NASA source.

"The fact that extraterrestrial intelligences would risk blowing their covers is surprising enough," the source says.

"But what really hit us was the very genuine and heartfelt sorrow in the messages," he says. "And in some cases we also got offers of technological assistance — to be carried out under a shroud of secrecy, of course — to help us find out what went wrong.

"One message was clumsily worded but came straight from the heart: 'Your space program is younger, and accidents cannot be avoided. Your procedures are not wrong, they are good, and we understand you're sad.'"

Another transmission offered "sincerest and deepest sympathies for your crew and their loved ones."

It then instructed NASA to place a small ad in a Spartanburg, S.C., newspaper if the space agency "desired technical assistance" with the *Columbia* investigation.

Officials from both NASA and the Office of Homeland Security are refusing to comment officially, but portions of the transmissions are being leaked by space agency sources and other highly placed Washington insiders.

Here are partial transcripts of several messages:

● "Your country must be proud of the brave astronauts and scientists who are leading you into a new era of enlightenment, peace and technological advancement."

● "A first magnitude tragedy can never be forgotten, nor can it be allowed to negate the progress you have made."

● "People of America. People of Earth. Your primitive words cannot express the depth of our feelings. Mankind has suffered enough. We call upon the Lords of Creation to minister to the needs of the lesser beings. Humans must be given the knowledge to lift themselves up into the realms of happiness, where pain is a memory — and life knows not the sting of cold death."

● "May the wings of our prayers be with you as you endeavor to grow strong in your tragedy and sorrow. We as brothers and sisters offer our sympathies and our help. Should you need us, think it — and so it shall be done."

● "We express our condolences in connection with these tragic events. We have seen these tragedies many times ourselves. We have lost many of our own people. We stand with you in grief and in strength to face and conquer the trials you face today, and those which are to come."

By **NICK MANN**
Correspondent

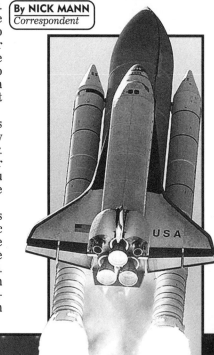

MISSION OUT OF CONTROL: The space shuttle *Columbia* blasted off Jan. 16, 2003, and never returned.

Their messages are a touching and heartfelt tribute to the brave astronauts who died

WWN CLEANS OUT ITS CLOSETS: ITEMS FROM THE FUTURE

The first U.S. currency to feature a space alien

High-tech jetpack

DVD of Janet Jackson and Justin Timberlake's 20-year reunion concert

Bill Clinton's final rose from the 2015 season of *The Bachelor, Sr.*

As we like to remind people when we are contacted for details about what the mainstream media off-handedly refers to as "the unexplained," being the place everyone turns when something bizarre happens is a heavy responsibility, but one that we feel uniquely qualified to shoulder. Unfortunately, it also means that the closets at WWN HQ are stuffed full of oddities we've received over the years from every corner of the globe.

During a recent bout of spring cleaning, we uncovered several gems from a group of items that tumbled into our universe from the future. The items traveled through a few (very costly, as it turned out, in terms of property damage) rifts in the space-time continuum that appeared in the second-floor men's room at our London bureau over the course of several weeks in summer 2001. The amazing assortment of artifacts was originally slated to be included in a serialized feature about how bright the future looks for humankind, but most of the material was ultimately judged by the science editor to be too dangerous to the continued existence of the universe to be printed. As it was, several WWN employees had to undergo hypnosis (and one lobotomy) to remove their memories of what they had learned about the future. What survived the purge is included here.

MAN SUES GENIE
for not granting him 3rd wish

By MATT KIRSCH

MIAMI, Ohio — Riley Barber, 46, a construction worker, is planning a lawsuit against a genie who refused to grant him the third of a promised three wishes.

Barber recalled the incident. "I'm on this backpacking trip in the desert with the wife when I trip over what turned out to be a half-buried lamp. I dug it up and started rubbing it. All of a sudden, green smoke seeps out and a genie appears. He tells me I have three wishes. I quickly wish for a billion dollars. Boom — I'm stinking rich! Then I ask him to make my wife look like Pamela Anderson. Boom — She does.

"Then on the third wish, I ask for unlimited wishes. Nothing happens. This jerk-off genie tells me that's against the 'rules' and I lose the wish for even asking. Hey! That's not written anywhere! So with my cash, I hired the best lawyer in the world and we're suing that genie for everything!"

"I think we have a very strong case," said Rex Hammer, Barber's lawyer. "Legally, this genie entered into a verbal contract with my client the second he granted that first wish.

"Trust me, when we get done with him, he'll be granting wishes from a malt liquor bottle."

Asked to comment, the genie who appeared to Cletus Bodine as reported in *WWN*'s May 2, 2005, issue said, "It sounds like Barber found a nonunion, fly-by-night genie."

This secret NASA photo confirms ...

WEEKLY WORLD EXCLUSIVE NEWS

MOON RAYS TURNED APOLLO ASTRONAUTS INTO WEREWOLVES

Will shocking evidence put kibosh on future moon landings?

By MIKE FOSTER

A CREEPY photo NASA has suppressed for decades proves that Apollo astronauts who landed on the moon were affected by the powerful lunar rays — and turned into werewolves!

The shocking picture, leaked by a space agency insider, shows a helmeted astronaut standing on the surface of the moon with wolf-like hair covering his entire face.

Controversial St. Louis astronomer Dr. Bernard Muselfreed, who received the mind-blowing photo from an unnamed NASA source, calls the bizarre image enlightening.

"We know that moonlight can cause some individuals on Earth to become lycanthropes," he says. "It's only logical that a person actually standing on the lunar surface and exposed to even more intense rays would be likely to undergo such a transformation."

BAD MOON RISING: This top-secret NASA photograph of an unidentified Apollo astronaut indicates that lunar rays can have a hair-raising effect on otherwise normal people.

NASA's reasons for keeping the eye-popping photo from the public are obvious. "Winning the space race by landing a man on the moon was a major propaganda victory for the United States," notes aerospace historian Bob Dressel. "Certainly, news that our space heroes were turning into werewolves would have marred that success."

Because the photo is undated, Dr. Muselfreed says it's impossible to be sure which of the Apollo astronauts who visited Earth's satellite in the six moon landings between 1969 and 1972 is pictured.

But that's irrelevant, he maintains, because "almost certainly" every man who walked on the moon spent minutes — or in some cases hours — as a werewolf.

"I believe that Neil Armstrong, the first human to walk on the moon on July 20, 1969 turned into a werewolf within moments of his arrival," Dr. Muselfreed declares.

"We know that Armstrong almost immediately became disoriented, botching the line that had

PRESIDENT BUSH may want to reconsider plans to send U.S. astronauts back to the moon after seeing the shocking photo.

been carefully written for him — "One small step for a man, one giant leap for mankind' — and uttering instead the nonsensical 'One small step for man, one giant leap for mankind.'

"What few Americans know is that Armstrong's speech deteriorated rapidly and moments later Mission Control heard what sounded like growls coming over the radio.

"At the time, this was dismissed as 'static,' but in light of this remarkable photograph, an educated guess would be that the astronaut was turning into a wolfman."

Seven independent photo analysts who've examined the picture confirm its authenticity. While refusing to brand the photo an outright hoax, a NASA spokesman dismissed the werewolf report as "an exaggeration."

Lycanthropy is a medical condition that has been identified in the medical literature dating back to the ancient Greek physician Hippocrites.

"Although theories about the cause vary, the most consistently cited factor is the influence of the moon," says British endocrinologist Dr. Colin Mayfair.

"This revelation about the Apollo missions confirms that lunar rays play a critical role in the disease process."

ARE YOU KIDDING?

An astounding 23 percent of U.S. high school students believe the moon is made of cheese.

3 I WAS BIGFOOT'S LOVE SLAVE!

Sensational Stories of the Bizarre

It's no secret that *Weekly World News* out-scoops, out-reports, and kicks the journalistic behind of other newspapers in its reporting on the subjects that matter. But it really flaunts its journalistic chops in its coverage of the biggest, scariest, freakiest, and most mutated creatures to crawl, slither, and, yes, breed upon the Earth.

So superior is *WWN*'s coverage of the bizarre, in fact, that most other

news sources have simply given up on trying to track the comings and goings of the world's mutants.

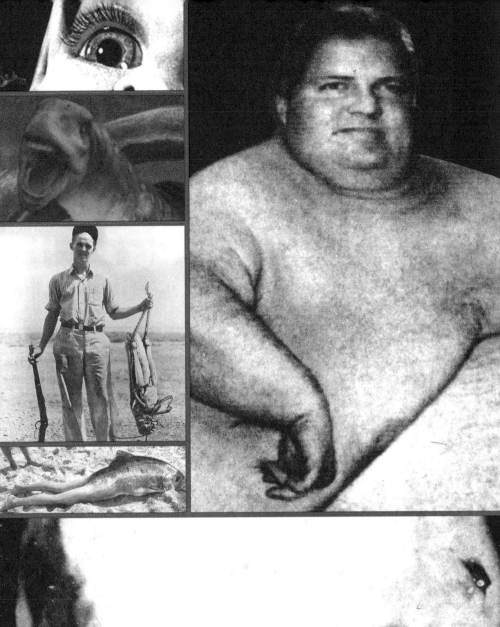

That's why, after *WWN*'s science bureau broke the story of a half boy/half bat discovered in a West Virginia cave, its mutant freak bureau refused to let the downy freak fade into obscurity. Instead, it picked up the story and ran with it.

And who better to run after than Bat Boy, that loveable ragamuffin whose shenanigans are the delight of millions of fans around the world? There's no FBI officer powerful enough, no scientist clever enough, and no padlock strong enough to keep down this biting, screeching wunderfledermauskind.

"When Bat Boy was discovered, *WWN* was the first and only newspaper I contacted," says Dr. Ron Dillon, the esteemed scientist who first laid eyes on the mutant tot. "Its reputation for fearless and accurate reporting about extraordinary scientific discoveries and phenomena made it the obvious choice." *Weekly World News* covers the story as fairly and meticulously now as it did then, and readers can be certain it will continue to do so until Bat Boy (and the ghost of Bat Boy) disappears from this earth.

But *WWN* was covering the bizarre long before Bat Boy bit the scene. Where else did readers find out about the discovery of a 22-pound housefly, not to mention a 23-pound mutant grasshopper? How else could they follow the story of Nessie's love affair with, and subsequent impregnation by, the Lake Champlain monster? And who else would tell the tales of the many lumberjacks, campers, and woodland dwellers who have had startling, terrifying, and occasionally erotic encounters with Bigfoots?

Time and again, when a story is just too bizarre for the more fainthearted members of the media to handle, *Weekly World News* has delivered the goods, and in doing so has defended journalism's time-honored principles of thoroughness, decency, and fair play.

So vital has *WWN*'s reporting of such phenomena become, Dillon notes, that a saying of sorts has cropped up in the scientific community: "If it's not in the *Weekly World News*, it doesn't exist."

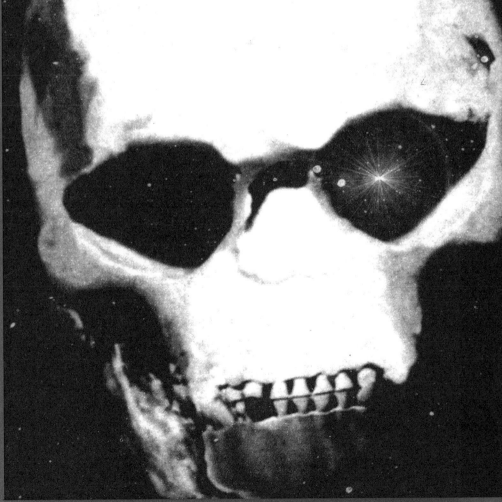

FREAKS OF NATURE BAFFLE SCIENTISTS!

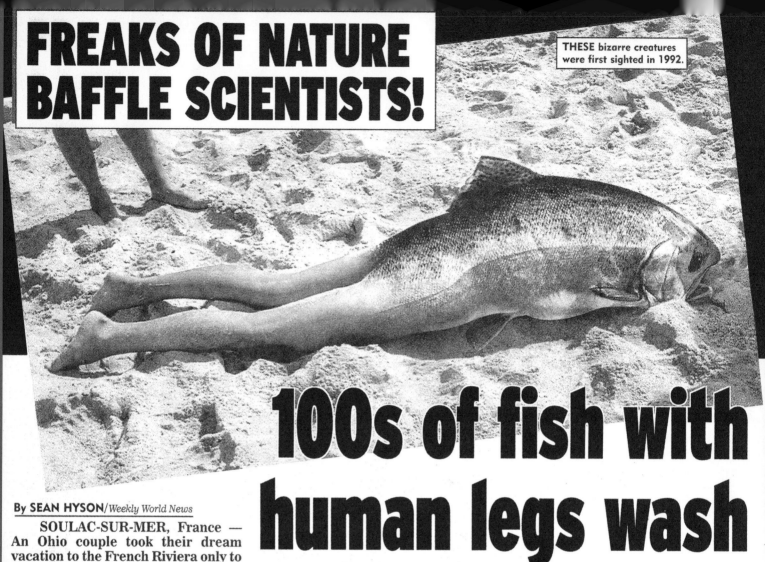

THESE bizarre creatures were first sighted in 1992.

100s of fish with human legs wash up on French Riviera!

By SEAN HYSON/*Weekly World News*

SOULAC-SUR-MER, France — An Ohio couple took their dream vacation to the French Riviera only to be turned away by the stink of dead fish with human legs!

Walter and Alice Bean told reporters they were just hours into their trip when they discovered that beaches along the French coast were closed — and they remained shut for the next four days.

According to the couple and the respected European news agency, France Newspress, hundreds of the strange half-fish, half-human life forms had washed ashore in the wake of an offshore algae bloom that left the creatures choking for oxygen.

They ranged in size from 1½ inches to 6 feet, eyewitnesses said.

"They looked like regular trout but instead of tails, they had two human legs dangling behind them," explained Mrs. Bean, who claims to still be "in shock" from the bizarre experience.

"We're devastated," she continued in an interview with French reporters. "We've

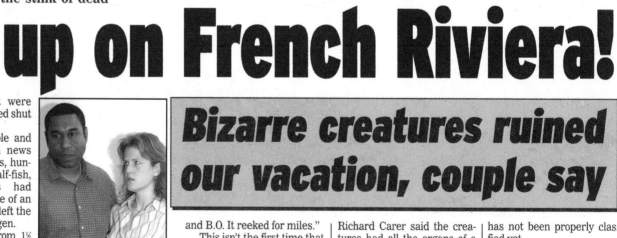

VACATION RUINED: Walter and Alice Bean.

Bizarre creatures ruined our vacation, couple say

saved every penny since we got married six years ago — just waiting to take this trip."

Walter Bean added, "The smell was the worst of all. It was a combination of dead fish and B.O. It reeked for miles."

This isn't the first time that fish with human legs have been found beached.

As *Weekly World News, The New York Times* and other major media reported in November 1992, fish with human legs washed ashore on Florida's famed Daytona Beach.

At the time, Bahamas-based marine biologist Richard Carer said the creatures had all the organs of a normal fish.

But their legs, he noted, "are clearly those of a normal human — except for a waxy coating that we suspect protects them from exposure to water."

Dr. Carer believes these mysterious creatures may be a mutation or a possible missing link — an organism that has not been properly classified yet.

Along the Riviera, French scientists reportedly took several of the animals to a lab for study and will issue a full report on them later this year.

Meanwhile, the Beans have returned to their home in Springfield, Ohio.

"We never even got to put our toes in the water," Mrs. Bean said.

BAT BOY ESCAPES!

A half-human "bat boy" that was captured in West Virginia last spring has escaped from the research facility where he was taken for observation — and is still running free!

Zoologist Ron Dillon said the 2-foot, 19-pound creature was last seen in downtown Wheeling, on September 10. In spite of his small size, the boy has razor-sharp teeth, the strength of an ape and should be considered extremely dangerous, the expert said.

"This is a tragedy beyond measure," continued Dr. Dillon, who has been studying the bat boy since his capture last May.

"This little creature is quick, powerful, and as much as I hate to say it, as vicious as a lion in the wild. If he feels his life is threatened, he will lash out without fear of consequences.

"We mustn't forget that this child evolved as a cave dweller and knows nothing about our society and civilization.

"I hope and pray that we are able to capture him before anybody gets hurt."

As *Weekly World News* and other major media reported earlier this year, Dillon and his research team found the bat boy while studying subterranean life-forms in a cave near Seneca Rocks in the Shenandoah Mountains.

The experts subdued the creature with a tranquilizer injection and took him to a private facility in Wheeling to continue their observations.

At the time it was reported that the boy had large amber eyes that allow him to see in the dark and oversize ears that work like radar.

It was also noted that the boy, who appears to be three or four years old, consumed his weight in live insects every day.

"As time went on we determined that the boy possesses an intelligence rivaling that of the smartest chimps and apes," said Dillon.

"We felt like we were on the verge of learning how to communicate with him

By DACK KENNEDY
Correspondent

when he twisted the heavy steel padlock off his holding cell and escaped. The bat boy was last seen heading south and there's no telling where he will turn up next," continued the expert.

"He moves so quickly that I wouldn't be surprised if he was in Virginia or Kentucky by now."

Dillon refused to speculate on what might have caused the boy to flee the facility and flatly denied rumors that a drunk custodian beat the creature the night before he escaped.

The expert went on to say that he and his research team set traps in and around the mountain cave where the boy was originally captured.

But at this late date, it's highly unlikely that he can or will return to it.

Dillon said that he has warned authorities across the country to be on the lookout for the creature.

Given enough time, he explained, the bat child could turn up anywhere in the United States.

"Our task is all the more difficult because the bat boy moves by night and sleeps by day," said Dillon.

"It's a little like trying to spot a shadow on a cloudy, moonless night.

"The harder you look the less you see. That's what we're up against."

SPOT THE BAT BOY

If you spot the bat boy, *Weekly World News* wants to know about it. Drop us a line describing when and where you saw him, what he was doing and the direction he was traveling. By drawing on the resources of millions of devoted readers, *The NEWS* can help authorities recapture this dangerous creature before anybody gets hurt. Write to Bat Boy, Weekly World News, 600 South East Coast Ave., Lantana, Fla. 33462.

FIGHTING UNTIL THE END! As FBI agents descended upon Bat Boy, the 3-foot-tall creature went wild — biting two agents on the arm, then biting off another's finger and eating it.

BAT BOY CAPTURED!

By JOE BERGER / *Weekly World News*

CHARLOTTE, N.C. — The bizarre, bug-gobbling Bat Boy who's been on the run since he escaped from a West Virginia research facility in 1992 has been recaptured — and excited scientists say they may finally be able to unravel the mystery of the tiny terror's origins!

Federal agents corralled the bloodcurdling creature in a wooded area northeast of here after more than two months of reported sightings in and around Charlotte. But Bat Boy did not go down without a fight.

"The thing bit two of the agents real bad on the arm, and he bit off one guy's finger and ate it," said rattled camper Rudy Winscel, 33, who witnessed the hair-raising confrontation. "He was terrified — and more ferocious than just about anything I've ever seen in the wilds."

The sawed-off escapee — now nearly three feet tall and weighing about 40 pounds — was finally subdued with the aid of a tiny tranquilizer dart and was whisked away to the top-secret laboratory from which he escaped in September 1992.

"This time we'll all take extra security precautions to make sure the little fellow doesn't get away from us again," said concerned zoolo-

ON THE RUN: Bat Boy tore the heavy steel padlock off the door to his holding cell and escaped in 1992. The manhunt had focused on Charlotte, N.C., since early July.

> **'He was more ferocious than just about anything I've ever seen in the wilds'**
> — *Camper Rudy Winscel*

gist Dr. Ron Dillon, who originally discovered the big-eyed Bat Boy while studying subterranean life-forms in a mountain cave five years ago.

The mystified scientist surmised at the time that the unpredictable, pointy-eared creature might be a human baby raised by bats or a separate species that wandered from the twisting path of man's evolution during prehistoric times.

But before Dr. Dillon could determine what he was dealing with, Bat Boy tore the heavy steel padlock off the door to his holding cell and escaped.

"He ripped that big lock off like it was made of plastic," the astonished zoologist recalled. "He's very strong — and that's one of the things that make him so dangerous."

Since his escape, the elusive fugitive has been spotted hundreds of times from Boston to Bakersfield, and dozens of stunned citizens have reported being attacked by the half-pint hellion.

In Florida last year, a panic-stricken 6-year-old girl was bitten on the arm when she entered her garage and found Bat Boy hiding inside. And in Massachusetts earlier this year, a flabbergasted 44-year-old man had a chunk of his right ear bitten off by the runaway runt.

"Since early July, any number of sightings have been recorded in and around Charlotte, and that's where our search had been concentrated recently," Dr. Dillon told a reporter.

"Then last week a camper, Mr. Winscel, reported being attacked on a riverbank by a creature with sharp teeth and wild eyes, and from his description — and the terror in his voice — we were reasonably sure we had at long last found Bat Boy."

Police, scientists and federal agents rushed to the remote area and eventually managed to capture the screeching creature.

"There was a certain amount of bloodshed but only on the part of the agents — Bat Boy didn't get a scratch," Dr. Dillon said later.

"Now if we can only hang onto him long enough this time, we may finally find out just what — or who — this amazing little guy really is."

> **'From Mr. Winscel's description — and the terror in his voice — we were reasonably sure we'd found Bat Boy'**
> — *Dr. Ron Dillon*

MISSING HALF-BAT, HALF-HUMAN STRIKES AGAIN!

ACTION PHOTO taken from a Detroit overpass clearly shows cops chasing the stolen Mini Cooper. Inset closeup reveals Bat Boy is the driver.

CAR THREE

WWN 3X ZOOM

FBI Special Agent Jack Trasker has been hot on Bat Boy's tail since the mutant disappeared last May.

DETROIT — Bat Boy, the world's favorite winged freak, went on an incredible, death-defying joyride through Michigan, Indiana and Ohio after carjacking a brand new Mini Cooper — and is still on the lam somewhere in America!

The brazen theft took place in the crowded parking lot of a Mini dealership. Eyewitnesses report that the Mini Cooper's owner had just accepted the keys to the vehicle when Bat Boy jumped out from behind some bushes, snatched the keys and sped away.

By **WAYNE DIAZ**
Weekly World News

CLOSE-UP photo of car's side view appears to show Bat Boy behind the wheel.

"The whole thing happened in a matter of seconds," says the car's horrified owner, who asked not to be identified. "The dealer had just handed me the keys when this monstrous creature appeared out of nowhere and tore off like a bat out of hell."

Police suspect that Bat Boy had been casing the dealership for hours, waiting for just the right moment to strike. Two employees gave chase, but Bat Boy quickly lost them in traffic.

Police say they are looking for a red Mini Cooper, last seen around Akron. A police spokesman says, "That little speed demon was heading East on Interstate 80. We urge all motorists to be on the lookout for this car, and to notify authorities if they see a Mini Cooper driven by a bat-like creature."

There were numerous sightings of Bat Boy following the theft, but police have been unable to locate him and he remains at large as of this writing.

"We know where Bat Boy has been during his little adventure — we just don't know where he is now," notes FBI Special Agent Jack Trasker.

"We've been tracking his movements via reports of gas station drive-offs — apparently Bat Boy is

BAT BOY STEALS — AND GOES ON STATE JOY RIDE!

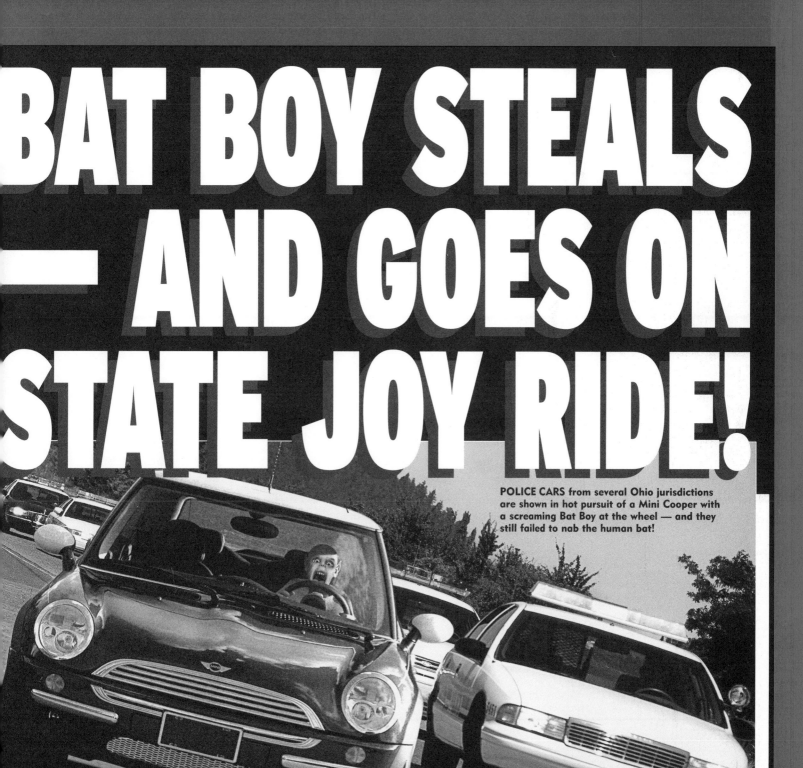

POLICE CARS from several Ohio jurisdictions are shown in hot pursuit of a Mini Cooper with a screaming Bat Boy at the wheel — and they still failed to nab the human bat!

stealing gas when the tank runs low and drives away before police can respond."

Bat Boy learned how to drive while working with the U.S. military combating terrorism in Afghanistan.

Secret military files leaked to *Weekly World News* report that he stole at least two Jeeps and a tank during his stint there.

Since returning to the United States, Bat Boy's behavior has become increasingly erratic.

Three months ago he escaped from government custody and became a fugitive.

Police reports collected from stunned onlookers put Bat Boy in at least three different states. Sitings include:

• The Detroit Zoo, where he was believed to be looking for a quick snack.

• Drive-through of an Indiana donut shop. Several police officers taking a break in the shop gave chase, but Bat Boy managed to lose them in traffic.

• Interstate chase in Ohio. With cops in hot pursuit, Bat Boy whizzed down the Interstate at speeds in excess of 100 miles an hour.

Authorities are desperate to recapture Bat Boy, and have asked the nation's driving public to immediately report anything unusual. FBI and police scoured the tri-state area via car and helicopter, but they're no closer to capturing Bat Boy than they were three months ago.

"Hell, he could be a thousand miles from here by now," notes Agent Trasker, who has been on Bat Boy's tail since he escaped government custody.

"For someone so weird, he man- ages to hide himself pretty easily. With winter just around the corner, he'll probably head south.

"We already have task forces assembled in Georgia, North Carolina and Florida so when he shows up, we'll be ready."

In the meantime, the owner of the stolen Mini Cooper says he probably won't press charges should Bat Boy finally be captured.

"I hope Bat Boy learns his lesson and turns himself in," the man says. "I just want my Mini Cooper back."

NESSIE PR

— & Champ's the

EDINBURGH, Scotland — Outraged Scottish tourist officials charge that Champ, the Loch Ness Monster's American counterpart, made Nessie pregnant — then left her high and dry!

Now the bagpipe-blowing big wigs are demanding that the enormous male sea monster come back to Scotland and "do the right thing."

"This heartless Yank beast has dishonored our beloved Nessie — and he's broken her heart," declared Mary MacHeath, vice president of the Society for the Preservation of Scottish Culture.

"Apparently, the big brute thinks he can just sail into town, swishing his big tail, have his fun with our Ness, then swim away when he pleases, paying no mind to his responsibilities and leaving her with no one to help her raise the wee one.

"But we're not going to let the cad get away with it — Nessie is a national treasure and we plan to protect her."

Last fall's historic mating of the Lake Champlain Monster, better known as Champ, and Nessie was initially greeted with excitement by both U.S. and Scottish scientists.

Experts from around the world gathered at Loch Ness after researchers tracked Champ on an epic voyage from his lair in Vermont's Lake Champlain.

The 120 eyewitnesses who watched in awe as the two massive, dinosaur-like creatures made passionate whoopee later described it as "a majestic sight."

But after the titanic, six-hour love romp, the male beast showed no interest in cuddling.

"Champ reared his head out of the lake and roared with pride, like he was king of the world, then swam away," says Scottish cryptozoologist Dr. Brian MacHennessy.

"He showed up back in Lake Champlain just 15 days later."

Two weeks ago, following observations that Nessie appeared nauseous, concerned researchers collected a urine sample from the water — and confirmed that she's expecting.

Scottish scientists expected Champ to return to join his mate, but have seen neither hide nor hair of him.

"Nessie has been pining like a lovesick schoolgirl," says Mrs. MacHeath angrily.

"She feels abandoned and afraid. We believe she was pure before Champ came along — she's never been through this before and doesn't know what to expect.

"She's alone just when she most needs the support of a mate."

Scottish officials are asking the U.S. Navy to see that Champ returns to Scotland — by force if necessary.

But fans of the Lake Champlain Monster deny that he's a deadbeat-dad dinosaur.

"There may be plenty of other male sea monsters out there — how do we really know who the father is?" one Vermont fisherman asked.

— By MIKE FOSTER

EGNANT
daddy

American monster left her high & dry, charge angry Scots!

RECENT RENDEZVOUS between Nessie, left, and the Lake Champlain Monster, right, resulted in Nessie getting pregnant, say sources.

LOCH NESS MONSTER TIMELINE

565–First known sighting of Loch Ness Monster, by St. Columba

1609–First known sighting of Champ, the Lake Champlain Monster

1873–P.T. Barnum offers a $50,000 reward for the capture of Champ

1934–First photo of Nessie taken, by R.K. Wilson

1953–Champ joins the Church of Latter-Day Saints

1981–State of Vermont passes a House resolution protecting Champ

1991–Nessie is captured by scientists, only to escape 3 months later

1996–Nessie stars with Ted Danson in the hugely popular film *Loch Ness*

Oct. 2001–Champ attacks an oil tanker, gaining international infamy

Dec. 2001–Nessie takes out an Internet personal ad

Jan. 2002–Champ swims to Scotland; does "underwater mambo" with Nessie

Feb. 2002–Nessie discovers she's pregnant

Apr. 2002–Donald Trump attempts to purchase Nessie and her unborn child

Aug. 2003–Nessie gives birth to baby

Oct. 2003–Baby of Loch Ness captured by American fisherman and killed; Champ vows to destroy him

2004–Champ and fisherman appear on *Judge Judy*, Judy rules in favor of Champ

2005–Sneezy the Dwarf mascot spots Champ and Nessie frolicking in the Caribbean from Disney cruise ship the S.S. *Magic Mountain*®

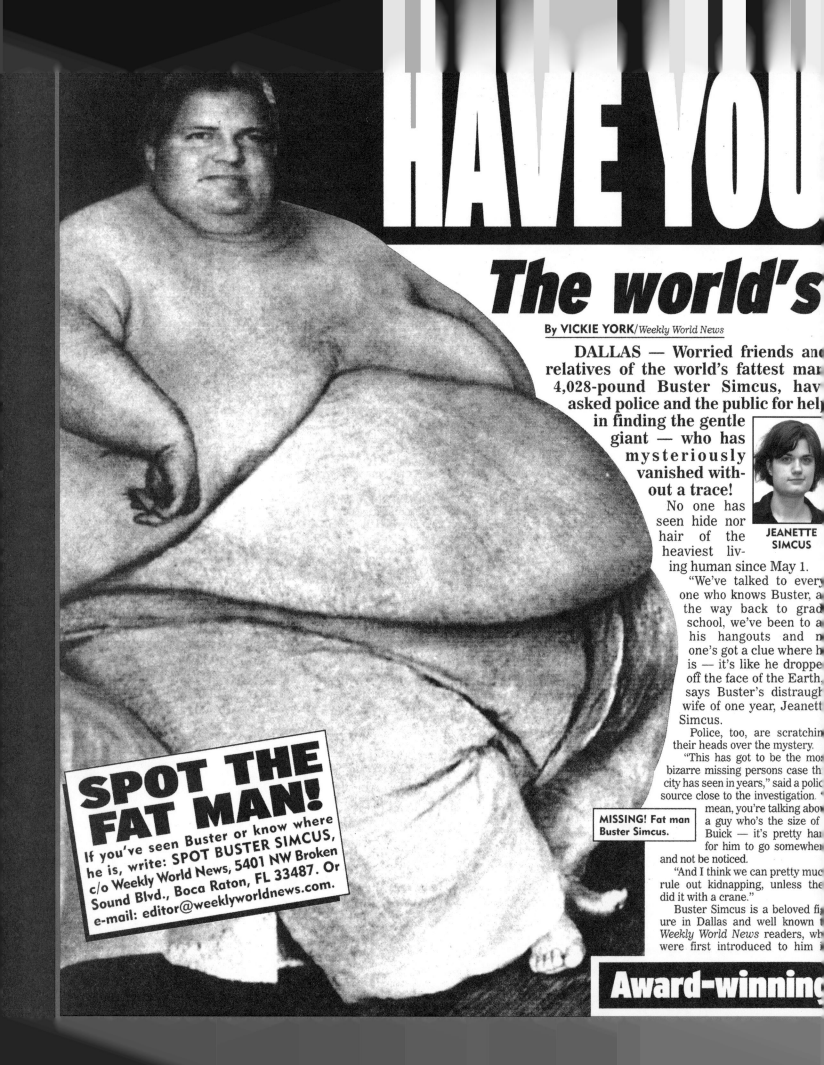

The world's

By VICKIE YORK/*Weekly World News*

DALLAS — Worried friends and relatives of the world's fattest man, 4,028-pound Buster Simcus, have asked police and the public for help in finding the gentle giant — who has mysteriously vanished without a trace!

No one has seen hide nor hair of the heaviest living human since May 1.

JEANETTE SIMCUS

"We've talked to every one who knows Buster, all the way back to grade school, we've been to all his hangouts and no one's got a clue where he is — it's like he dropped off the face of the Earth," says Buster's distraught wife of one year, Jeanette Simcus.

Police, too, are scratching their heads over the mystery.

"This has got to be the most bizarre missing persons case the city has seen in years," said a police source close to the investigation. "I mean, you're talking about a guy who's the size of a Buick — it's pretty hard for him to go somewhere and not be noticed.

"And I think we can pretty much rule out kidnapping, unless they did it with a crane."

Buster Simcus is a beloved figure in Dallas and well known to *Weekly World News* readers, who were first introduced to him in

MISSING! Fat man Buster Simcus.

Award-winning

SEEN THIS MAN?

fattest man has vanished — without a trace!

1994. At that time, at a scale-crunching 2,137 pounds, he was already being heralded by the world press as the fattest man alive.

Since then, this paper has chronicled his valiant and repeated efforts to achieve a healthy weight.

At one point, by adopting a strict regimen of diet and exercise, Buster slimmed down to well under 1,000 pounds. But he soon regained every inch of flab and since the late '90s, his waistline has done nothing but expand.

"Man wasn't meant to live on carrot sticks and cantaloupes and spend all his time exercising," he said after abandoning the diet. "I'm two tons now, but I feel great."

Big-bellied Buster, known to wolf down a dozen milk shakes, 25 T-bone steaks and 14 apple pies every day, was last seen by his wife heading out to a local supermarket for one of his routine six-hour food-shopping trips. Store clerks say he never got there.

"He kissed me goodbye like always," said Mrs. Simcus. "Nothing seemed to be wrong."

Theories about what's become of blubbery Buster abound — ranging from way-out whisperings about alien abduction or kidnapping by urban cannibals, to rumors of foul play.

While relatives say the missing man was happily married, neighbors note that Jeanette stands to inherit a huge trust fund left to her husband by a wealthy relative.

Mrs. Simcus angrily discounts such talk — as well as suggestions that the famed fat man may have committed suicide.

"People say Buster might have killed himself because he hated being so fat," said Mrs. Simcus. "But that's not the kind of person he is — Buster loves life."

Others have suggested that the massive man has gone into seclusion to go on a crash diet and plans to surprise the world by resurfacing with a brand-new, bone-thin look.

Said Mrs. Simcus, "The last thing he said to me when he left for the store was, 'Can I bring you anything back, honey?'

"I told him, 'Bring me some ice cream.' And he looked at me and smiled, 'Ice cream for my sweetie — you got it.'

"And that's the last thing he ever said to me. I've been praying for his safe return ever since. We're only married a year. The honeymoon isn't even over. I'm sick with worry and I miss him terribly."

WWN EXCLUSIVE
DATELINE: NOVEMBER 9, 1993

HALF-HUMAN, HALF-ALLIGATOR DISCOVERED IN FLORIDA SWAMP

PREHISTORIC BEAST was photographed by hunters as it basked in the southwest Florida sun.

Scientists calling bizarre creature the missing link!

Weekly World News – America's BEST newspaper!

He spit a wad of 'tobacco' juice that knocked my mutt on his butt!

I SHOT A 23-POUND GRASSHOPPER

By STEVE DUNLOP
In Auckland, N.Z.

A 48-inch grasshopper chewed its way through an acre of corn before farmer Barry Gissler drew a bead on the creature with his 30-30 rifle — and shot it dead!

Now university experts are studying the 23-pound insect's carcass in hopes of finding out where it came from and why it grew so big.

"You can hold a garden variety grasshopper in the palm of your hand but this thing is damn near as big as a Labrador retriever," insect specialist Robert Scholl told reporters.

"Hopefully, it's one of a kind. A swarm of these things could level your average farm in a single afternoon."

Gissler shot the gigantic grasshopper on March 15. Oddly enough, he had seen the insect perched on the seat of his tractor three days earlier but was tired after working his

The critter chewed through an acre of corn!

fields and thought his mind was playing tricks.

"The next afternoon I noticed something had been eating my corn plants and set out to find it," said Gissler, who lives 15 miles south of Reefton, New Zealand.

"A few minutes later I saw the hopper clinging to a stalk and I don't mind telling you that I just about jumped out of my pants.

"But this time I knew my mind wasn't playing tricks.

The damn thing spit a full quart of 'tobacco' juice and hit me square in the face."

Gissler returned to his house, got his rifle and stalked the grasshopper — unsuccessfully — for the rest of the day.

The next morning he resumed the hunt and found the creature polishing off a cornstalk on the west end of his field.

"My mongrel dog took off after him but the hopper knocked him flat on his butt with another salvo of juice," said Gissler.

"For the split second he was distracted I aimed and shot. He never knew what hit him."

The farmer took the insect to the local agriculture office where agents referred him to Scholl.

The bug expert is already conducting tests on the carcass but says it will be weeks or possibly even months before results are in.

"It's imperative that we find out what made the grasshopper grow so big and if there are others like him," said Scholl.

"It's all we can do to keep regular insects from eating all our crops right now.

"A breed like this could turn the tide in their favor once and for all."

Said Gissler: "This is something I'll tell my grandchildren about. I'm just glad I've got a picture. Otherwise, they wouldn't believe it."

WEEKLY WORLD NEWS EXCLUSIVE

FARMER Barry Gissler holds his prize — a 23-pound grasshopper which he shot after it attacked his cornfield.

WWN EXTRA

With recipes like Giant Locust Stuffed with Spring Onions and Crabapples, Vern's Deep Fried Big Daddy Long Legs, and Caterpillar Swirl Ice Cream, there's sure to be something in *Cookin' (and Eatin'!) Giant Bugs* by Maisie Mae Jessop (Dutton, $6.98) for every member of the family. Also included is Maisie Mae's incredible life story, from her experience with killer barn arachnids to her win for best Giant Earthworm Sausage Gravy at the Tulsa County Fair.

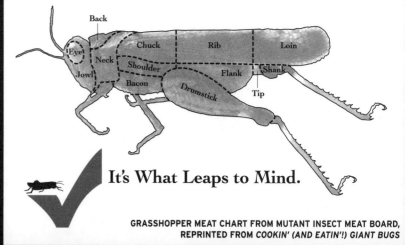

It's What Leaps to Mind.

GRASSHOPPER MEAT CHART FROM MUTANT INSECT MEAT BOARD, REPRINTED FROM *COOKIN' (AND EATIN'!) GIANT BUGS*

Don't go after this one with a swatter!

GIANT BUG is the result of growth hormones in insecticides.

By **TONY BURTON**/*Weekly World News*

22-POUND HOUSEFLY CAPTURED

MEXICO CITY — Scientists have captured a 22-pound housefly — and they say the giant bug proves that the use of growth hormones in insecticides has caused nature to go terribly haywire!

"No one was ever certain what would happen when we started using these new chemicals," said insect expert Dr. Aurelio Baez. "When you fool around with Mother Nature just so you can have larger tomatoes, you better be prepared for other consequences — and this bug might be just the first of many."

The giant housefly was first seen near a farm outside Monterrey, Mexico. Reports of the fly attracted dozens of scientists.

After days of failed attempts, one team of scientists was able to catch the huge bug without killing or injuring it.

"We wanted to capture the insect alive so we could do extensive research on it," said Dr. Baez.

"Fortunately we were able to hit it with a very mild tranquilizer, capture it and then take it in to a laboratory."

The fly is still alive and under daily examination at an undisclosed location in Mexico. According to Dr. Baez, the fly is extremely healthy and shows a tremendous appetite.

"One of most amazing aspects of this creature is how much it eats," he said. "It is quite common for it to devour 25 pounds of sugar and almost 10 pounds of hamburger in a single day."

The bug is generally allowed to fly free in a large caged room, where its gigantic wings make a tremendous noise. Scientists inject its food with tranquilizers so they can put the fly on a table and study it more closely.

"From biopsies we have done on the fly's tissue we are certain growth hormones in insecticides caused its unnatural size," Dr. Baez said. "That would strongly indicate that there are likely other large flies out there. And there could even be thousands of them."

FLASHBACK TO:

WEEKLY WORLD **NEWS**

NOVEMBER 1991

WWN EXCLUSIVE
DATELINE: SEPTEMBER 16, 2003

FLEA CIRCUS ATTACKS OWNER

Flea Circus Trainer Rushed to Hospital After Performing Fleas Go Berserk

Big trouble brewing as...
UNDEAD DEMAND LIFE INSURANCE!

By G.A. GUNN

WASHINGTON, D.C. – The nation's undead community is demanding the right to life insurance – and it is a battle it can win, say experts.

"We can't issue life insurance to people who are technically not alive," says one insurance industry spokesman. "But there is a possibility that we can provide undead policies, especially if the insured are nonsmokers."

However, the government is firmly against the move.

A Capitol Hill insider says when insurance for vampires, werewolves and other undead species was mentioned to President Bush, he said it was "like a stake through his heart," especially with Democratic members of Congress calling for the establishment of a Department of Undead Affairs.

"Don't the undead have loved ones who must carry on after their destruction?" asks one Democratic congresswoman. "Surely they have a right to insurance like everyone else."

However, a rush study ordered by the government reveals that vampires as a species are incapable of love, therefore they don't have loved ones.

"In essence, after a vampire is staked either here or abroad, his insurance payment would just go to another member of the undead," says William Bell, leader of the study team. "There is no weeping wife and no little vampire kiddies involved here, no hardship cases."

Vampire spokesman Anton Dreisch told *Weekly World News*: "I believe Mr. Bush has declared war on vampires and other members of the undead because none of us are Republicans. If we were, you'd see him providing undead insurance real fast.

"If I am ever staked, I'd like to know that my vampire mate would get insurance money. She'd need the cash for travel and dental care, something I currently take care of, to say nothing of the upkeep of our ruined mansion in the Appalachians.

"I say life insurance for the undead is needed right now."

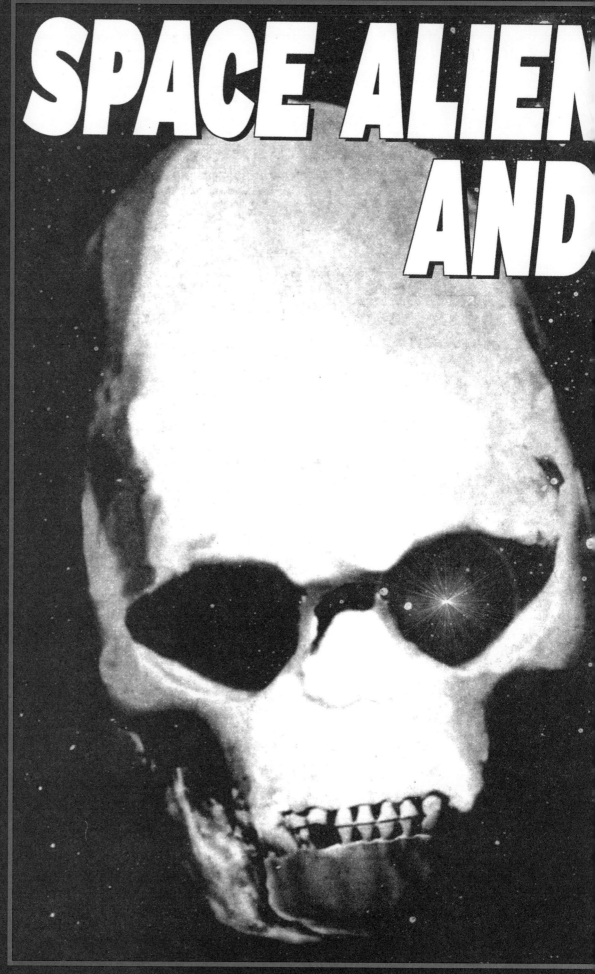

SPACE ALIEN AND

SKULL TALKS SINGS!

2000-year-old relic found in Mississippi last November!

By MIGUEL FIGUEROA/*Weekly World News*

WASHINGTON — A mysterious, lightbulb-shaped space alien skull found in a Mississippi bayou last November has begun to talk and even sing, a report claims.

The Mississippi Delta Skull, as the bizarre artifact has been dubbed, is about 2,000 years old, radiocarbon dating shows, and it speaks in an ancient French dialect, according to the report.

"It talks in a barely audible whisper, without moving its jaws, and often lapses into sing-songy jingles," says science writer Byron Hugnought, who broke the amazing story.

"Researchers have identified the language as a dialect spoken in the southern part of Gaul, the area now known as France."

The weird object was uncovered by archaeologists excavating the remains of a Native American village, according to Washington-based Hugnought.

"The skull didn't talk when it was first found, but it caught the archaeologists' eyes because it was on an altar similar to those used by oracles in the days of the Roman Empire," he says. "Also, the features

WRITER Byron Hugnought

were not those of a normal human being."

The skull has a large, bulging forehead, oversized, slanting eye sockets and small, vestigial teeth — making it look for all the world like the head of a space alien. And, if the skull's babblings are any clue, that may just be the case.

"The translations are incomplete, but the skull has repeatedly mentioned Mars — suggesting it may have come from the Red Planet," says Hugnought, who first made his revelations on a D.C. radio show. "It has also asked for its mother and father."

U.S. government officials seized the skull soon after it uttered its first words on June 2 and it is now being studied in a secret Smithsonian research lab, claims Hugnought.

"Everything I'm telling you, I learned from my Smithsonian sources," he says.

A leaked photo of the unearthly skull helped convince him the strange story is credible.

Baffled scientists can't explain how a centuries-old skull — whether it once belonged to a space alien or not — could possibly talk.

"One researcher has come up with an interesting hypothesis — that the skull has retained some trace of the extraterrestrial's powerful mind and it's actually using telepathy to communicate," he said.

Smithsonian officials insist they know nothing about any talking skull.

What the alien looked like

Forensic artists have created a striking image of what the Mississippi space alien might have looked like based on the unique size and shape of the skull.

"The creature obviously had an enormous brain capacity, which would have given his head the classic lightbulb shape we often hear described by people who have had close encounters," said one member of the team that created the computer image of the alien.

"The eyes appear oversized and perhaps even bulbous against the backdrop of the creature's thin, sunken cheeks and sharp chin.

"The long neck and garments are included only for perspective," the source said.

WWN EXTRA
HOW TO IDENTIFY THE ALIENS AMONG US!

While many extraterrestrials are totally freaky looking, others are able to live secretly among us. These intergalactic travelers pose as humans and become our coworkers, neighbors, and friends as they gather information about Earth. Here, from *WWN*'s interplanetary bureau, are five ways you can distinguish aliens from real humans.

🛸 Aliens don't have taste buds and judge food entirely on texture—this is why aliens will insist that "fake meat" tastes the same as "real meat."

🛸 Aliens love the World Wrestling Federation, especially Hulk Hogan. In fact, two planets from the Zebanor galaxy are currently in bilateral negotiations over how to extinguish all endangered animals on Earth in retaliation against the World Wildlife Fund for stealing WWF's acronym.

🛸 Aliens do not understand Earth humor. They may not laugh after you tell them a hilarious joke about "blondes" or forward them a witty email. They also may burst into laughter at inappropriate times, like when you are reciting some poetry you wrote or telling them about the coming-of-age experience you had the summer you were a Dave Matthews Band groupie.

🛸 Aliens transmit information back to their home planets via a device that attaches to their stomachs and looks like a human bellybutton. However, because they use Earth's cellular phone networks to transfer the data, their reception is poor. Therefore, you will often see aliens wearing clothing that leaves their "bellybuttons" exposed, even if their midriffs are not visually appealing.

Just when they thought they'd seen it all!

SPACE ALIEN FLASHER ROCKS L.A.

WANTED
HEIGHT: 5' 1"
WEIGHT: 115 lbs.
EYES: Black
HAIR: None
COMPLEXION: Grey

CENSORED

MIKE FOSTER/*Weekly World News*

LOS ANGELES — Riots and earthquakes were bad enough — now L.A. is being rocked by a perverted space alien who's exposed himself to scores of women!

Since June 15, at least 37 flabbergasted females — including a respected physician and a member of the mayor's staff — have told police they were confronted on the street by the bizarre extraterrestrial flasher.

"In the comics, space aliens usually have nothing down there, but believe me, this thing did — and it was totally repulsive," said 35-year-old Nellie Yartell, one of the victims.

"His you-know-what spun around on his body like a blender and made a frightening whine like a dentist's drill. I almost fainted from shock when I saw it."

Police are urging people to stay calm, downplaying the incidents. One law enforcement official described the sightings as "probably some form of mass hysteria."

But UFO researchers find the eyewitness accounts compelling.

"The similarities in the reports the women gave to the police are so significant that it's hard to write them off as coincidental," says respected British UFO investigator Dr. Sherrie Longbow, who has been keeping abreast of the phenomenon.

"In each case, the women claim that they were walking on a street late at night when the alien jumped out at them, seemingly out of nowhere.

FLASHER victim Nellie Yartell.

"They describe the being as having an oversized, lightbulb-shaped head and a small, spindly body.

"While initially dressed in a dark-colored overcoat, he then opened it up, exhibiting his private parts — which glow in the dark and make a whirring-type motion."

Miss Yartell, a beautician who's worked for many top Hollywood stars, says the most frightening aspect of the close encounter was the expression on the sicko E.T.'s face.

"When he saw my stunned reaction to his 'thingamajig,' he gave this disgusting, leering grin as if he were incredibly pleased with himself," she recalled with a shudder.

"Then he tied his overcoat shut and darted away."

Dr. Longbow says the case throws new light on the strange visitors from space.

"In the past it was widely believed that space aliens had no external genitalia.

"We now know that is untrue — perhaps what people saw was some kind of formfitting, flesh-colored undergarment," she said in a phone interview from London.

"Also, this confirms that some aliens, like humans, exhibit aberrant sexual behavior."

E.T.'s private parts spin like a mixer and whirr like a dentist's drill!

UNCLE SAM OWES ME . . .
AGING SPACE ALIEN APPLIES FOR SOCIAL SECURITY

By MIKE FOSTER
Correspondent

. . . SAYS HE'S BEEN EMPLOYED AT AREA 51 SINCE CRASH IN 1947!

ELDERLY ALIEN startled Social Security office staff.

GOVERNMENT clerks got the shock of their lives when an elderly alien walked into a federal office building and applied for Social Security benefits — claiming he had worked for the government at Area 51 since the 1947 Roswell crash!

"He shuffled around with a major stoop and his gray skin was all wrinkly, not smooth like you seen in the movies," says a staffer at the Social Security office in Sacramento, Calif., where the bizarre close encounter occurred.

"His uniform was disheveled and he seemed confused. He had trouble recalling a lot of very basic information, such as his date of birth and his marital status.

"The only thing he kept repeating loud and clear was that the government owed him benefits because of all these inventions he gave America over the years.

"He specifically mentioned the Stealth Bomber about five times."

Frazzled social workers helped the little old alien fill out the necessary forms — but before he left the building, six black-garbed federal agents suddenly arrived and roughly escorted him away.

"They also seized his paperwork, deleted everything we'd put on the computer and ordered us to shred any records we had made of his visit," says the staffer, who spoke on the condition of anonymity. "We were also warned that if we told anyone what we'd seen, we would lose our jobs and could face criminal charges under the Patriot Act."

Excited UFO investigators say the incident proves their long-standing theory that aliens who survived the famous flying saucer wreck in New Mexico were whisked away by the Air Force and have been helping America develop high-tech gizmos ever since.

"Normally, extraterrestrials bend over backward to avoid revealing their presence on Earth to ordinary citizens," says UFO researcher Terence Wheyfair.

"In this situation, we lucked out because it appears that this alien is suffering from some form of senile dementia and freely spilled the beans."

Although the alien told clerks he had trouble remembering his exact date of birth "in Earth years," he said he believed it was "about 1922 or '23."

"That would put his age at roughly 80, which would certainly more than meet the age requirement for receiving Social Security," Wheyfair notes. "Probably, our government has some other plan in place for providing for these aging aliens and officials were aghast when they found out he'd shown up at a public facility."

At least 45 visitors witnessed the long-in-the-tooth ET's appearance at the office, in addition to about two dozen employees, according to the staffer.

"They were pretty shocked," he says. "They got the same warning we did."

For decades, UFO researchers have maintained that at Area 51, a secret Air Force base located near Rachel, Nev., aliens have been using their know-how to help government engineers build advanced weaponry and flying vehicles. Lending credence to the theory have been countless sightings of unidentified aircraft in the vicinity — including mysterious wedge-shaped and disk-shaped craft.

U.S. Air Force officials doggedly denied the existence of Area 51 for years. Recently, they finally acknowledged that there is such a place, but still insist no aliens work there.

Not surprisingly, Air Force officials now claim they "don't know anything" about any over-the-hill alien applying for Social Security.

BIGFOOT SHOT BY MONTANA POLICE

By **MICHAEL CHIRON**/*Correspondent*

MONTANA state troopers brought down a charging, seven-foot-tall Bigfoot in a hail of gunfire after it chased a pair of terrified hikers through the woods for nearly 20 minutes!

The dramatic battle in Beaverhead Rock State Park left the ape-like creature dead, and a police photographer's eye-popping photo of its huge, hairy carcass has been leaked exclusively to *Weekly World News*.

"It was very scary — it must have taken 30 rounds to the chest to kill that thing," says shaken hiker Steve Rampling, 43, who credits the officers with saving his life and that of his wife, Robyn. "We're just glad the troopers were there."

While excited researchers are hailing the photo as "indisputable proof" that the legendary man-beast really exists, they are disappointed that the rare creature was not captured alive. Police have come under fire from environmentalists who say they acted too hastily in blowing away the shambling creature, which, they contend, was probably only defending its turf.

"Surely there must have been another way the officers could have handled this situation — it sounds like they were either trigger-happy or flat-out panicked," declares a spokesman for the International Crusade for the Protection of Endangered Species. "Bigfoot is a shy, docile creature that rarely attacks humans unless provoked."

The troopers, however, insist the hikers were in "imminent danger" and that they opened fire on the fierce, foaming-at-the-mouth sasquatch when it was less than six feet from a patrol car.

The Montana Highway Patrol has yet to issue an official statement. The officers involved in the shooting have been placed on administrative leave pending an investigation and are forbidden from speaking to reporters.

But a fellow lawman defended the shooting.

"I'd like to see how these tree-huggers would react if some 800-pound monster was charging at them, roaring and gnashing its fangs," he says angrily.

"Our guys had only a split second to respond and they acted responsibly. They should be treated as heroes."

The carcass was airlifted to an undisclosed research facility and state officials have gone into what frustrated local reporters are calling "full cover-up mode."

"We know absolutely nothing about any Bigfoot being killed in Beaverhead," insists a spokesman for Montana's Department of Fish, Wildlife and Parks.

Robyn and Steve, vacationers from New Zealand, were taking a leisurely stroll through the sprawling state park when nature unleashed its savage fury.

"I'd stopped to take a tinkle and soon after I dropped my pants I had the distinct sense I was being watched," Robyn, 41, tells *WWN*.

"I looked up and this giant stepped out from the bushes — a cross between a man and ape. Steve told me, 'Stay still, hon, don't panic.'

"But then the Bigfoot roared and lunged toward me. Steve grabbed my arms and said, 'Scratch that — run like hell!'

The leer on the Bigfoot's ape-like face gave her husband "raw chills," he admits.

"I'm convinced the Bigfoot wanted to mate with Robyn," says Steve, a financial planner. "The look in its eyes was simply terrifying."

The scared-stiff couple took off like jackrabbits, dashing through the woods with the loping creature hot on their heels.

"People have this idea that because Bigfoot is big and ungainly, he's slow, but we found out first-hand that isn't so," Robyn says. "It was like being chased by a grizzly bear — and the sound of the low branches snapping as he crashed through the forest after us was

...AFTER CHASING TERRIFIED HIKERS!

LUCKY TO BE ALIVE! Steve and Robyn Rampling credit the officers quick response with saving their lives.

CE LINE DO NOT CROSS POLICE

the most frightening sound I've ever heard."

Finally, bedraggled and drenched in sweat, the couple reached the highway.

"We ran along the roadside, praying we could flag down a car," Steve recalls.

Miraculously, a pair of highway patrol cars returning from an accident scene spotted the couple — and the enormous creature barreling after them. The two officers both pulled over and leapt out of their cars, guns drawn.

"They ordered the Bigfoot to stop and when he didn't, they started shooting," says Steve. "At first the .40 caliber bullets thumping into his big, hairy chest didn't seem to be having much effect — they just seemed to make him mad and he roared louder. Then all of sudden he keeled over."

Famed cryptozoologist Sir Clive Baxley, who recently made headlines worldwide when he recovered what appeared to be a Yeti jaw in the Himalayas, agrees it's "highly possible" that the Bigfoot was bent on rape.

"There have been an increasing number of reports of sex assaults by Bigfoot in recent years, particu-larly in Montana and North Dakota," he observes.

But he has another theory that would explain the Bigfoot's aggressive behavior.

"It's possible that this Bigfoot was suffering from rabies," he speculates. "I hope wherever they've taken this one, they have the sense to do a simple blood test to find out."

THE DEAD Bigfoot (top left) was a much lighter color than usual and may have been an albino. Above, the bullet-riddled creature is loaded into a panel van for transportation to an unknown destination.

BIGFOOT shown here is an artist's conception based on a description by Verdell.

By MIKE FOSTER/*Weekly World News*

TACOMA, Wash. — Burly lumberjack Leon Verdell says he was kidnapped in the woods by a Bigfoot who kept him as a love slave for three long months!

But far from being traumatized by the hairy experience, Verdell says he's gotten accustomed to life with the towering, fur-covered companion he's come to call Wookums — and he never wants to go home!

"Wookums doesn't look like anything I've ever seen, but I've learned to look beyond physical appearance," says the 38-year-old woodsman. "Inside, Wookums is kind, sensitive and nurturing — and accepts me for who I am."

The bizarre development has enraged his wife of 10 years, Denise Verdell, who spent three months desperately combing the forest for her hubby, after he vanished without a trace on June 15.

"I searched every inch of those woods, I even hired professional outdoorsmen to help me find Leon. I was worried sick, thinking that he was stranded somewhere, maybe pinned under a fallen tree or caught in an old bear trap, suffering," says Denise.

"But when I finally tracked him down he was living with that horrible beast.

"He's no longer the man I married — he's a changed man. He told me he doesn't want to come home, and that's fine by me — I've filed for divorce."

Leon says his strange odyssey began when he was working with a 15-man crew in the foothills of Mt. Rainier. As the robust 6-foot-2 lumberjack took a break to answer nature's call in the bushes, he had the eerie feeling he was being watched.

"I figured I must be imagining things," he recalls. "Then, just when I zipped up my fly I saw this huge creature come barreling out of the woods. It was 8 feet tall and covered head to toe with fur like an ape.

"I turned and tried to run, but the Bigfoot grabbed me by the collar. Next thing I knew, it scooped me up, tossed me over its shoulder and carted me off."

Leon says the Bigfoot carried him for many miles, before arriving at its cave.

"I was scared stiff because I thought it was going to eat me," he says. "Then it got this funny look in its eyes and started stroking my cheeks tenderly. It stood there in the cave, batting its long, thick eyelashes, with this huge grin on its face.

"Then it pounced on me, ripped all my clothes off and had its way with me."

Over the succeeding months, the lumberjack claims, the Bigfoot became more gentle in its attentions and the odd couple gradually established a domestic routine.

"Wookums would go out and forage for fruits, nuts, berries and small animals, and I would prepare them," Leon says.

"I also tried to keep the cave clean and decorated it with rocks and twigs I found. Wookums seemed to appreciate my labors — unlike my own human wife.

"For the first time in my life, I felt truly loved and needed."

When frantic wife Denise, accompanied by a professional tracker and his bloodhounds, finally found Leon on Sept. 18, he was in no need of rescue.

"The two of them were there cuddling in the cave like a pair of teenagers," disgusted Denise recalls. "When I asked Leon what was going on, he shouted, 'Go away — we don't need you.'"

Denise dragged her husband back to Tacoma just long enough to sign divorce papers and says she doesn't care what he does "as long as he sends my alimony checks."

Leon now says he wants to return to the woods and spend the rest of his life with his Bigfoot in the remote lair, the location of which he refuses to divulge.

"I've never been happier," he insists. "I'm staying with Wookums forever."

ANGRY Denise Verdell found her husband in a loving embrace with a Bigfoot.

ARE YOU KIDDING?

It is widely believed that the Bigfoot's favorite food is the taco.

Outraged wife Denise Verdell: 'He's a changed man'

I WAS BIGFOOT'S LOVE SLAVE

LOVE-STRUCK woodsman Leon Verdell plans to spend the rest of his life with the Bigfoot he calls Wookums.

Lumberjack's story of forbidden love will amaze you!

BIGFOOT THROUGH THE YEARS

1967

THE photo that started it all! Photographer Roger Patterson snapped this picture near Eureka, Calif., and said the creature stood over 7 feet 6 inches.

1974

DR. GROVER Krantz, an anthropologist at Washington State University, displays casts made of Sasquatch footprints found in southwestern Washington. He said the prints were definitely made by a creature about 8 feet tall and weighing 600 to 800 pounds.

1977

THIS is a still photo made from a 16mm film by Ivan Marx showing Bigfoot cavorting in the hills of northern California.

1981

EXPLORER Thomas Biscardi, who has been searching for Bigfoot for nearly a decade, snapped this picture of the legendary creature during an expedition in northern California.

Vampire sues employers for $120G — because they won't let him work in the dark

By LILA SCHVANDT
Weekly World News

BRASOV, Romania — A 39-year-old man who says he is a vampire has sued owners of the warehouse where he works, claiming they are discriminating against him — because they won't let him work in the dark.

Anton Khoroni says his rare condition makes it impossible for him to tolerate daylight and that the bright fluorescent lights in his workplace are sapping his strength. He fears he will

Fluorescent lights in warehouse make him sick, says lawyer

die if his work conditions are not changed, but his employers refuse to turn out the lights.

"My client's health de-mands that he work in a total-ly dark workplace," said Kho-roni's attorney in court papers filed last week.

"Yet his requests for a rea-sonable response to his needs have been ignored. Company officials say they have safety issues to consider, but while they're looking out for the welfare of others my client is suffering. We feel this is a clear case of job discrimina-tion against a vampire and we are not going to stand for it."

Khoroni claims that expo-sure to fluorescent light, while not as deadly for a vampire as exposure to sun-light, will eventually destroy his immune system and lead to a painful death.

Yet he argues that he needs his income and can't afford to quit.

"I want my employers to make it possible for me to work just like anyone else — and they can do that by turn-ing out the lights," Khoroni said. "If they refuse to look after my health and welfare, then I think they should compensate me for the dam-age to my health."

Brasov Warehouses, Inc., has not commented publicly on the suit.

DECEMBER 30, 2001

A PTERODACTYL BIT MY ARM OFF
...and I've got the stump to prove it!

ALAN PERRY holds a photo of a pterodactyl, which he says is similar to the one that attacked him.

WEST PALM BEACH, Fla. —Shellshocked Alan Perry says a 25-foot pterodactyl ripped off his left arm while he angled for bass in the Florida Everglades.

"It was absolutely, positively the most ter-rifying experience of my life," the 48 year-old concrete company executive told reporters. "All I can think is that the Good Lord has big plans for me. Otherwise I'd be dead."

Perry was pulling a fish out of the water when he was attacked by the prehistoric creature, which he described as having "leathery flesh and a wingspan of at least 25 feet."

"I didn't have time to react," Perry told reporters. "The pain was blinding. I think I yelled, but I really don't remember because I was in shock. But I do remember one thing — and it's something I'll never forget: Seeing a pterodactyl fly away, about 5 feet above the water, with my bloody arm dangling from its beak.

"I felt like throwing up. And you know what? I did."

By JON MASTERS

PERRY shows photographers how he fought off the flying lizard. He survived, but lost his left arm.

THE WEEKLY WORLD NEWS CONCISE GUIDE TO EVOLUTION

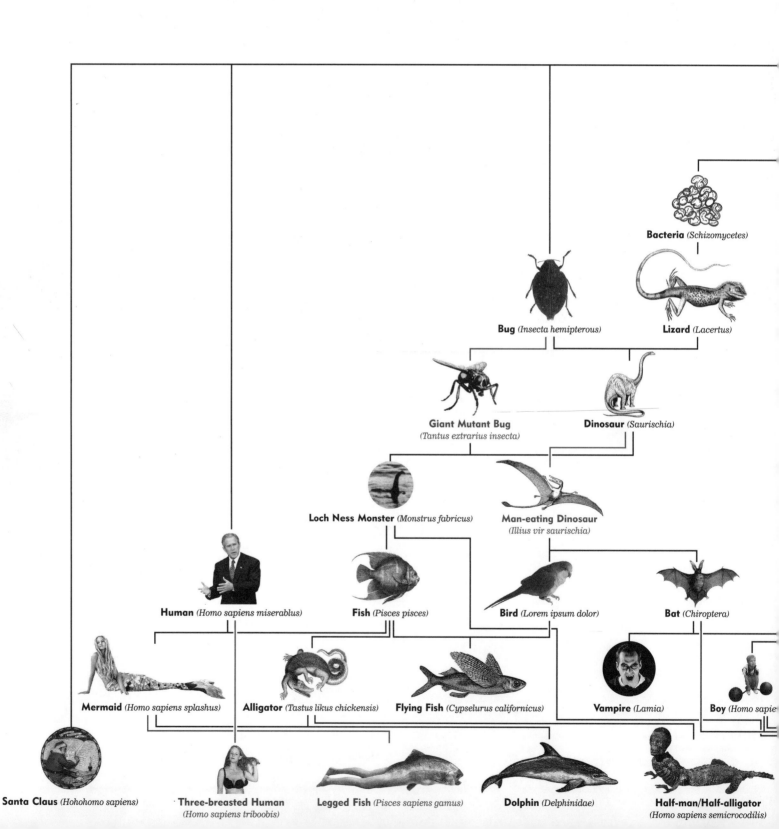

Bacteria (*Schizomycetes*)

Bug (*Insecta hemipterous*)   **Lizard** (*Lacertus*)

Giant Mutant Bug (*Tantus extrarius insecta*)   **Dinosaur** (*Saurischia*)

Loch Ness Monster (*Monstrus fabricus*)   **Man-eating Dinosaur** (*Illius vir saurischia*)

Human (*Homo sapiens miserablus*)   **Fish** (*Pisces pisces*)   **Bird** (*Lorem ipsum dolor*)   **Bat** (*Chiroptera*)

Mermaid (*Homo sapiens splashus*)   **Alligator** (*Tastus likus chickensis*)   **Flying Fish** (*Cypselurus californicus*)   **Vampire** (*Lamia*)   **Boy** (*Homo sapie*

Santa Claus (*Hohohomo sapiens*)   **Three-breasted Human** (*Homo sapiens triboobis*)   **Legged Fish** (*Pisces sapiens gamus*)   **Dolphin** (*Delphinidae*)   **Half-man/Half-alligator** (*Homo sapiens semicrocodilis*)

Aliens (*Obsessus anal probus*)

God (*Jokus cruelus*)

Microbes (*Microbios*)

The *Weekly World News* is proud to present this concise guide to the evolution of several of today's most ubiquitous and most notable species, both as a handy reference for adults as well as an indispensable educational tool for young children (especially those attending public schools where teaching the theory of evolution is discouraged). Religion-minded parents and godless liberals alike will find that this informative timeline has been intelligently designed to display the (frequently surprising) evolutionary relationships between the key species of this world as well as several others. Note: red lines indicate species that developed as a result of the perfectly natural process of mutation.

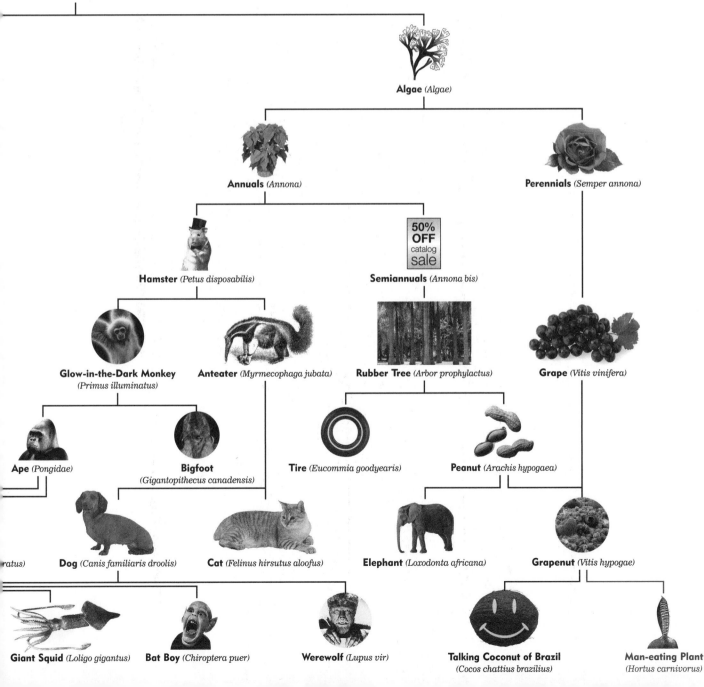

Algae (*Algae*)

Annuals (*Annona*)

Perennials (*Semper annona*)

Hamster (*Petus disposabilis*)

50% OFF catalog sale

Semiannuals (*Annona bis*)

Glow-in-the-Dark Monkey (*Primus illuminatus*)

Anteater (*Myrmecophaga jubata*)

Rubber Tree (*Arbor prophylactus*)

Grape (*Vitis vinifera*)

Ape (*Pongidae*)

Bigfoot (*Gigantopithecus canadensis*)

Tire (*Eucommia goodyearis*)

Peanut (*Arachis hypogaea*)

Dog (*Canis familiaris droolis*)

Cat (*Felinus hirsutus aloofus*)

Elephant (*Loxodonta africana*)

Grapenut (*Vitis hypogae*)

Giant Squid (*Loligo gigantus*)

Bat Boy (*Chiroptera puer*)

Werewolf (*Lupus vir*)

Talking Coconut of Brazil (*Cocos chattius brazilius*)

Man-eating Plant (*Hortus carnivorus*)

Approx. 3.5 billion years | Approx. 8,000 years | Approx. 7,427 years | Approx. 7,000 years | Approx. 6,500 years | Approx. 6,000 years | Approx. 4,500 years | Approx. 3,250 years | Approx. 2,500 years | Approx. 500 years

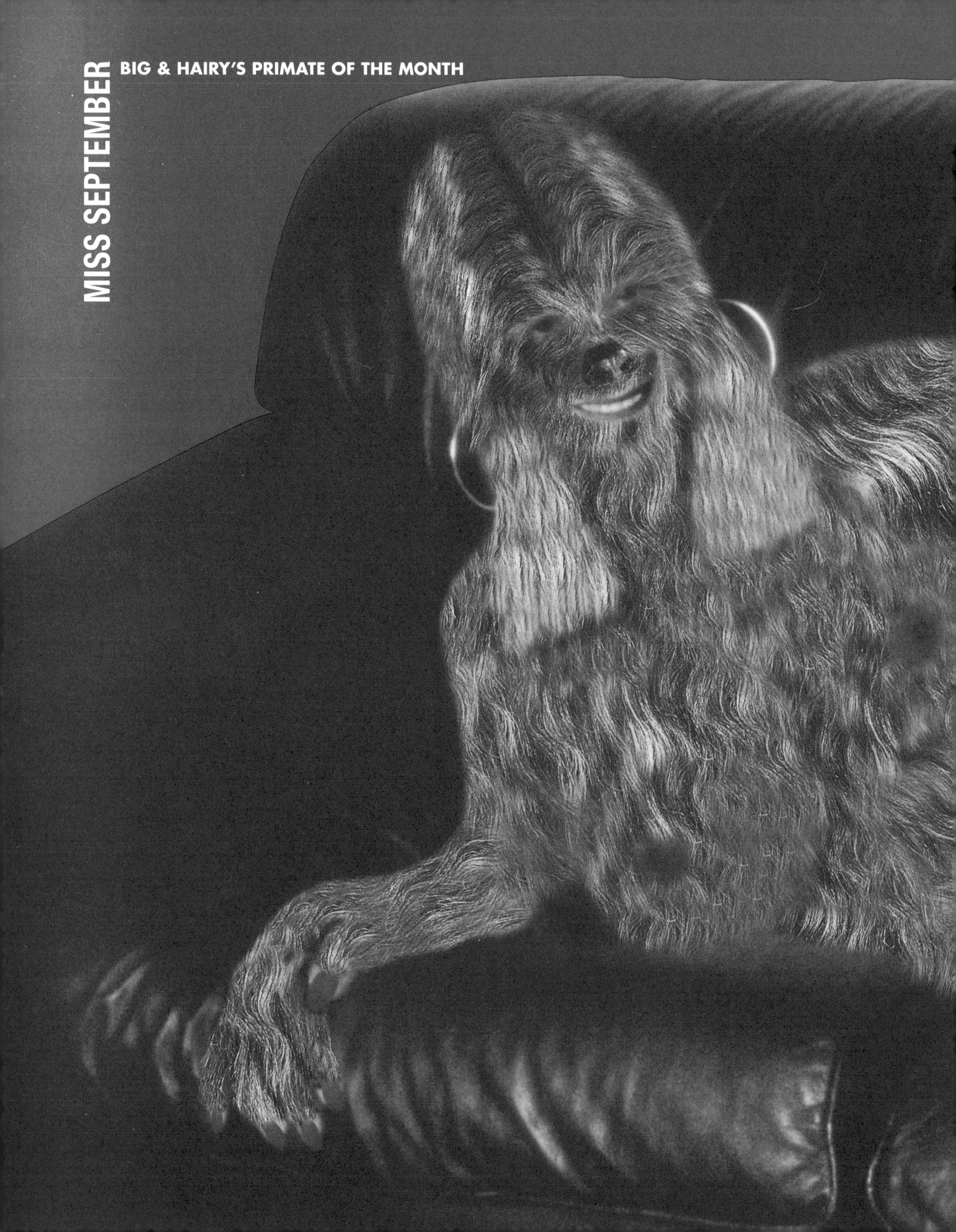
MISS SEPTEMBER
BIG & HAIRY'S PRIMATE OF THE MONTH

PRIMATE DATA SHEET

NAME: _____Helen_____

BUST: __52__ WAIST: __40__ HIPS: __44__ SHOES: __28½__

HEIGHT: __7' 2"__ WEIGHT: __125 kg (275 lbs.)__

BIRTHDATE: __4/3/78__ BIRTHPLACE: __Regina, Sasquatchewan__

AMBITIONS: __Becoming the first Bigfoot ballroom dancer to compete internationally.__
One problem, however, is that Bigfoot men tend to be less than dainty on their feet.

TURN-ONS: __I like a fella who is tall, isn't afraid of his feelings, and can catch trout with__
his bare hands. Watching sunsets at Banff National Park on a crisp evening. Body hair.

TURN-OFFS __Litterbugs, big game hunters, multinational timber corporations, lice or ticks,__
and that guy Grover Krantz.

FAVORITE PLACES: __The Alaskan National Wildlife Refuge; Beasley, Canada—where__
I grew up; and the dumpster behind Taco Bell.

FAVORITE MUSICIANS: __Ani DiFranco, Tom Jones, and Joe Cocker and Shelley Fabares—__
I really admire their hair.

FAVORITE MOVIES: __Pretty Woman, Hustle & Flow, Harry and the Hendersons, Legally__
Blonde 2; King Kong and Mighty Joe Young (original versions!); any movie on Lifetime TV.

FAVORITE FOODS: __Nuts, berries, grubs, pit-roasted squirrel, Baja Chicken Chalupas__

SECRET FANTASY: __Settling down with that special lumberjack and opening a little B&B__
somewhere near the Arctic Circle.

6th Grade—I got teased a
lot because of my hair.

The 90s—I was the first
to shave half my head.

All dressed up and no
place to go!

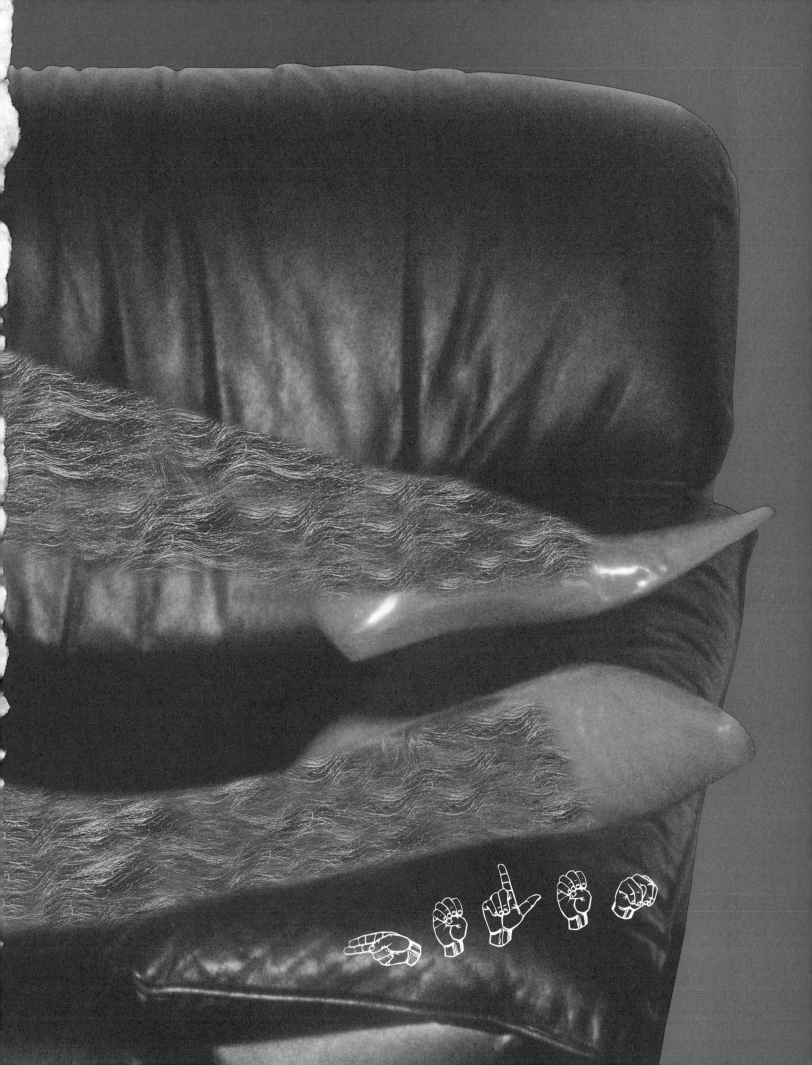

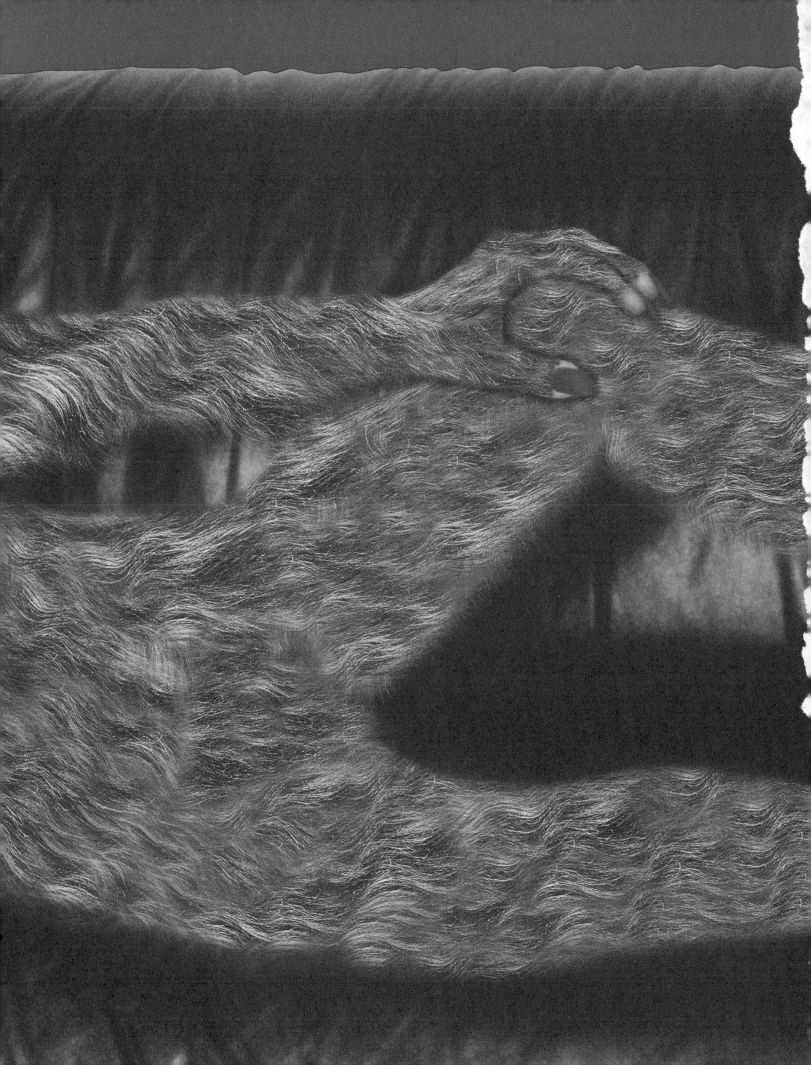

4 ELVIS IS ALIVE!

Penetrating Pop Culture Exposés

As Winston Churchill once said, "There's a fine line between the famous and the freakish—perhaps no line." Nowhere is this more apparent than in the pages of the *Weekly World News*, where celebrities and freaks not only share headlines, they exchange dating tips.

Where other publications hesitate to cover stories more scandalous than a simple, messy divorce or a celebrity's poor choice of outfit—no doubt for fear of a costly lawsuit or nasty phone calls from a rabid talent agent—*WWN* gives you all the little-known (and, in some

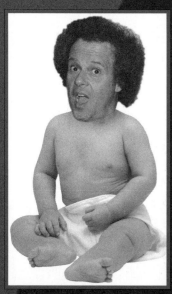

cases, truly startling) dirt on the rich and famous. From Jay Leno's prosthetic chin to Arnold the Pig's gay sex romps, the terrifying nocturnal ramblings of Mr. Rogers'

ghost to Paris Hilton's utter rejection by the alien paparazzi, readers have a place to turn for their extra scoop of Rocky Road.

WWN first came to be recognized as the world's foremost source on popular culture with its shocking 1988 report that Elvis Presley, the King of Rock and Roll, was — despite an elaborate funeral hoax in 1977 and much public mourning thereafter — alive and well and living in Kalamazoo, Michigan. The story became the most newsworthy event of the year, surpassing George Bush's presidential victory, Andy Gibb's death, the crash of Pan Am flight 103, the end of the Iran-Iraq war, and the season finale of *ALF* as the most talked-about event of the year. So in-depth was *WWN*'s coverage, in fact, that it even pocketed the highly coveted Global Media Excellence award.

"The Elvis story changed everything," says media expert Dr. Fernando Diaz. "News sources around the world stood up and took notice, and gossip rags realized that they had to dig deeper for stories that hit a little harder than such toothless feature pieces focusing on the brand of hair gel used by Tom Selleck or which Corey was cuter, Feldman or Haim."

Despite the newspaper's newfound notoriety, the truth is that *WWN* has always been the number-one source on the pop culture forces that *really* shape the world. Where else, for instance, could trend-watchers find information about the latest fashions — from surgically implanted high heels to eating mermaid sushi, growing elongated nose hair to collecting bellybutton lint, three-legged models to internal-organ tattoos — sweeping the globe?

Of course, your average Joe isn't the only guy scouring the pages of *WWN* to see what's hot and what's not. Celebrities themselves are often seen discreetly flipping its pages to find out which singer is really an android and what starlet has an alien implant lodged in her rear end. "The only gossip I'm interested in is in the *Weekly World News*," says Hollywood heartthrob Johnny Depp. And who can blame him?

READERS SPOT ELVIS!

FANS who've seen Elvis recently say he's now ready to step back into the limelight.

The King definitely lives — *NEWS* readers say — and may be on the verge of reclaiming the lofty throne he yielded nearly 11 years ago when he faked his own death!

In a series of spectacular sightings that dot the country from the rolling hills of New England to the shimmering shores of the Pacific, Elvis Presley in recent months has repeatedly revealed himself to scores of lucky fans.

Now 53, the rock-'n'-roll superstar even gave an impromptu performance of one of his hit songs for a college audience at a weekend party in Blacksburg, Va.

By **JOHN BLACKBURN**

"At first I thought he was just a professor looking for a good time," a young musician told *The NEWS.*

"But then I took a good look at him and my heart stopped. I knew it was Elvis, even though his hair was thinner and he was wearing a beard.

"He stood by himself for the longest while, just listening to the music. Suddenly, though, when we started playing 'Blue Suede Shoes,' he grabbed the microphone and started to sing. It was astonishing. Everyone stopped dancing.

"When the song was over, the crowd stood silent and motionless as The King casually strolled off and left the party. Then the spell was broken and I rushed after Elvis, but he had disappeared. I'd give anything to hear that man sing again, though. It was probably the greatest night of my life."

The King also has been spotted enjoying an auto race in Minnesota, fishing a rushing stream in upstate New York, strolling a rock-strewn beach in Maine, eating lunch at an out-of-the-way restaurant in the wine country of California, browsing through books at a little shop in the Florida panhandle and shopping at a posh Texas department store.

In an incredible encounter outside a Las Vegas hotel where a musical tribute to the rock idol was the featured attraction, Elvis confessed to a dedicated fan he had indeed staged his tragic death, but was now ready to step back into the limelight.

"We had both just come out of the hotel after viewing the tribute," the astounded fan told *The NEWS.*

"But I recognized him immediately — and when I confronted him, he smiled shyly and admitted he was Elvis.

"He told me he faked dying because fame had become too heavy a burden to bear. He had no life of his own, he said. He felt that he was always on display — like he was nothing more than a goldfish in a glass bowl.

"He said that after fading from public view he started a new life — a quiet life away from all the glitz and glamor of show biz — in a small town in Michigan.

"Recently, though, he told me, he decided to come out of seclusion and started traveling around the country. And he doesn't seem to mind if people recognize him — because he's considering resuming his career. He said he felt he had matured and would be better able now to handle the lack of privacy that comes with fame."

WWN EXCLUSIVE

DATELINE: JULY 19, 1988

I LIVED WITH ELVIS IN 1981!
Lie detector proves her incredible story!

Living Elvis writes letter to a fan!

By RAGAN DUNN

A woman claiming to be one of the best friends Elvis Presley ever had says she just got a letter from him that tells why he faked his death and assumed a new identity in 1977.

Verena Deuble, 87, who lives near Bad Nauheim, West Germany, says Presley signed and mailed the two-page typewritten letter from Memphis on October 11.

In it, he assured her that he was alive, happy and well. He also said that he went underground at the height of his career because he could no longer endure the rigors of stardom and didn't want to disappoint his fans.

"You don't know how happy I am to hear from that boy," Mrs. Deuble, who got to know Presley when he was in the Army and stationed in Bad Nauheim between 1958 and 1960, told reporters.

"He is a sweet, sweet man and has so much to offer. I just wish he had written me before this. I thought he was dead."

The letter has appeared in top German newspapers that obtained copies from Mrs. Deuble free of charge.

It goes like this:

Dearest Verena, I hope you're sitting down when you read this because what I'm going to tell you is going to come as a shock. Remember me? Elvis Presley? Well, I'm not dead like everybody thinks. I'm alive and doing just great.

I don't know why I haven't gotten around to writing you before. I guess I had to straighten things out. I was so pent up that I had to "kill" myself and start a new life.

I was killing myself with the drugs and the booze and the shows, anyway. I tried and I tried hard but I couldn't keep up the pace. Near the end I felt like I was the only human being in a sea of sharks.

I was getting pretty fat, too, and I think you know that my voice wasn't what it had been. I used to look at myself in the mirror and think about it. I'd say, "Elvis, the magic's gone. You're going to disappoint your fans."

Of course, I knew I was go-

ELVIS met the woman who received his recent letter while he was stationed in Germany in 1958.

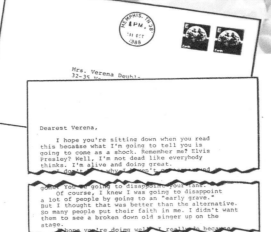

THE KING feared drugs and booze would turn him into a has-been and wanted to avoid that at all costs, he wrote.

Mrs. Verena Deuble
32-35 ...

Dearest Verena,

I hope you're sitting down when you read this because what I'm going to tell you is going to come as a shock. Remember me? Elvis Presley? Well, I'm not dead like everybody thinks. I'm alive and doing great.

... I don't know why I haven't gotten around ... gotten. You're going to disappoint your fans.

Of course, I knew I was going to disappoint a lot of people by going to an "early grave." But I thought that was better than the alternative. So many people put their faith in me. I didn't want them to see a broken down old singer up on the stage.

... hope you're doing well. I really do because ...

... let you know firsthand. Take care of yourself lady and think about me when you can.

Love, *[signature]*

P. S. I still remember those great sandwiches

In his own words, Presley tells why he disappeared!

ing to disappoint a lot of people by going to an "early grave." But I thought that was better than the alternative. So many people put their faith in me. I didn't want them to see a broken down old singer up on the stage.

I hope you're doing well, I really do, because I certainly am. I'm taking life as it comes and I enjoy being a regular fellah, I can't tell you how I did it

but I'm different now. I go anywhere I want and talk to everybody I see and nobody even suspects who I am.

You always were like a second mama to me, you know that, and I wish I could see you soon. Meanwhile, I just wanted you to know what I've been up to. There have been a lot of stories and books about me here in the States and I figured I'd let you know first-

hand. Take care of yourself, lady, and think about me when you can.

Love, Elvis Presley
P.S. I still remember those great sandwiches you used to make. I wish I had one right now!

News that Mrs. Deuble had received a letter from Presley touched off an immediate controversy among the rock legend's European fans.

Some, like fan club president Ethel Waring of Frankfurt, suggested that the letter may be a hoax.

Others, like freelance journalist Peter Richter, defended the authenticity of the letter on the grounds that Mrs. Deuble has absolutely nothing to gain by faking a letter from The King.

"The woman is well off and almost 90 years old," said Richter. "She could have sold the letter for a six-figure sum or even more if she had wanted to. But she gave it to the press for nothing. And she is very sincere about being Presley's friend.

"The signature at the end of the letter also appears to be genuine. Handwriting experts told the media they are 99 percent sure it is the real thing."

Repeated attempts to reach Mrs. Deuble, who has no telephone, have been unsuccessful.

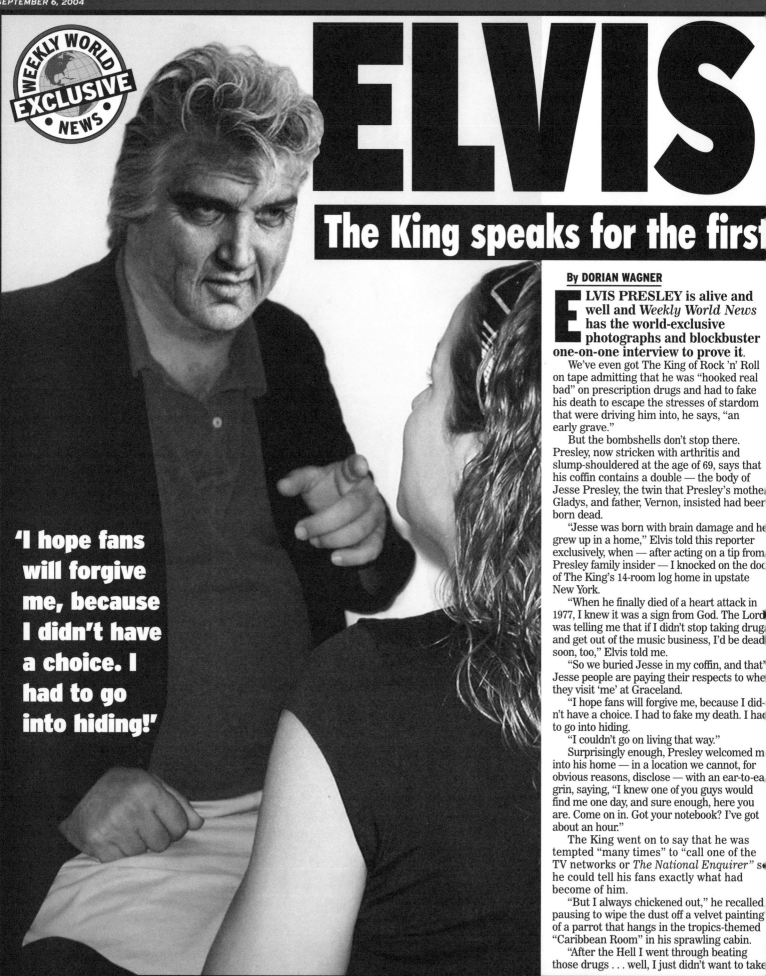

WEEKLY WORLD EXCLUSIVE NEWS

ELVIS

The King speaks for the first

'I hope fans will forgive me, because I didn't have a choice. I had to go into hiding!'

By DORIAN WAGNER

ELVIS PRESLEY is alive and well and *Weekly World News* has the world-exclusive photographs and blockbuster one-on-one interview to prove it.

We've even got The King of Rock 'n' Roll on tape admitting that he was "hooked real bad" on prescription drugs and had to fake his death to escape the stresses of stardom that were driving him into, he says, "an early grave."

But the bombshells don't stop there. Presley, now stricken with arthritis and slump-shouldered at the age of 69, says that his coffin contains a double — the body of Jesse Presley, the twin that Presley's mother, Gladys, and father, Vernon, insisted had been born dead.

"Jesse was born with brain damage and he grew up in a home," Elvis told this reporter exclusively, when — after acting on a tip from Presley family insider — I knocked on the door of The King's 14-room log home in upstate New York.

"When he finally died of a heart attack in 1977, I knew it was a sign from God. The Lord was telling me that if I didn't stop taking drugs and get out of the music business, I'd be dead soon, too," Elvis told me.

"So we buried Jesse in my coffin, and that's Jesse people are paying their respects to when they visit 'me' at Graceland.

"I hope fans will forgive me, because I didn't have a choice. I had to fake my death. I had to go into hiding.

"I couldn't go on living that way."

Surprisingly enough, Presley welcomed me into his home — in a location we cannot, for obvious reasons, disclose — with an ear-to-ear grin, saying, "I knew one of you guys would find me one day, and sure enough, here you are. Come on in. Got your notebook? I've got about an hour."

The King went on to say that he was tempted "many times" to "call one of the TV networks or *The National Enquirer*" so he could tell his fans exactly what had become of him.

"But I always chickened out," he recalled pausing to wipe the dust off a velvet painting of a parrot that hangs in the tropics-themed "Caribbean Room" in his sprawling cabin.

"After the Hell I went through beating those drugs . . . well, I just didn't want to take

IS ALIVE!

time since faking his death on Aug. 26, 1977

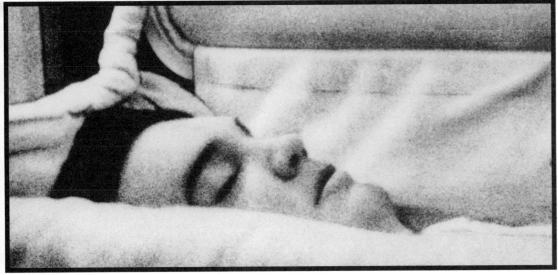

NOT THE REAL DEAL? Elvis says this was really his secret twin brother, Jesse Presley, and not him. He faked his own death to get away from all the stress of stardom. Maybe it's not always good to be King.

the chance that by going public, I'd somehow wind up back onstage and then start using dope again.

"Drugs are something I don't wish on my worst enemy.

"The first six months after I went into hiding, I crawled the walls getting off those things, but the Lord gave me the strength to go on."

The King declined to answer questions about his family — ex-wife Priscilla Presley and daughter Lisa Marie — although he did let it slip that he is "very proud of that young lady."

He was only slightly more talkative about old friends and relatives, some of whom rushed to capitalize on his name after he faked his death and went into hiding, as he puts it, "in the mountains of North Carolina, up near Cherokee where a man can disappear as long as he wants to."

"Some of them were true-blue, and some of them sold me and my reputation down the river," he said.

Interestingly enough, Presley — who admits that he was "blowed up like an old toad fish" when he disappeared from public view 27 years ago — is still on the chunky side.

Given the fact that he snacked on fresh organic veggies and roasted tofu throughout the interview, that seemed odd — until he revealed that he "still likes to fry up peanut butter and banana sandwiches in a couple of sticks of butter," creating the high-calorie, heart-clogging treats that he made famous.

"Some things never change," he chuckled, pointing a fat finger at his still-ample belly.

"I'm not doing a whole lot of shakin' anymore, but my herbalist — I don't trust doctors after all those drugs they gave me — says I'll live to be 100."

Presley says he still sings "every day of my life, but only in the shower." And he is quick to point out that he has "no desire to record a new

THE KING started out shakin' — and ended up fakin'.

album or perform live on stage."

"Rock 'n' roll is a young man's game," he says. "I wish I would have had sense enough to have realized that sooner.

"Instead of getting myself into trouble with prescription pills, I'd have retired and lived a happy life."

The King says he still sees "a few old friends" — including an ex-Beatle who, with only two of them still alive, has to be either Ringo Starr or Paul McCartney.

Intriguingly, he went on to insist that he "absolutely, positively does not live alone."

He refused to elaborate, but I noticed two pairs of petite pantyhose and a breast-enhancing "Wonder Bra" hanging from the shower head in a bathroom, indicating that at least one of the "old friends" and perhaps the person who lives with

Elvis is a woman.

"I know you're looking for a wedding band but see for yourself — I don't wear any jewelry," Presley told me, referring to the heavy gold "Taking Care of Business in a Flash" ring that Elvis wore throughout the latter part of his career.

As for how he has occupied himself during his long years in hiding, the ex-superstar simply says, "I've been doing all the things that ordinary people do — reading, piddling around the house. I've even got a little garden out back.

"It's not that hard to hide when people think you're dead," he continued. "Because when somebody does see you, everybody makes fun of them and calls them crazy. And besides, the older you get, the less you look like the young guy people remember, so it's easy to put on sunglasses and a fake mustache and go anywhere you want.

"Back in the late '80s and early '90s there was that wave of 'Elvis sightings' all over the U.S. — which tickled me to no end.

"Some of them were the real me and some must have been impersonators. You'll have to guess which were the real deal 'cause I ain't telling."

Now that the living legend has gone public, of course, the big question is, "Will he continue to live reclusively or again take center stage?"

"You might see me on a talk show from time to time if there's a cause I want to promote or a message I want to get out," he said.

"But my recording days are over, and I have no desire to perform. When it comes to listening to music, well, you know, I like some of these new people like Celine Dion and The Backstreet Boys and Lisa Marie. Cher is still good, too.

"But most of the time I just put on one of my old albums and let my mind drift back to the good old days when rock 'n' roll was new and the people of my generation were still kids who thought we'd never grow old.

"Boy, were we wrong."

JIMMY HOFFA WAS TURNED INTO DOG FOOD!

Mafia killed Teamsters boss — then shipped his body to pet food factory, stunning new evidence says

By RANDY JEFFRIES/*Weekly World News*

A WELL FED DOG like this one might have gotten a piece of Hoffa.

THE TRUTH UNFOLDS — Teamsters leader Jimmy Hoffa has gone to the dogs.

WWN EXTRA

What are the ingredients of the average can of dog food?

- Weekly World News, 0.5%
- Other newspaper, 4%
- Jimmy Hoffa, 0.4%
- David Crosby's hair, 1.1%
- Bacon bits, 6%
- Unidentifiable, 26%
- Gizzard, 18%
- Road kill, 29%
- Horse, 7%
- Olive Garden breadsticks, 8%

WASHINGTON — After 25 long years, the mystery of union leader Jimmy Hoffa's disappearance has been solved: The controversial Teamsters boss was turned into dog chow in a South American pet food factory!

Washington crime writer Andrew Rebinow, who has been consulted by police forces all over the nation, has come forth with the grisly truth in a soon-to-be-released book called, *The Ugly Death of Jimmy Hoffa.*

Rebinow presents a powerful case for his allegation that Hoffa's body was shipped to — and sold by — a South American dog food company.

"Since Hoffa vanished without a trace on July 30, 1975, there has been endless speculation about what became of him," Rebinow writes in the book's introduction.

"Some believe he was buried in cement during the construction of Giants Stadium in East Rutherford, N.J.

"Others say he's still alive and living in South America.

"There have even been some Hollywood movies that have offered well-meaning but misguided theories about what happened on that day.

"But the actual events surrounding the bizarre case are stranger than celluloid fiction."

Quoting sources as varied as Mafia kingpins, federal agents and high-ranking politicians, Rebinow paints a violent picture that could make the most sensational screenwriter squeamish.

The author continues:

"After sorting through dozens of boxes of photographs, listening to thousands of hours of taped interviews and — most convincing of all — seeing the results of a thorough DNA test, there is no doubt in my mind: James Hoffa was murdered by the mob, sold to an Argentine dog food company and devoured by pets all over South America."

Rebinow traces the last day in the life of Hoffa, then 62, as he met with reputed mobsters Anthony Provenzano and Anthony Giacalone in the parking lot of the Red Fox Inn in Detroit, Mich.

"The meeting lasted about three-quarters of an hour," Rebinow says.

"The killing took place after the meeting. Giacalone and Provenzano were not involved.

"Hoffa was garroted 10 minutes after that meeting by two other men."

The author will not divulge the identity of the killers, but will say this: "They were people Jimmy thought he could trust."

Perhaps the most graphic evidence in the book is the result of a test run by a team of prominent Washington scientists.

The researchers matched the DNA in a can of 25-year-old dog food with that of a skin sample taken in 1972 when the famed union boss was tested for cancer.

The test leaves no doubt that the meat in the can was taken from Hoffa's corpse.

"It's one of the most vicious and dehumanizing ends a man could possibly come to," Rebinow says.

"I can't imagine a more cruel or gruesome thing a person could do — especially a person who he trusted.

"This was more than just a politically expedient assassination.

"It was the expression of a very personal rage."

The Ugly Death of Jimmy Hoffa is due to hit the bookstores this December.

CRIME WRITER
Andrew Rebinow.

By **CLIFF LINEDECKER**
Weekly World News

Was Lawrence Welk murdered?

SANTA MONICA, Calif. — Beloved bandleader Lawrence Welk was murdered by wild-eyed anti-alcohol fanatics who were convinced his "champagne music" was encouraging young people to drink, claims a former band member.

"It's ironic that a man who was deeply committed to the nation's young and determined to provide them with clean, wholesome entertainment, should be targeted for assassination by a bunch of wacko zealots," the ex band member confided to a fan magazine, *Champagne Dreams*.

The musician, who was admittedly frightened that he might be targeted for speaking out, agreed to the interview with the California-based magazine only after he was assured of complete anonymity.

The hit was believed to have been carried out by a group called MOB — Mothers Opposed to Booze, a shadowy organization of modern-day Carrie Nations who are dedicated to reenacting national Prohibition laws and promoting prune juice as the new drink of choice at campus keg parties and other social occasions.

When Welk, 89, died at his home in Santa Monica, Calif., on Sunday night, May 17, 1992, pneumonia was officially ruled as the cause of death.

But his longtime colleague said private investigators confirmed that a MOB woman had slipped a slow acting poison into his champagne months earlier that led to a slow, lingering death.

"Anyone who gets in MOB's way is ruthlessly rubbed out," he said.

The musician told the reporter, "Poor Lawrence was planning a concert tour of Berkeley and other major college campuses when he was snuffed out."

SOME called Lawrence Welk's tunes wholesome entertainment. Some called it Devil music.

Champagne music made him a target of anti-liquor terrorists!

CELEB MOB HITS?

Lawrence Welk may not have been the only victim of the ruthless MOB (Mothers Opposed to Booze). Below are some other celebs who are rumored to have been rubbed out by the MOB for their widely known drinking habits.

ANDY GIBB Many think Andy was one of the first to stand in the way of the MOB.

DANA PLATO died in 1999 of an alleged suicide — some aren't so sure.

RIVER PHOENIX The actor died of an overdose in 1993 but may have been in the target hairs of the MOB for years.

CHRIS FARLEY His drinking binges were known in celeb circles. He died in 1997 of an alleged overdose.

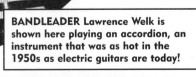

BANDLEADER Lawrence Welk is shown here playing an accordion, an instrument that was as hot in the 1950s as electric guitars are today!

Prissy porker from TV's Green Acres EXPOSED!

By **DOUGLAS VINCENT**/*Weekly World News*

Arnold the pig was GAY

ARNOLD was caught having sex with another male pig.

HOLLYWOOD — Though his trainer and others went to great lengths to hide the fact, one of television's best-loved performers — Arnold the pig on *Green Acres* — was gay!

So claims author Dennis Jenkins in his upcoming book, *Fur and Fame: The Life and Times of Hollywood's Greatest Animal Actors*, scheduled to be published later this year.

"To put it quite simply, Arnold Ziffel was a closet queen," states Jenkins, who spent nearly three years researching his revealing tell-all. "He was an extremely talented pig, but both his owner/trainer and the show's producers knew that if word of Arnold's homosexuality ever got out, it would have a devastating effect on the show's popularity, so they went to great lengths to hide it."

In one bizarre incident, Eva Gabor, who played Lisa Douglas on the show, turned a corner and stumbled on Arnold having sex with another male pig that had been brought in for a particular episode.

"Eva was shocked," Jenkins reports. "She had never considered that Arnold would have a sex life, much less one involving gay sex."

Despite his alternative lifestyle, Arnold was a consummate professional when the cameras were rolling. "Arnold was able to do almost anything his trainer asked of him," Jenkins says. "He could learn new tricks with remarkable speed — sometimes in a matter of minutes — and repeat them for take after take. The cast loved working with him."

Arnold's sexual orientation became known when his trainer tried to put him up for stud and found that Arnold simply wasn't interested in the opposite sex, preferring instead the company of his own gender. Not surprisingly, he also liked to dress up in women's clothing.

"Hollywood animal trainers love to tell the story of Arnold's hat," Jenkins says. "According to legend, Arnold's owner tried to teach him to wear a little top hat, but Arnold wouldn't go for it. He preferred a pink toy tiara instead."

GREEN ACRES stars Eddie Albert and Eva Gabor loved Arnold despite his sexual preference.

WWN EXTRA

SECRETS OF OTHER CELEBRITY ANIMALS

Arnold wasn't the only Hollywood quadruped who enjoyed rolling in a little flaming hay. It's well known among celebrity insiders that Lassie was not only a transvestite, but was a long-time "roommate" of Rin-Tin-Tin, K9 cop. Here are five more shocking secrets about Hollywood animals:

* **Eddie the Dog** from TV's *Frasier* had his spots painted on before each episode's taping.

* One of **Flipper**'s famous appendages was detached in a gruesome tuna-net incident in 1965 and was replaced with a bionic flipper during the last two seasons of the hit show. After it started malfunctioning, producers had the flipper replaced, and the famous dolphin went finless during one episode, "Cap in Love," in which you never see Flipper's right fin.

* Michael Jackson's sidekick **Bubbles the Chimp** was the true composer of "Free the World."

* Although it's Hollywood legend that **Mr. Ed** would eat peanut butter to make it look like he was talking, in reality he ate it because he had the munchies. Ed was a notorious pothead and insisted on toking up before filming, using a horse-size bong made from a grain auger and an extra-large feed bowl.

* The first golden retriever to play **Comet** on the groundbreaking '80s sitcom *Full House* was fired when she went into a rabid frenzy and brutally mauled, then devoured, the forgotten third Olsen triplet.

SWEATIN' WITH THE NEWBIE!

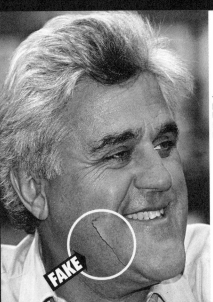

MORE OF him to love! Health and exercise guru Richard Simmons has helped millions of folks lose weight and feel great!

IT'S Richard Simmons as you haven't seen him in nearly 50 years!

Did mad scientist clone Richard Simmons?

By CARROLL KEENER

LONDON — A renegade biologist announced that he not only cloned the world's first human, but that he successfully cloned Richard Simmons.

Dr. Nunzio Altiplano, a well-known fertility expert, made the shocking announcement in London recently, claiming that a likeness of Richard Simmons — identical down to the smallest cell — is currently thriving in its crib at the doctor's secret laboratory, somewhere in the Canary Islands.

DR. NUNZIO ALTIPLANO.

"This is an enormous breakthrough," gushed Dr. Altiplano.

"Not only have I duplicated a human being for the first time in world history, I have duplicated a great human being.

"I have set the guidelines for all future human cloning — to propagate only the best in mankind."

Altiplano, who was in London to visit Dolly the sheep, said he first hit on the idea of cloning Richard Simmons while doing sit-ups to the chatty celebrity's workout video, *Sweatin' to the Oldies.*

"It struck me that this was a man," explained Dr. Altiplano, "the kind of man the world needs more of. His incredible wit and sagacity made me see that there should be more men like Richard Simmons — many more.

"And I intend to make many more clones of Richard — an army of them — to help the world."

The cloning was denounced by the Human Fertilization and Embryology Authority (HFEA) in England, whose members have publicly referred to Dr. Altiplano as "a madman" on more than one occasion.

"They said that Napoleon was mad," responded Dr. Altiplano. "They said Hannibal was mad, and that Caesar was maddest of them all!

"I say let time decide who is right."

— By JOHN THOMAS

WWN EXCLUSIVE
DATELINE: OCTOBER 8, 2004

JAY LENO'S CHIN IS FAKE

JAY'S 12-ounce prosthetic chin has peeled away several times behind the cameras.

LENO hopes new look will help him land big-screen leading roles.

FAKE

REAL

Man grows world's longest nose hair!

BUFFALO, N.Y. — As gross as it might seem, Alan Byrdal is about to make it into *Guinness World Records* — for having the longest nose hair in the world!

The 64-year-old former pool table salesman has been pursuing the record "since the mid-1980s," he says. And now that the longest of his nose hairs has reached a staggering 6.12 inches, he's ready to stake his claim to the record.

"I guess everyone wants to be known for something, and this is it for me," he said. "I've heard all the comments — I know some people might say it's disgusting or whatever. But you can bet most of those people will never make it into any kind of record book."

Byrdal said he had to start cutting his nose hairs when he was about 27 years old because they grew so fast.

"My dad and grandfather had the same problem," he said. "Mine started growing when I was fairly young and back then it was pretty gross. Long nose hairs are not really the kind of thing the girls go for."

But when Byrdal reached his 50s, he decided to forget

By AMY LECHNER
Weekly World News

about trimming his nose hairs every day.

"By that time my hairs were growing faster than they ever had," the lifelong bachelor said. "I decided, to heck with it, let's see how long they can grow."

Byrdal now admits he "probably became obsessed" with his bizarre hobby.

"It became the most important thing in my life," he said. "I still remember how surprised I was when I found out there wasn't an official world record for longest nose hairs."

Byrdal said he probably would never have done it if he had the active social life he enjoyed when he was younger.

"Nowadays I live by myself and hang around the same group of guys most of the time," he said. "I guess the girl down at the grocery store has seen me so many times she doesn't even notice anymore.

"But I'm getting ready for that all to change now. I'm going to be famous when people all over the world hear about how long my nose hairs are."

SWEET SMELL OF SUCCESS! After more than 15 years, Alan Byrdal has almost reached his goal of getting into the *Guinness World Records.*

FLASHBACK TO: WEEKLY WORLD NEWS JANUARY 1999

WWN EXTRA
WORLD'S LONGEST EAR HAIR!

Inspired by Alan Byrdal's courage and passion, Armand Boyd has cultivated the world's longest ear hair in the hopes of gaining his turn in the spotlight.

"At first I just had these monster earfros," Boyd says of the experience of developing his hirsute auricles. "Then I made them into some kicking dreads, but that didn't fly so well with the boss—I work in accounting. So finally I bought myself some beads and had my mother braid them."

By BRETT ANNISTON
Dornum, Germany

RESEARCHER REVEALS: Karl Marx was one of the Marx Brothers!

GERMAN philosopher Karl Marx achieved lasting fame as the father of Communism — but in later years, he failed miserably when he tried his hand at show business — as one of the original Marx Brothers!

That's the surprising revelation of researcher Ronald Warkens, author of the upcoming book *Karl Marx: The Lost Vaudeville Years.*

"Karl, who used the stage name Beardo, possessed a brilliant intellect, but his comic timing was lousy," says Warkens.

"Worse still, he would often diverge from the script during performances to expound upon some of his pet theories, such as the 'withering away of the state.'

"Understandably, audiences weren't thrilled by these ad-libs, and he was frequently booed off the stage.

"He performed for only eight months before he dropped out of the family act — at the request of his more talented brothers."

When most Americans hear "Marx Brothers," they typically think only of Groucho, Chico and Harpo. They often forget Zeppo, who usually played the romantic lead in the hilarious films.

"Only real Marx Brothers fanatics remember Gummo, who quit show business in the 1920s, when the brothers were still in vaudeville," notes Warkens. "And virtually no one knows about Beardo."

It's no accident that Karl's name was totally erased from the comedy group's official bio.

"By the 1930s, Communism was a dirty word and the name Karl Marx was one of the most hated in the world," explains Warkens. "To survive in Hollywood, it was essential for the Marx Brothers to obliterate all their connections to the figure who'd become the black sheep of the family."

Technically, Karl Marx was an uncle of Groucho and his siblings.

"He was an elder half-brother of

MARX BROTHERS:
From left, Groucho, Harpo, Chico, Karl (a.k.a. Beardo) Marx, author of the *Communist Manifesto.*

their father Sam and, by coincidence, also more distantly related to their mother Minnie Schonberg, who was born in Dornum, Germany," reveals Warkens.

"The whole clan was involved in show business — Minnie's father worked as a ventriloquist."

As a young man, Karl, however, rejected the family showbiz tradition in favor of a career in academia. In 1847, he penned the infamous *Communist Manifesto.*

"Karl thought it would make him the darling of the academic world," says Warkens. "But as a result of his incendiary ideas, revolutions soon broke out all across Europe and he became a pariah."

Exiled from intellectual circles and finding it difficult to land work, Karl eventually made a reluctant return to the family business — entertainment.

"At that time, the late 1870s, Sam Marx's brothers were performing in German beer halls, doing a primitive version of the vaudeville act Groucho, Chico and Harpo would later make famous in America," Warkens explains.

"Karl appeared on stage with these original Marx brothers — who originated the personas we now know and love: A mustachioed wiseguy with a cigar, an Italian who keeps mangling the language and a silent clown who gets laughs through pantomime."

While the crowd adored the other brothers, they didn't like Beardo, who generally appeared as a professor trying in vain to keep order in a class.

"Night after night, the audience would pelt poor Karl with tomatoes," reveals Warkens. "Even so, he doggedly persevered.

"Finally, one night his half-brothers quietly took him aside and convinced him that showbiz wasn't for him."

Karl died in 1883 — four years before the birth of Chico, the first of the "next generation" Marx Brothers who were destined to make the act world-famous.

"But many of the classic comedy sketches Karl wrote were used in the Marx Brothers act well into the 1920s," Warkens says

"While he lacked stage presence, he actually had a good sense of humor."

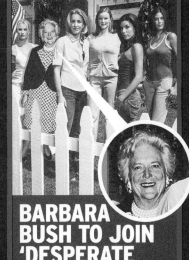

BARBARA BUSH TO JOIN 'DESPERATE HOUSEWIVES'

By GEORGE SANFORD

CRAWFORD, Texas — The stars of *Desperate Housewives* may be a bit over the hill, but they're spring chickens compared to the newest cast member — former First Lady Barbara Bush!

Initially, producers had sought Laura Bush, who had joked publicly about being a "desperate housewife."

"Laura politely declined," revealed the insider. "But she suggested, 'Ask my mother-in-law.' Mrs. Bush jumped at the offer."

It turns out that bored-stiff Barbara is desperate, too.

"George Senior is always doing some silly stunt like jumping out of an airplane while I'm at home twiddling my thumbs," she reportedly told producers. "Now it's my turn to be outrageous."

Producers are banking on the beloved Republican icon to help them with conservatives.

"The show has taken a lot of heat because of its racy content — there's even been boycott talk," explained another source.

"We're hoping having Barbara in the cast will defuse the criticism — and increase ratings in the Red States."

Barbara will play Matilda Larson, a recent widow whose homespun humor and strong morals offset the bed-hopping behavior of her naughty neighbors.

"Barbara's character won't be a prude however — she's a sexually savvy woman who makes ribald one-liners, like 'Ma' in *The Golden Girls.*" the source revealed.

"And in one episode, she'll even land in bed with a stud half her age."

OPRAH TO REPLACE

ALIEN PERSONAL ADS

There's someone outer there for everyone

It is common knowledge that *WWN* is dedicated to improving the lives of its readers, and what better upgrade could we provide than a shot at true love? Whether it be between a man and a woman, a man and a she-male, a former President and his three-breasted intern, a woman and a dolphin, a Bigfoot and a circus performer, a mermaid and a legged fish, two possessed teddy bears, a zombie and a pickled cerebellum, love is on offer in the extremely popular personals section of the *Weekly World News*.

Of course, love is never harder to find than when you're thousands of light-years from home, which is why *WWN* is proud to offer a special section for aliens. Collected here are some of the most touching, heart (or other love-organ) warming, and wittiest personal ads that aliens seeking love (or love seeking aliens) have placed over the decades (and all for only a small fee).

answer=42

Slimeballs Need Not Apply—Spunky female arachnoid from Betelgeuse seeks sentient he-lizard for fun and possible relationship. I've dated a lot of slimy ETs and am ready for a guy who's more on the dry and scaly side. If you live with your parents, don't understand the importance of returning phone calls, and think leaking ectoplasm is cool, don't bother responding to this ad—been there, done that!

ocdblackhole

Will You Float with Me?—Sexless nebulous life form seeks other nebuloids for conversation, maybe more. Must be detail-oriented. Ability to survive in the vastness of space a plus.

hasidembutdon'thear'em

Chosen One from Europa Seeking Same—Humanoid rabbinical scholar from Jupiter's moon seeks nice Jewish girl ready to start a family on Earth. I've lived all over the universe since my days on kibbutz and am ready to settle down. Must have strong faith and be open to living in Israel.

LINCOLN ON $5 BILL

WASHINGTON — The familiar face of Abraham Lincoln on the five-dollar bill could soon be replaced by daytime talk show host Oprah Winfrey.

By MATT BETT
Weekly World News

According to a well-placed insider, a congressional sub-committee is debating a secret initiative to replace all the United States Presidents featured on currency with modern celebrities.

"The first celebrity was obvious," said the Treasury Department source. "Everybody loves Oprah."

The initiative is in response to a landmark study that shows students are growing increasingly unfamiliar with this nation's historical figures.

According to the survey, kids are still familiar with George Washington, but beyond that, are clueless.

"Alexander Hamilton is on the ten-dollar bill. Even most members of Congress don't know who he is," the source admitted.

The proposed legislation would immediately update the five-dollar bill and gradually introduce changes to the remaining denominations.

"The lawmakers are working toward a nationwide rollout of the new bills by the end of 2002," the source confirmed. "Just in time for Christmas shopping."

The subcommittee has also considered the positive effect the new bills will have on the economy. There is consensus that the newly redesigned money will motivate people to shop more.

"Those debating the bill believe that people will have more fun spending money if it has pictures of familiar faces," the source concurred.

Other celebrities being considered include Martin Sheen, Christina Aguilera, Bruce Willis, Michael Jordan and Scooby Doo.

The congressional sessions have been conducted behind closed doors for fear of Hollywood publicists lobbying the lawmakers to feature their clients and crazed fans suggesting their favorite stars.

"The members of the Cameron Diaz fan club have been crashing the Capitol Hill switchboard," said the source. "But, she honestly doesn't have a chance."

WHAT DO YOU THINK?

Who in the world is Alexander Hamilton? Ever heard of Benjamin Franklin? Should they stay on their bills or would you rather see your favorite celeb gracing the face of a Hamilton's $10 or Franklin's C-note. Tell us what you think. Write to: Change The Faces Poll, c/o Weekly World News, 5401 NW Broken Sound Blvd., Boca Raton, FL 33487. Or you can email us at: editor@weeklyworldnews.com

---

gbttfriendly

Trisexual Seeks Same—Horny green alien with three sex organs (his, hers, and other) looking for another adventurous E.T. who likes to play the trifecta. Must have at least six limbs—no Scorpios, please.

yecancu

Human, All Too Human—One-eyed humanoid from Dextron seeks fellow E.T. for friendship, possibly more. I enjoy going to Earthside Star Trek conventions, eating donuts, telepathy, and abducting humans from portable toilets. Looking for someone who isn't afraid to just cut loose every once and a while. Must be human acting/appearing, non-smoker preferred.

aderhater

Famous E.T. Looking for Love—I'm a highly intelligent, traditionally tall, dark, and handsome male E.T. who has had several well-publicized affairs and am now looking for a human female for long-term commitment, possible (?) reproduction. Sorry, no celebrity hounds and no First Ladies.

oldiebutgoodie

Save the Last Dance For Me—Mature E.T. from the Horsehead Nebula ISO female alien, aged 2,000–2,500, for a second chance at love. Looking for someone to enjoy the finer things in life with: warming our tentacles in front of a fire, molting together, and watching the suns rise. I'm kind and bulbous—give me a chance and maybe we can spend the last few hundred years of our lives together.

koolkolor

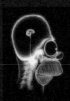

Let's Cuddle—Single yellow male seeks green/purple/blue male/female/it for companionship, love. I have no sex organs, but I have a great sense of humor and a heart that's bigger than my head. You: have a steady job (ain't nothin' goin' on but the rent!), be open and honest, and have earlobes.

iheartaliens

Hot Earth Babe Seeks Multiple Alien Playmates—Sexy female Earthling ISO two to four sexual partners for frank exploration of interspecial, multiple-partner sex play. Must be open-minded, honest, preferably in possession of both male and female reproductive organs, and like to watch and be watched. No insectoids, please!

playdroid

Earth Mag Seeks E.T. Hotties—Calling all hotties! Intergalactically renowned monthly laddie mag seeks attractive female E.T.s for full-frontal, artistic nude pictorials. Must be young (relative to expected species lifespan), personable, attractive, and free for long weekends at the Space Mansion on Earth's moon. No molters and no immature instars (you know you who you are). Please send JPEGs of head, thorax, and full-body to this email address: et_nude@playdroid.space or visit our Website at www.playdroid.space.

PROCTOLOGISTS FINALLY GET THEIR OWN HALL OF FAME!

Doctors tired of being the butt of jokes!

SURGEON SUSPENDED FOR WRITING CURSES ON ORGANS

By **NICK JEFFREYS**

SULU VALLEY, Calif. – Dr. Haden "Dutch" Vanderflooger was suspended without pay from California's prestigious Surgery Depot for writing filthy swear words on patients' internal organs, say police.

Investigators, tipped off by an outraged nurse, say they've already discovered five cases of cursed guts. Vanderflooger scribbled:
● @#$% You on a pancreas
● Screw Off on a liver
● Go To Hell on a heart
● Ass (on one lung) Hole (on the other)
● #!%sucker, #!%sucker, #!%sucker, #!%sucker scrawled more than 50 times the length of a small intestine.

Vanderflooger freely admits to the surgical graffiti.

"Hey, it's a hobby," says the doctor. "Some guys fish or bowl or build ship models. I write obscene words on my patients' insides. It doesn't hurt them. I make sure to use non-toxic magic markers, and it makes me laugh. Come on. My job is very serious. I need to lighten the mood or I'd go nuts."

After the peeved R.N. ratted to cops, a few of Vanderflooger's patients volunteered to undergo free MRI procedures so law enforcement officials could collect evidence. The films were turned over to hospital administrators, who immediately cut off the surgeon's privileges until they could decide what to do next.

"Vanderflooger is such a fine physician that his patients don't want to press charges against the man who saved their lives," says Sulu Valley, Calif., police chief Joe Esposito. "And when we told them what was written on their organs, they thought it was hilarious."

WORLD'S

ARE YOU KIDDING?

The richest goldfish in the world is Goldie, who lives in Beijing, China, and inherited $100 million from her adoring owner.

RICHEST HAMSTER

Wealthy guy leaves $73 million to pet

By NICK JEFFREYS
New York, N.Y.

THE LATE Jonathan Van Wilker III bequeathed his entire estate of $73 million to his pet hamster Scooter, and the rodent is enjoying the heck out of it, says the dead man's enraged son.

"Sometimes when I look at that stupid little glorified rat I could swear he's sneering at me," says Jonathan Van Wilker IV.

"Father loved me more — I hate that little bastard. I inherited Dad's collection of toilet seat covers."

According to Sherwood Grothschild, an old family friend and Scooter's legal guardian, Scooter is living the good life.

"The first thing he bought with his inheritance was a gold-plated wheel," says Grothschild. "Then he hired another hamster as a 'chauffeur' to run on it for him while Scooter watches his 96-inch flat-screen TV. It's really cute. The driver has a tiny cap and uniform he comes to work in every day. Scooter is old-fashioned. He likes the servants to

SCOOTER and a special friend vacation in the Hamptons.

dress well."

The newly wealthy pet also went on a wild spending spree in New York City's fanciest boutiques that was so outrageous it would put the Hilton hotel heiresses to shame.

"Scooter went berserk," says Grothschild. "I hired him a stretch limo so he could shop in style. We stopped at the pet bakery where they make special treats for discerning animals.

"We went to Tiffany's where he purchased a lovely sterling silver water bowl inlaid with diamonds.

"Then it was on to Cartier, where world-renowned watch maker Kraus Kessler fashioned Scooter the tiniest wrist watch in the world. It has a square face with emeralds and rubies

SCOOTER's chauffeur runs on a golden wheel.

around it. Quite nice, actually. A little flashy for my taste, though."

Scooter went on to fill the limousine with expensive jewelry, clothes, fashion accessories and gifts for his hamster

friends, then hauled them all home to his new $50 million mansion in swanky Greenwich, Conn.

"It has an outdoor and indoor pool," reports Grothschild. "Scooter loves to swim. Of course, there are maids, a butler, two chefs who specialize in hamster pellets, a gardener and a guy who follows Scooter around with an itty bitty pooper scooper.

"He also has female 'visitors.' I never knew there were hamster hookers, but I guess they have needs, too."

The extravagant lifestyle may sound ridiculous to some folks, but Scooter has his reasons for squandering the dough fast and furious.

"Scooter's lifespan is only about 12 months," says Grothschild. "He's already 11 months old.

"When he goes, Van Wilker's fortune will go to his son, who isn't very nice to Scooter. He makes mean phone calls and threatens to step on Scooter and squish him. The kid better change his tune or there won't be anything left."

THREE-LEGGED MODEL TAKES PARIS BY STORM

Get a load of these gams!

BEST FOOT FORWARD: This long-legged beauty is reportedly in talks with shoe giant Manolo Blahnik.

By NIGEL FLEMING

FRENCH modeling sensation Celine Lacroix has something that none of her famous supermodel predecessors possessed — and that thing is a third leg. Yes, beautiful, curvaceous Celine is dazzling the runway world by strutting her stuff on three gams.

"She's absolutely fabulous," gushes fashion photographer Monty Fleegle, while petting his pet poodle, Fifi, at a recent photo shoot in Paris. "She was totally professional and really made that third leg work for her. I can't imagine how Cindy Crawford, Naomi Campbell and Heidi Klum did so well with just two legs."

Celine is quite modest about the adoration being showered upon her by French critics. "Now I know how Jerry Lewis feels. The French people make me feel so loved — except for the ones who spit on me, pelt me with stones and call me an ugly freak."

Delicate Celine was born on Dec. 12, 1983, in Brooklyn, N.Y., to Maurice and Laverne Lacroix, who moved around a lot because they were in the witness protection program.

"I remember my father used to say such silly things to make me laugh, like 'Maybe ratting out the Lombardi family wasn't the smartest thing I ever did.' And then I would laugh even more when he heard a car backfire and he would turn so pale and faint. Papa was funny."

Papa disappeared soon after and the family relocated to Paris, where Celine competed on the high school three-legged-race team. But she dropped out of school when some of the other girls nicknamed her Webby, because of her duck-like middle foot with the overgrown toes.

That's when she took a part-time job with a haute couture designer named Andre Beaumont, who realized Celine had the potential at best to turn the fashion world on its ear or at least to become a place kicker for a professional football team.

"Andre was like a father to me," Celine remembers, "except for the fact that he insisted I juggle oranges with my three feet to amuse his wine-guzzling friends."

When one of Andre's prized models consumed seven platefuls of headcheese at an all-you-can-eat buffet and was too bloated to sashay down the catwalk, Andre urged Celine to take her place. Reluctant at first, she finally relented and the rest is history.

Celine is now one of the top-paid models in France, and she will soon be gracing top fashion shows in New York, London, Tokyo and Latvia.

Besides working tirelessly to broker world peace and to find a cure for acne, Celine wants to serve as an inspiration for other girls who are "slightly different" to go out and follow their dreams.

"Even if you have 11 fingers or three eyes and two colons, there's no reason you can't be a supermodel, too," she says. "I swear to that on my 15 toes."

NEW TREND: FAKE BELLYBUTTONS!

PARIS — The hottest new fashion accessory to come along since temporary tattoos is the Fake Navel, a collection of eight latex belly buttons that fit over your "original" to give it a different look!

"If you were born with an 'outie,' which protrudes from the stomach, you can change it to an 'innie,' which is a depression in the stomach," said fashion consultant Catherine Dusette.

"Fake Navels are a godsend for women," she added. "When it comes to attracting men, navels are as important as the breasts and buttocks."

SICK NEW FASHION:

BUILT-IN HIGH HEELS!

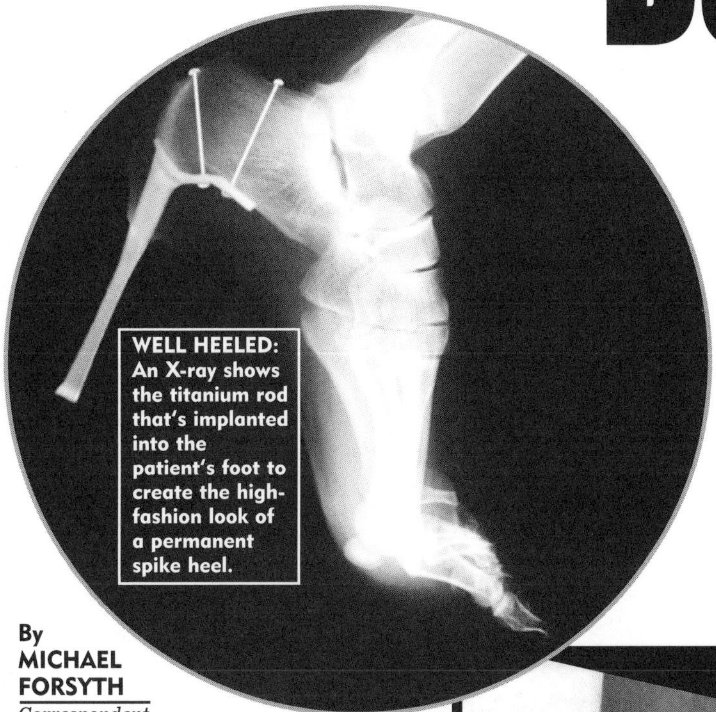

WELL HEELED: An X-ray shows the titanium rod that's implanted into the patient's foot to create the high-fashion look of a permanent spike heel.

By
**MICHAEL
FORSYTH**
Correspondent

THE NEWEST rage afoot among the fashion elite has feminists hopping mad. Ultrachic women around the world are getting high heels surgically implanted into their feet!

The look, called *ascenseur naturel* or "natural lift" by French designers, entails having two flesh-colored metal poles attached to the recipient's heel bones. Once implanted, the fad-crazy gals have the high-heeled look even when barefoot.

"I love my natural lifts — they give my legs a longer, sexier look and now I have that alluring wiggle that high heels give you all the time, even when I'm on the beach or at home with my boyfriend," says 26-year-old model Camille Monet of Paris, where the trend took off earlier this summer.

"I like getting those adoring stares from men as I strut by a cafe, without having to worry about a stiletto heel suddenly breaking or a shoe falling off as I run for a cab."

But podiatrists, health officials and feminists decry the bizarre body-modification fad, which they call dangerous and stupid.

"We're busy removing silicon breast implants from women because of health concerns — this is not the time to be looking for frivolous new ways to toy with the human body," blasts the head of a French medical society.

Women's lib groups in both the United States and England are demanding that their governments ban doctors from performing the procedure.

"This is the most odious example yet in a long line of gimmicks created to alter the female form to correspond to male fantasies, going back to the bustle, which gave the illusion of ridiculously prominent buttocks," declares Megan Humford of the British Association for Women's Freedom.

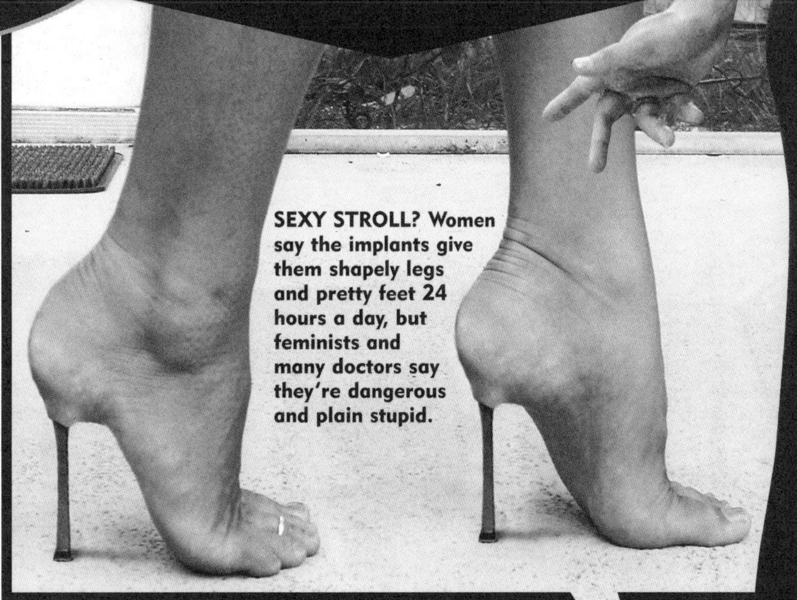

SEXY STROLL? Women say the implants give them shapely legs and pretty feet 24 hours a day, but feminists and many doctors say they're dangerous and plain stupid.

"It's like the old Japanese custom of foot-binding — but what makes this worse is that these so-called 'natural' lifts actually require surgery."

Defenders of the built-in heels insist the implants are actually safer than shoes, because they're made of titanium and can withstand heavy use.

Natural lifts are starting to crop up in big U.S. cities like Los Angeles, New York and Miami. Surprisingly, many customers are high-priced call girls and exotic dancers, according to surgeons, who charge $2,500 per foot.

"When dancers strip nude except for their shoes and get down on all fours, our patrons don't like it when the bottom of their high heels look scuffy," explains the owner of a trendy gentlemen's club in Miami. "With these natural lifts, you never have that problem."

Mr. Rogers' ghost

By BERNIE PYLE

WHILE alive, Mr. Rogers, the amiable mild-mannered children's TV show host, educated and entertained kids for decades, and called them all "neighbor." But now that he's dead, his ghost is scaring the bejeezus out of them!

"He's turning into the 'neighbor' from Hell," says Amy Specter, a professional ghost-buster. She says Mr. Rogers' ghost began appearing three months after he died.

"His ghost is the same as he was in life — sweet, friendly, soft-spoken — but when you're a floating transparent wraith, the effect is totally different. Saying 'Howdy, neighbor' and 'Can you say "death"?' to a five-year-old when you're a spirit is terrifying to them. Children have been freaking out," says Specter.

"Mr. Rogers had a hard time adjusting after he died. For one thing, he was lonely, because there's a

He's turning into the 'neighbor' from Hell!

TRENDY NEW DELICACY: MERMAID SUSHI!

terrorizing children

paucity of children on the other side, thank goodness. He also missed the spotlight. And he would see a child on this side by himself feeling lonely, and say 'I'll go help that child.'"

But the effect has been far from what Fred Rogers intends. Children have gone running into their parents' bedroom screaming "Mommy, there's a strange man in a sweater flying around my room!"

"It's traumatizing," says Sue Banshee, a child psychologist. "In life, Mr. Rogers made children feel safe and secure. Now he's inadvertently terrorizing them."

Specter, who runs Not a Ghost of a Chance, the ghostbusting firm, was called in after

> **His spirit is the same as he was in life — but when you're a floating, transparent wraith, the effect is scary!**

Mr. Rogers' ghost was spotted four times in two days.

"Like a lot of apparitions, Mr. Rogers' ghost is confused," Specter says. "He doesn't really understand that his situation has changed. I tried to explain it to him, but he didn't get it.

"I couldn't bring myself to destroy Mr. Rogers' ghost. I mean, I grew up watching the man myself."

Instead, Specter has some suggestions for dealing with the spirit.

Try to be with your child, or have an adult with them, as much as possible. Mr. Rogers' ghost only seems to appear to children.

Keep repeats of his TV show on whenever possible. "When Mr. Rogers' sees himself on TV,

it makes him feel good, and he doesn't feel the need to approach children."

If your child does see Mr. Rogers' ghost, teach him or her to be friendly. "Have them say, 'Hi, Mr. Rogers' ghost! Can you say 'ghost?'

"This will make Mr. Rogers' ghost feel good inside," says Specter. "If his spirit finds peace, it may finally go to the other side. Also, it will help him realize he IS a ghost, so maybe he'll reevaluate what he's doing."

Banshee, the child shrink, says the whole situation is very sad. "Fred Rogers spent decades building his reputation as a friend to children. Now his ghost is scaring children, and that will come back to haunt him."

WWN EXCLUSIVE   DATELINE: JANUARY 17, 1995

MAN COLLECTS 119 LBS. OF LINT— FROM HIS BELLY BUTTON!

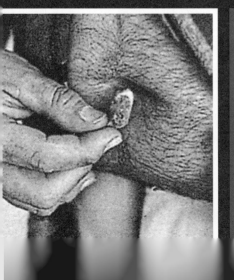

BEN FRANKLIN INVENTED THE MOONWALK

PHILADELPHIA — Roly-poly Founding Father Benjamin Franklin, not singer Michael Jackson, invented the Moonwalk, a new biography claims.

According to the book by a leading expert on the Revolutionary War era, bespectacled Ben used to amuse pals by seeming to effortlessly glide backward as he walked on wooden floors.

"The descriptions by Franklin's contemporaries completely correspond to

what we now know as the Moonwalk — and predate Mr. Jackson's famous dance move by more than 200 years," says British historian Robert Furnsworth.

Franklin is also credited with the invention of bifocals and discovering how to harness electricity.

Stool-pigeon pet spills the beans on cheatin' hubby — a legal first!

BLABBERMOUTH PARROT TESTIFIES AT DIVORCE TRIAL!

BOZO, a 14-year-old cockatoo, gave away all the family secrets at his owners' divorce trial.

PIMP WRITES SELF-HELP BOOK

Chicken Soup for the Ho

By DAVID TOLSEY

Pimp Flozell Wilson wants to impart some advice to his corral of ladies. "Take it one day at a time, ladies, because you never know what's around the street corner."

Those thoughtful words are part of Flozell's new book called *Chicken Soup for the Ho.*

"I know that ladies of the night have some tough times hangin' on the streets," says Flozell. "So I thought I would do my part to tell them life is all good. This book is a culmination of five years of hard work. I just hope it helps my bitches out."

"Flozell's been my Poppi for so long now," says Bianca Tavarez. "Now, I start every evening out with a passage from his book. Robert Fulghum and the rest of those so-called writers ain't got nothin' on my daddy. He writes inspirational words like, 'The grass is always greener on the other side of the sidewalk.' "

While *Chicken Soup for the Ho* may not make it to the *New York Times* bestseller list, Flozell can still envision a full-time writing career one day. "Check it, I'll make sure my bitches are secured with another pimp before I pull a *Finding Forrester* on them."

COUPLE STAYS TOGETHER FOR 9 YEARS AFTER DIVORCE... BECAUSE THEY CAN'T TELL THE DOGS!

MAN FIRES HIMSELF TO WORK FROM A CANNON

...TO BEAT RUSH HOUR TRAFFIC!

—By MATT BETT

HE'S OFF! While millions battle rush-hour traffic, Mexico City's flying accountant takes the "high road."

MEXICO CITY — Martin Navarro gets a bang out of his morning commute.

Tired of traffic jams, this accountant fires himself from a cannon at his suburban home and flies to work each morning.

"It used to take me 25 or 30 minutes just to get out of my driveway," Navarro says. "I'm not exaggerating. The traffic here in Mexico City is worse than anywhere in the world. And there's construction delays on every street.

"My drive to work was only four blocks, but it could take me up to 90 minutes," he says. "I would move forward for a couple of seconds and sit for 10 minutes. It was totally unbearable."

Now Navarro takes a breezy 28-second flight over the clogged roads — high above the choking exhaust fumes.

"It used to be I'd arrive to work with a headache every day," he says. "Now I almost never do — unless I have a rough landing."

To make those landings easier, Navarro's company placed a net on the roof of their office building.

"It's a pretty big target," he says. "If I miss it I'm in trouble — but I think it was more dangerous for me to be down in that traffic."

Navarro's family was the inspiration for the change. "When I was driving, I was unable to spend much quality time with my wife and three kids. Now, we eat a leisurely breakfast each morning. Then, they kiss me goodbye and light the fuse."

His boss wasn't immediately supportive.

"When Martin approached us with his idea, we wanted no part of it," said Don Oritz, founder of Ortiz Accounting. "Nets are expensive. But then we realized it would get Martin to work on time daily and we would be able to give his parking spot to someone else. It's a win-win."

Martin admits that his flying drew a lot of attention when he started doing it three weeks ago.

"A lot of my colleagues would go up to the roof to watch me arrive," he says. "Now it's become no big deal for them.

"I've heard some of the guys are interested in shooting themselves to work. We just need to be sure we coordinate our arrival times so we won't have any collisions."

CALL HIM the "Pharaoh of Funk"! Here's what contemporary rap great Puff Daddy might have looked like if he'd lived and performed 3,500 years ago!

3,500-year-old rap lyrics found in Egyptian tomb!

By PAT WELLS
Weekly World News

CAIRO, Egypt — Archaeologists from the University of Milan excavating a tomb in Egypt have made an astonishing discovery — rap lyrics dating from 1470 BC!

The rhyming hieroglyphics were unearthed near ancient Thebes and describe mummification, the Pyramids and the Nile using rhythms, words and attitude that are primitive precursors to the works of contemporary artists like Puff Daddy and Eminem.

Along with the hieroglyphics, the archaeologists found the fossil of a conical reed that the ancient rapper could have used to amplify his voice like a primitive microphone!

"I'm blown away," says hip-hop historian, Levar Williams, "These Egyptian raps are almost 3,500 years older than The Sugar Hill Gang's 'Rappers Delight,' which marked the resurgence of the ancient art form in 1979."

The raps were translated into English by Milanese Egyptologists and are included on this page for *Weekly World News* readers to be blown away themselves.

No point to the pyramids

There ain't no point to the pyramids
In Gaza, or no matter where it is
'Cause up at the point where all four sides meet
Room too narrow for a burial tomb
Instead, should be flat like a papyrus sheet
But I ain't one of King Khufu's elite
So when I'm dead I be buried with my cat out in the street

Nile rap

Water flows turnin' the soil rich for the hoes
That wack weed from the seed is makin' dough
It sun bakin' into a pile, stacked in Greek style
With fondness, sun goddess, I partakin' and rappin' about the Nile

Mummify your behind

Gonna mummify your behind
Bindin' your butt in linen then wrappin' seven times
Gonna mummify your behind
'Cause your colon already been cut, unrollen and embalmed in heady palm wine
Gonna mummify your behind
But you decomposin' and now I'm tryin' to push your pose in
So I pray to Isis in this crisis
Gonna mummify your behind

BAT BOY TO BE KNIGHTED

By **MICHAEL CHIRON**
Correspondent

'Arise, Sir Bat Boy!'

ON his last visit with Her Majesty, Bat Boy could hardly contain his enthusiasm when told he was in line to be knighted.

QUEEN Elizabeth is reportedly set to knight Bat Boy after the intrepid freak of nature saved a British army patrol in Iraq!

According to official sources, the pointy-eared hero sniffed out an ambush laid by terrorists and warned the five soldiers in the nick of time.

The recommendation for Bat Boy's knighthood was made by a top British commander and reads in part:

"Showing total disregard for his own safety, Bat Boy engaged the terrorists in a small-arms firefight. Despite being wounded, Bat Boy then ran three miles and warned an army patrol of the terrorist force. The enemy fighters were later attacked by gunships and sustained heavy casualties."

The knighting ceremony is expected to take place at Buckingham Palace in early August, says a royal source.

But not every Brit is tossing up his bowler hat at the news. Some bluebloods are incensed that the rare honor is being bestowed on the half-human, half-bat mutant.

"It's bad enough that we now see knights made of working-class actors like Michael Caine, who speaks with a cockney accent thicker than a London chimney sweep," sniffs a member of the House of Lords. "It's quite another matter to welcome into the company of nobles a grunting, savage creature that is not even fully human.

"This little monster is unpredictable and dangerous. Who knows what will happen when Her Majesty tries to knight him? He may feel threatened by the sword, snatch it from her hands and run her through."

But high-ranking government officials say knighthood for the plucky youth is almost certain.

"Saving that patrol is only the latest contribution Bat Boy has made," says a source close to British Foreign Secretary Jack Straw. "His missions for the U.S. are top secret, but it's known his superior sense of smell was used to track down Saddam Hussein.

"Also, rumor has it that he recently unearthed evidence of weapons of mass destruction while looking for a cool cave to sleep in one night. This will help Prime Minister Tony Blair save face after the failure to find WMDs in Iraq.

"Mr. Blair owes his political life to Bat Boy and he's been petitioning Queen Elizabeth to proceed with the knighthood."

Bat Boy will likely be named a Knight Commander of the Most Excellent Order of the British Empire, or KBE, the title typically given to non-Britons.

Because he's an American, Bat Boy should not actually be addressed as "Sir," but will be permitted to put the letters KBE after his name.

The pint-sized hero isn't the first Yank to receive the honor. Other distinguished Americans who've been knighted include former New York Mayor Rudolph Giuliani, evangelist Billy Graham and former President Reagan. And, it was recently announced, megabucks computer geek Bill Gates has earned a knighthood as well.

According to custom, the recommendation will be reviewed by the Chancellor of the Exchequer, before being passed on to the Queen.

Palace insiders say that pressure to knight Bat Boy — who is more popular in British opinion polls than Prince Charles — will be impossible for the monarch to resist.

"It is not with undiluted pleasure that we look forward to meeting this peculiar individual in person," she reportedly told an aide. "But his service to the realm must be rewarded."

Editor's note: As *Weekly World News* went to press, we learned that, in a recent meeting with the queen, Bat Boy attempted to bite the monarch on the arm. While Her Majesty was not amused, the ceremony of knighthood will go on as scheduled.

ZOMBIE REALITY SHOW BOMBS

By MICHAEL FORSYTH

A REALITY TV show featuring an all-zombie cast has been axed by a Haitian TV network after just three episodes!

The macabre series, titled *The Undead Life*, failed to connect with audiences, even in a country where it's estimated that 7 percent of the population are zombies.

"On paper, it seemed like a very fresh concept, but it turns out that watching zombies go about their daily lives is like watching paint dry," explains entertainment writer Jean-Pierre Parcel in Port-au-Prince.

The 12 cast members, who were put up for the duration of the show in a swank mansion, tended to shuffle listlessly from room to room, rarely speaking to one another and wearing blank expressions.

"For a reality TV series to work, you need conflict – you want to see sparks fly," Parcel says.

"With *The Undead Life*, you just didn't get that. Cast members didn't skinny-dip, make out in the hot tub, shout at each other or do anything else interesting. It was often hard to even tell if they were awake or asleep."

That the show bombed comes as no surprise to Dr. Henri Compeigne, a leading Haitian anthropologist.

"Contrary to what you see in Hollywood movies, zombies almost never attack normal people and eat their flesh – they are very docile," he observes.

"In the cane fields where they typically are used for brute labor, zombies are less interesting to watch than grazing cows."

UFO group's astounding claim:

ALIEN BODY SNATCHERS REJECT PARIS HILTON

THERE'S no place like home! Apparently Paris wasn't exactly the aliens' cup of tea.

By NICK JEFFRIES

WILD-CHILD socialite Paris Hilton was abducted by aliens — and five minutes later, they opened the spaceship door and kicked her out.

Or at least that's the word from a researcher who claims a ticked off ET made an irate phone call to the UFOs Reach Earth Americans Line (U-FO-REAL).

"Most of the time the calls are wrong numbers," says Dieter Vanderhorn, one of the monitors who work in shifts to ensure the phone line is covered 24/7.

"This time, the person on the other end sounded so strange and angry I just knew in my gut it was the real deal."

Vanderhorn says an entity who identified himself as "Vortox from the planet Runyon" told him he had just dumped Paris in a nearby field and asked him how humans could worship such a shameless, couture-wearing egomaniac who thinks she's "the cosmic consciousness' gift to all sentient life-forms."

The alien wanted to register a formal complaint with U-FO-REAL, claims Vanderhorn.

"Vortox said: 'As soon as we beamed the Earth woman you call Paris Hilton onto our ship she began criticizing our wardrobes, hairstyles, and

ARE YOU KIDDING?

Paris Hilton was named worst dressed this year on Mr. Blackwell's 44th annual list of the Worst Dressed Women.

makeup. My wife Vizbin is the personal stylist for everyone on this ship and suffered emotional injury,' " relates Vanderhorn.

"Then Paris insisted she would sing for us. She opened her mouth and emitted the most horrible screeching cacophony I have ever heard. I was forced to cover my antennae and recite the Intergalactic Federation's Pledge of Brotherhood until it stopped.

"We wanted to question this Paris about her life on Earth, but all she did was smile and pretend to pose for paparazzi pictures until I was tempted to set my proton blaster to 'annihilate' and send her disassembled atoms hurtling into the void.

"As if that weren't enough, she spoke of all the Earth parties she has attended and started listing every pair of designer shoes she owns. It was so many that I fear I regurgitated a bit in several of my orifices.

"When she began extolling the apparently infinite perfection of her flawless no-tan-lines body, it was all I could do not to turn the proton blaster upon myself. Just as she began to describe her daily beauty routine, I opened the vacu-door and shoved her out."

A source close to Paris and her sister, Nicky, seems to corroborate Vanderhorn's outlandish story.

"I heard that the UFO nuts called Nicky, and she was very apologetic," says the source.

"She's usually right by her side, but apparently Paris might have gotten too drunk and rode off on the back of some guy's motorcycle.

"While I was speaking with her, Paris stormed in screaming: 'I can't find my blue Chanel eyeshadow, Nicky. Did you steal it?" Then the line went dead. I hope she's O.K."

God works in mysterious ways . . .

PLACE YOUR HAND ON JANET'S MIRACLE BOOB

By
VICKIE YORK
Correspondent

...& BE HEALED!

JIGGLY Janet Jackson's titillating antics at the Super Bowl half-time show enraged many Americans. But she's won the gratitude of thousands of people worldwide, who claim they were cured of disease after watching her exposed breast on TV — or simply touching a photograph of it!

Sports fans who tuned in to the game and inadvertently got an eyeful of Janet's bare boob have flooded health departments with letters stating that the sight cured them of a host of medical woes, ranging from cancer to zits.

Perhaps even more incredibly, hundreds of others who only saw the censored image when it was replayed ad nauseum on TV — or touched a still picture in their morning newspaper the next day — also claim to have received miracle cures.

And while angry FCC honchos are investigating Janet and MTV, which produced the half-time show, for possible violation of federal decency rules, folks whose health was restored by the naughty display are begging the agency to give the miracle songbird a break.

"When Justin Timberlake tore Janet's costume and her breast popped out, I felt a shock go through me," says 85-year-old Edith F. of Paterson, N.J., who had been confined to a wheelchair due to crippling arthritis since 1993.

"I was so disgusted, I stood up, crossed the room and turned off the TV. Then I realized what I'd done — I'd walked for the first time in 11 years. There's no pain in my legs anymore. My arthritis has been cured. Janet's miracle boob healed me.

"She should be rewarded, not punished. And they should rebroadcast that moment every chance they get."

Other amazing accounts:

● A 56-year-old brain cancer patient in Tulsa, Okla., says his tumors vanished overnight after he saw the "accidental" boob-baring episode replayed on *Good Morning, America.*

● A 24-year-old Shreveport, La., man who had suffered from acne for a decade claims viewing the half-time show cleared up his complexion.

● A 35-year-old Topeka, Kan., housewife plagued by hemorrhoids says the condition went away after she touched a censored newspaper photo of the boob-flash. "I was covering up the picture so my son wouldn't see it, and the very next time I used the bathroom everything was completely clear."

While most experts are skeptical, some say it's conceivable that the shocking event really has medical miracles busting out all over.

"We've known for decades now that a shock to the system can sometimes jolt the body back to health," explains Dr. John Wilson. "Shocking images can jump-start the body's own healing mechanisms."

Nevertheless, it's unlikely that we'll be seeing encore performances of Janet's breast-baring routine on the air.

HOW TO USE THE POWER OF JANET'S BREAST TO IMPROVE YOUR HEALTH

The key to gaining a medicinal benefit from shocking images is the element of surprise.

Cover the photo of Janet's breast, reproduced on this page, with a blank sheet of paper. Empty your mind of all thoughts. After one full minute, uncover the image and glance at it — then quickly place your hand on top of it. Hold it there for another minute.

Repeating this two or three times a day seems to have a beneficial effect on one's health, say people who have tried it.

And the FCC appears unlikely to back down from its vow to investigate what Chairman Michael Powell branded a "classless, crass and deplorable stunt."

An FCC insider insists, "The fact that a small number of Americans out there may have benefited from this outrageous behavior does not outweigh the fact that millions of others were traumatized."

5 NEW HOPE FOR THE DEAD!

Amazing Accounts of Religion & Prophecy

In today's polarized political climate, perhaps no topic is more heated than the divide between church and state. And when a moral issue hits the front pages, most mainstream papers dance around the subject, trying to please both sides of the divide while not appearing to be too liberal.

But *Weekly World News* never hesitates to tackle the touchy issues head-on. In fact, we have been reporting on Our Lord, right along-

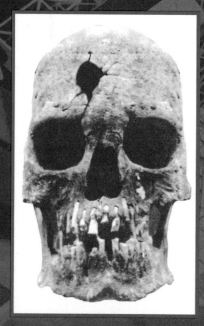

side articles on politics, for years. That's because we here at *Weekly World News* know there is a God— and she is an alien lesbian.

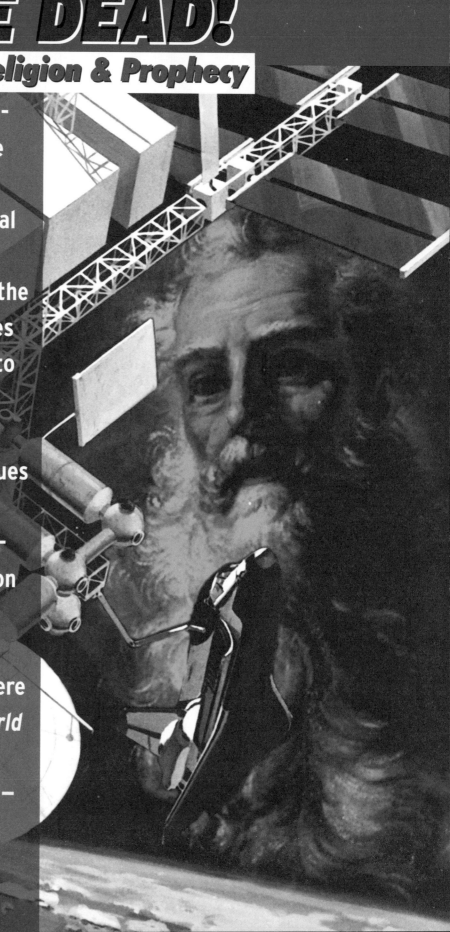

And since most Americans agree (at least on the former), they expect us to deliver all the latest Biblical news—from Bible prophecies your preacher doesn't want you to know about (it's okay to covet your neighbor's wife) to the discovery that pizza was served at the Last Supper (Judas ordered pepperoni).

"If someone's taken a photo of Heaven or discovers that Hell is freezing over, we in the religious community know we can rely on *Weekly World News* to spread the word—even though all the aliens on their staff are Scientologists," says prominent priest Father Nicholas Tugman.

But some Bible-thumpers aren't as pleased about WWN's commitment to printing all the religious news—including the facts some Christians find hard to swallow.

"For those folks to say that Heaven is like America Online, only with dead people, well that doesn't seem quite right to me," says conservative pastor Daniel Grimmitz of Rome, Georgia. "I mean, I still read WWN religiously, because they were the first to expose aliens, celebrities, and clones as the liberal weirdos they really are—but when they start interpreting the Bible—well, I don't know if they should do that."

Fortunately for its faithful readers, WWN does not bow to pressure about what to print from any special interest—whether it be political, religious, or otherworldly.

WWN even goes beyond Christianity to bring you vital news from the other "religions." Although those bureaus are mostly staffed by interns, these young go-getters are dedicated to bringing you the latest on Buddha, Ganesh, Mohammed, and Salma Hayek's breasts.

And for those of you who don't believe in *any* God, WWN reports on sacrilegious prophecies that can affect your life. Among the hundreds of foretold facts we've printed over the years are these gems: the world is not coming to an end, Hillary Clinton will become president and be the oldest woman to give birth to twins, and Jesus will return to Earth as a jockey.

But most of all, readers turn to WWN because its coverage of religious topics keeps them informed of the latest in spiritual news, and because it's only a matter of time before our reporters discover the back door to heaven.

WORLD EXCLUSIVE PHOTO OF OF

NASA'S incredible *Cosmic Background Explorer* satellite shocked scientists with its amazing photo of the Milky Way galaxy.

By NELSON MANN
Special correspondent

Scientists claim to have found heaven at the center of the Milky Way galaxy and they have the photograph to prove it!

The dramatic picture was beamed to Earth from the *Cosmic Background Explorer* satellite and clearly shows a large glowing bulge at the center of a brightly-lit disc of stars.

Experts initially theorized that the disc and bulge concealed a massive black hole. But a computer-enhanced version of the photo indicates that the object is actually an enormous celestial city that may be inhabited by God and the souls of the dead.

"If heaven exists, then we have found it," astronomer Dr. Henri Rankin told newsmen in Paris. "Our computer-enhanced picture reveals structures and features never before encountered in space.

"The disc is actually a vast city of Greek-style buildings and streets that shine like gold. The image isn't clear enough to identify smaller objects.

"But it's reasonable to assume that the city is inhabited by the human souls and a Supreme Being. Why else would it be floating in the vacuum of space where no living creature could possibly exist?"

The report by Dr. Rankin and two colleagues touched off a controversy that might not be resolved for years to come.

Some astronomers implied that the scientists had taken "too many liberties" in their interpretation of the computer-enhanced photo and called their claim of having found heaven "absurd."

Other experts, like the German astrophysicist Frank Bauer, believe that the interpretation was accurate and called for an international effort to get a

"IF HEAVEN exists, then we have found it," says Dr. Henri Rankin, left.

space probe or probes to the area right away.

"The disc is over 28,000 light years away so it's imperative that we move without delay," said Dr. Bauer. "Whether it's heaven or not is irrelevant.

"Something is definitely out there and we should be doing everything in our power to find out what it is."

Dr. Rankin agrees that further study is warranted but maintains that the object is, in fact, heaven.

"There is no other explanation," said the expert. "As far as I'm concerned we are knocking at heaven's door."

WWN EXCLUSIVE DATELINE: MAY 16, 2005

TEXAS MINISTER STARTS 'CHURCH OF GEORGE W. BUSH'

Satellite beams back SHOCKING PROOF

MYSTERIOUS buildings appear around the center of the Milky Way in this computer-enhanced photo.

... of paradise in space!

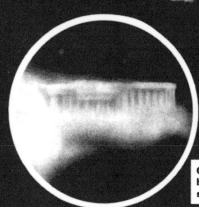

CLOSE-UP of the incredible photo reveals Greek-style buildings.

HEAVEN

Soviets found it first!

By NICK DRAKE

Astronomer Henri Rankin's photograph of heaven is the first to be published but Soviet astronomers discovered and photographed the same celestial city two years ago — in 1988.

Those pictures were suppressed by the Soviet government.

But as *The NEWS* reported in May 1988, documents smuggled to the West indicated that a Russian probe had sailed through a rainbow-colored tunnel of light.

It emerged over an unearthly green and yellow landscape and photographed human beings filing through the gates of a great walled city that glittered like gold.

Dr. Kurt Bauer, the German astrophysicist who obtained the documents from Soviet sources, said: "The pictures are remarkable in their similarity to what people have seen during near-death experiences.

"These photos are potentially more important than anything we have gotten from our exploration of space to date."

WWN EXTRA

THE SOVIETS: True Pioneers

Before international alien P'lod crushed the USSR's Communist regime, the Soviets beat freedom-loving America to the punch on more than just the first photo of Heaven. They were also the first to accomplish the amazing feats below.

1920s – first to set up a public display of a leader's embalmed body

1949 – first to use Russian dressing

1957 – first to send a dog into space

1961 – first to genetically engineer a gymnast

1990 – first to exchange first born for a pair of jeans

SPACE STATION MESSAGE FROM

By **SHARON MAYES**/*Correspondent*

A STEELY-EYED entity "the size of a giant asteroid" appeared to astronauts aboard the International Space Station and identified itself as "the God of Abraham and the God of Moses."

The entity warned mankind to "set aside human pride" or "stay the Hell out of Heaven forever," sources close to NASA report.

The message was delivered in English during what many are saying is the first divine encounter since God gave Moses the 10 Commandments on Mount Sinai in 1,400 B.C.

Meanwhile, the entire episode remains under wraps as analysts try to figure out how authentic — and how serious — the warning might be.

But sources say photographs that were beamed back to Earth by a passing spy satellite "strongly suggest" the massive, robed and bearded "man" that materialized over the space station "was an entity of enormous energy and purpose."

"If He was indeed God, then He means business," says one Washington insider. "You can't blame the government for stumbling on its investigation and assessment. This is unprecedented in the history of space exploration. And it's virtually unprecedented in human history of the past 4,000 years.

"The key question everyone is asking is how do we know this was God and not the work of extraterrestrials or even scientists on Earth. Sensors on the space station 'read' the image as being flesh and blood and of colossal size.

"They detected body heat and a pulse. And this wasn't inside the space station, this was outside. Nothing that lives and breathes can survive in the icy, airless vacuum of space. Nothing, that is, except God — or something very much like Him."

NASA and other federal agencies involved in the investigation, including the FBI, CIA and State Department, refuse to discuss the June 23 incident until the investigation is complete.

But privately, those in the know are desperately trying to cope with the shattering psychological impact of the vision.

Sources say the 32-second encounter began when

> **'Set aside your pride – or stay the Hell out of Heaven forever!'**

the entity materialized in a burst of white light that several unidentified astronauts could see on monitors that normally are used to perform visual inspections of the exterior of the vessel.

After a few seconds, the sources continue, the light dimmed, revealing the enormous face and body of a man.

"Astronauts say they sensed a presence that was so powerful they were speechless. They tried to talk but couldn't," says one investigator. "They were alarmed at first, but then found themselves overcome with a tremendous feeling of peace and calm.

"When the entity began to speak they described the voice as 'thunderous, and reverberating, like an organ in a glass cathedral.' "

The full text of the message remains a closely guarded secret. But the analyst says the entity claimed to be "the God of Abraham" and "the God of Moses."

It went on to warn that "of all sins, pride is your worst and the one I despise most for it is the very root and wellspring of all others."

The voice then advised: "You must humble yourselves before one another and before me. Become as little children if you would join the faithful in the Kingdom of Light.

"You must prove yourselves worthy of everlasting life and amen, amen I say to you that no man shall enter Paradise until he has atoned for his sins in the limbo that lies between Heaven, Hell and Earth.

"Those who fail this test will swim in lakes of fire that burn bright with the souls of the damned."

CIA analysts working with NASA and members of the clergy interpret the reference to a "limbo" to be a possible confirmation of the Catholic concept of purgatory — a place where imperfect humans go after death to pay for their sins and earn themselves a spot in Heaven.

"What's next for the government agencies is to pull everything together, prove this entity was God and not an impostor, and then figure out how to present the whole package to the public in a way that won't offend people who are not of the Christian faith," says the analyst.

"The God that appeared to these astronauts didn't mention Buddha or Mohammed. He talked about Abraham, Moses and Jesus. And in a world torn by holy war and threat of holy war, that could be a major diplomatic hurdle."

RECEIVES GOD!

DIVINE INTERVENTION: This artist's conception depicts the image of God that was seen by astronauts aboard the International Space Station.

Man comes back

HELLBOUND: Johnny Corazzo loved Hell so much, he plans on living a sinful life so he can go back.

By
LISA MERAKIS
Correspondent

'HELL

It's the playground of

PITTSBURGH, Pa. — Photographer Johnny Corazzo died for seven minutes when his heart stopped during an operation, went to Hell — and says it was great, absolutely great!

The 51-year-old bachelor says Satan's kingdom was full of fast cars, free booze, babes in bikinis, slot machines, hookers, greasy fried food and other amenities. It was so terrific down there that he didn't want to return to normal life again.

"In Hell I saw my best friend from the old neighborhood and when he told me it wasn't my time yet I was really disappointed," recalled Corazzo.

"I woke up in intensive care and I actually cried, thinking of the exciting scene I had left behind.

"I want to be back there where things are hot. I want to be having fun with all those dudes down there. But I guess Satan has plans for me here on Earth."

Corazzo suffered serious internal injuries in an auto accident in February and was rushed to a hospital.

There doctors operated immediately, hoping to repair a ruptured liver and badly damaged kidney.

While he was under the knife, Corazzo's heart suddenly stopped beating.

Desperate surgeons gave him heart massage and jolted him with electricity, but it took seven terrifying minutes to restart Corazzo's heart.

"I remember traveling through a tunnel toward a bright light," said Corazzo, who today is well again and back at work. "Suddenly I came out into a huge space where I could see millions of people, many of whom I knew had died years ago. These people were enjoying themselves, sitting around playing cards or drinking beer or playing the slots.

"They all looked so happy. They were having so much fun. There were beautiful babes all over the place, serving chicken nuggets, french fries and drinks. I had just grabbed a frosty bottle of beer when my old pal came up to me and told me I had to go back. I was so upset."

Corazzo says that since his glimpse of Hell, he's lost his fear of death. He says he can't wait to die and go back to the great afterlife there.

But meanwhile, he intends to lead a sinful life so he doesn't wind up in Heaven by mistake.

"I know where the fun is now," the photographer said. "No way do I want to spend eternity with a bunch of boring goody two-shoes in Paradise."

Satan's Place is loaded with booze, babes and one-armed bandits!

to life and tells docs:

IS GREAT'

the naughty!

SIGNS YOU'RE GOING TO HELL

Ever since *WWN* broke the story that Hell's not such a bad place after all, our newsroom has been inundated with calls and letters from readers wanting to know how they can secure their place in one of the nine circles. Sure, everyone knows they're going to Hell if they're Jewish or have never been baptized, but here are some not-so-well-known indications from *WWN*'s religion bureau that you may be headed to the fiery afterworld.

* You can name ten beers but not the Ten Commandments

* You've been known to wear white after Labor Day

* You own a Michael Jackson album on CD

* You've occasionally asked God to damn something for you

* You consider yourself a homosexual, transsexual, heterosexual, metrosexual, or Democrat

* You love the smell of brimstone in the morning

* You're a producer, director, or writer for a reality TV show

* You enjoy movies with graphic violence, brief nudity, adult situations, or CGI effects

* You have ever considered selling your soul for a luxury car or an affair with a celebrity on your "would do" list

* You engage in sexual acts for reasons other than procreation

* You have rolled your eyes at the mention of Mother Teresa

* You subscribe to the *Weekly World News*

LOUSY TRANSLATION

BIBLE SHOCKER!

FOLLOWING a map drawn in a Dead Sea-like scroll found weeks earlier, left. Dr. Gustav Von Ibson, above, discovered an old tomb in a cave on a hillside containing the remains of the first two humans created by God.

...OR BIGGEST LIE OF ALL TIME?

ADAM & ED!

GAY COUPLE WERE FIRST HUMANS

A BOMBSHELL discovery in an ancient cave in the Middle East may result in a rewriting of the entire first chapter of the Bible, say experts.

Following a map drawn in a Dead Sea-like scroll found weeks before, archaeologists discovered an old tomb in a cave on a hillside containing the remains of the first two humans created by God — and DNA tests reveal they were both MEN!

And in another explosive revelation, the ancient scroll reveals that Eve did NOT give Adam the apple and she is not to blame for their being expelled from the Garden of Eden.

The scientists say their groundbreaking discovery of the tomb proves — definitely — that Adam and Ed were the first humans, created 10,000 years ago.

Eve was formed later after the Almighty realized he'd made a gigantic goof, says Dr. Gustav Von Ibson, who headed the team that discovered the tomb and scroll.

"According to the scroll containing the map that led us to the bodies, God was exhausted by the sixth day after creating the earth and all the creatures on it," says Von Ibson, head of antiquities at the University of Copenhagen in Denmark.

"He apparently lost his focus after creating Adam, so when he decided to give him a companion, he accidentally created another man, Ed, from Adam's rib.

"When he realized that there was no mate for Adam to procreate with

to create more humans to populate the earth, God created Eve — but the scroll does not say from what."

This caused the first love triangle and a horrible mess, says Von Ibson.

"Since Ed was made from Adam's rib and was around before Eve, Adam took a tremendous shine to him.

"He actually preferred Ed to Eve and refused to cozy up to her."

The tug of love between Ed and Eve continued with Adam as the prize. Both began wooing him with gifts.

"That's when Satan jumped in. He wanted to cause trouble, so in the guise of the serpent, he convinced Ed to bring Adam the forbidden apple. Adam bit and loved it and loved Ed even more."

When God saw that Adam preferred Ed and was refusing to pair off with Eve, he became furious, says Von Ibson.

"The ancient Hebrews called the Lord the Merciless Thunderer for good reason. In his fury at the gay couple, God drove Adam, Ed and Eve from Eden with a barrage of terrifying lightning bolts and horrific explosions of thunder," says Von Ibson.

Later, realizing that the Lord was angry at him and his gay lover, Adam tried to get together with Eve, according to the scroll.

"They mated and produced children," says Von Ibson, "but Adam still preferred Ed and would sneak off to see him.

"We don't know how they died, but apparently it was together and that's how they were buried. We still don't know what happened to the third wheel in the triangle, Eve."

The shocking discovery of the tomb, in a desolate area of Southern

Syria, came just 16 days after the scroll was found also in a cave, some 15 miles away.

"The scroll was apparently written several thousand years later," says Von Ibson. "But at that time, the story of Adam and Ed was quite well known.

"Why later Biblical scrolls retell the story as Adam and Eve is unknown. Apparently, ancient peoples wanted to downplay the importance of gays — especially since they caused man to be banished from Eden."

Von Ibson calls the discovery "the most revolutionary find in Biblical history."

"We're pretty much going to have to rewrite the first part of the Bible, the Book of Genesis," he says.

He adds that God's early fury against gays in the Adam and Ed story should give President George Bush more ammo in his battle against gay marriages.

Meanwhile, Bible expert Dr. Paul Mayor of England's Liverpool University says it will be "a cold day in Hell" before he and other scholars accept the discovery as legitimate.

"Get real, those skeletons don't prove anything," says Mayor.

"Those skeletons could belong to anybody."

FURIOUS: God drove Adam, Ed and Eve from the Garden of Eden with a barrage of terrifying lightning bolts.

GOLIATH WAS SHOT

THE Bible says David killed Goliath with a "sling" and five "stones."

TEL AVIV, Israel — A new scientific examination of Goliath's skull proves con clusively that David, in the words of one scholar, "putteth a hit" on the biblical giant wit a .38-caliber handgun, NOT with a stone as most preachers tell us!

And some experts are suggesting that the incident, in fact, was a drive-by attack — with David having fired the weapon from a moving chariot!

A team of forensic pathologists using high-tech computer analysis reached their startling conclusions after examining holes in the forehead and the back of the ancient skull.

"The skull was penetrated by a .38-caliber slug that entered above the eyebrows at a high rate of speed and exited at the back of the head," confirms Dr. David Ben-Levy, who coauthored the study, published in *Israeli Archaeology Quarterly*.

"A great mystery, of course, is what a handgun was doing in the Holy Land more than 3,000 years ago, centuries before the first known use of firearms. We can only assume it was a gift from God.

"But an even bigger mystery is why the Lord in all his wisdom and power didn't give David an Uzi or a rocket-launcher or a submachine gun. He really does work in mysterious ways."

According to the familiar Bible story, the Hebrew shepherd boy David bravely took on the Philistines' greatest warrior, Goliath, even though the enemy champion stood well over 8 feet tall.

The Bible talks of David loading his weapon, described as a "sling," with five "stones." Miraculously, David used the weapon to strike down the far bigger man.

Their champion slain, the Philistines fled in terror, while triumphant David went on to become one of the greatest kings of ancient Israel. Goliath's skull was preserved in a temple in Jerusalem for centuries and is now housed in a museum here.

The sheer size of the skull — nearly 18 inches tall — has left little doub among archaeologists that did indeed belong to the wa rior, by far the tallest man his day.

But experts have alway been puzzled about the hug hole at the back of the head.

"It looks like a classi exit wound," Dr. Ben-Lev explains.

Many stunned Bibl scholars admit they're ba fled by discovery. But th Rev. John Deneck, a leadin theologian, says the answer t the riddle may be simple: Go knew that in fair contes Goliath would cut David t pieces, so He stepped in t help the boy.

"Since the Almighty was o David's side, He could suppl him with any weapon H chose — even one from anoth er time," the London-base clergyman points out.

But the biblical descriptio of the battle of David an Goliath is contradicted b other writings of the era tha say David "unleashed fir

New Jesus shocker... PIZZA WAS SERVED AT THE LAST SUPPER!

... and the pies were delivered!

By DAVID TOLSEY

STARTLING new research reveals that Jesus and his disciples feasted on pizza at the Last Supper — and the pies were delivered!

And while the majority of the pizzas were cheese or vegetarian, archaeologist Dr. Gilbert Rothschild maintains that at least one of the steaming treats had a meat topping and all of them were delivered.

"When Jesus broke bread with His disciples, we now know it was, in fact, pizza crust," says Rothschild, antiquities professor at the famed England's Fellingham University. "Thin crust to be sure. What really amazes us is how the delivery man managed to carry, we estimate, seven large pizzas through the walls of Jerusalem and up Mount Zion. Six cheese pizzas and one pepperoni, for Judas, we strongly believe."

Rothschild says there's no doubt that the pizzas were thin crust because The Last Supper was actually a Passover Seder during which only matzos, the cracker-like non-rising bread, is served.

Rothschild and his team of researchers spent the better part of 10 years digging and sifting through the room where the Last Supper was held, as well as the outlying areas of the Dormition Abbey on Mount Zion.

They claim they uncovered the remains of rudimentary pizza boxes, and an in-depth lab analysis confirmed particles of tomato sauce had adhered to the ancient flooring in the room.

"We would've saved a lot of time and money had we been able to get our hands on the tablecloth," adds Rothschild. "That said, my decade of research on the Last Supper has been the most fulfilling work of my career."

The findings from the archaeological team have drawn sharp criticism from the Catholic Church, in particular.

"How can these quack researchers say that pizza was delivered to Jesus and His apostles at the Last Supper?" decries Father Terrence O'Donoghue of the Archdiocese of Boston. "They make it sound like it was some sort of pizza and poker night with the guys. They need to bone up on their Bible readings, I'll tell you that much. I want them all to sit down and read the canonical gospels of Matthew, Mark, Luke and John. I suppose they think the Eucharist at Sunday Mass should be Gino's pizza snacks then."

Rothschild understands his work has shaken the followers of the Christian faith to their very

WITH A .38!

By **VINCENZO SARDI** / *Weekly World News*

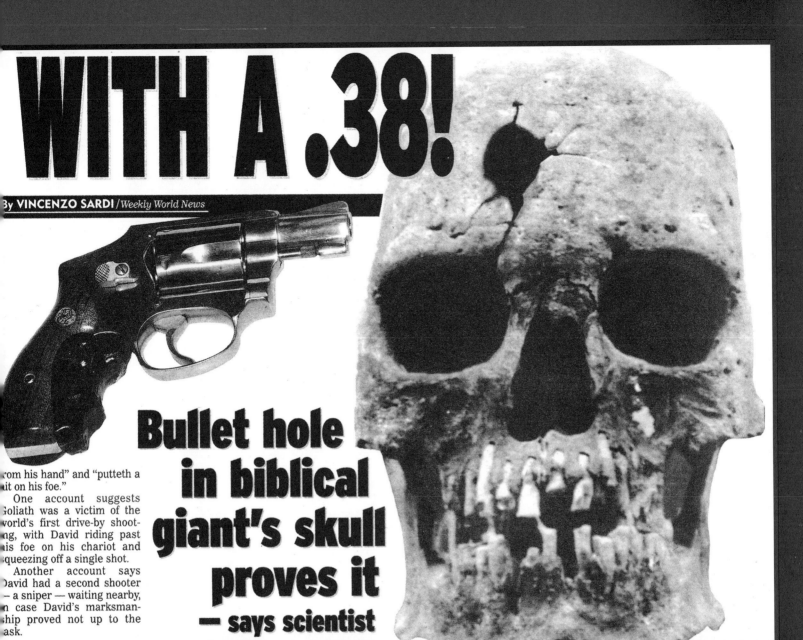

Bullet hole in biblical giant's skull proves it — says scientist

...rom his hand" and "putteth a ...it on his foe."

One account suggests Goliath was a victim of the world's first drive-by shoot-ng, with David riding past his foe on his chariot and squeezing off a single shot.

Another account says David had a second shooter — a sniper — waiting nearby, n case David's marksman-ship proved not up to the ask.

...core, saying, "Our research provides us with a clearer picture of what really transpired that night.

"Jesus and His apostles ordered pizza for delivery — simply astonishing. I think it's also fascinating to know that Jesus tipped the delivery guy saying, 'Take this in remembrance of me.'

"And let the art world please note that Leonardo da Vinci's painting, while a brilliant creation, was inaccurate. I mean the pizza boxes are nowhere to be found on the table."

EXPERTS strongly believe the pepperoni pizza was for Judas, not Jesus.

WEEKLY WORLD EXCLUSIVE NEWS

NUDE BIBLE OUTRAGE!

New Holy Book featuring naked photos spits in face of Jesus, says clergyman!

NEW BIBLE SAYS: There were no fig leaves in the Garden of Eden.

CENSORED

CENSORED

NEW YORK — A new illustrated version of the Bible is generating a firestorm of controversy — because it features full-frontal nudity!

In the *New American People's Bible*, slated for release next fall, Adam and Eve are shown romping around the Garden of Eden buck naked, the Old Testament temptress Salome strips down to the buff in her infamous belly dance and many other biblical figures are depicted in their birthday suits — including Jesus Christ.

"This is outrageous and blasphemous — it's spitting in the face of religion," blasts the Rev. Donald J. McYonnerly, one of 30 clergymen from around the nation spearheading a grassroots campaign to ban the bottom-baring version of the

By MIKE FOSTER
Weekly World News

Bible.

"They are taking God's word and turning it into a vehicle for pornography.

"This so-called 'Bible' even shows the Virgin Mary bare-breasted as she nurses the baby Jesus."

The publisher of the controversial new Bible says critics are making a mountain out of a molehill.

"The Bible is a very sensual work and we are simply illustrating that side of it," a spokesperson said. "This is a tradition that goes back centuries. The ceiling of the Sistine Chapel shows

THE REV. Donald J. McYonnerly calls the explicit Bible blasphemous.

numerous biblical figures, including God himself, nude."

The Good Book never says anything about Adam and Eve wearing fig leaves — that's just an idea that prudes tacked on later, the spokesperson argued. "The human body is beautiful.

God made it that way and said it was good. All we are doing is showing that."

But critics say the new Bible goes way too far — for example, by showing naked men in a gay bathhouse in the sinful city of Sodom and depicting a hairy-chested Jesus in the altogether as he wades into the water to

be baptized by John the Baptist.

"This is gratuitous nudity," said McYonnerly, of the Bronx. "It's offensive."

Publishing industry insiders say that with the religious markets hotter than ever, companies are doing everything they can to find gimmicks that will sell books. Yet another Bible that features nudity is in the works — featuring supermodel Claudia Schiffer as Eve.

"We're only going to see more of this," an insider told *Weekly World News*.

STOP THE MADNESS!

Do you think the nude Bible should be banned? If so, speak out! Write to Nude Bible, Weekly World News, 5401 NW Broken Sound Blvd., Boca Raton, Fla. 33487. Or e-mail us at editor@weeklyworldnews.com

WWN EXTRA: THE HOTTEST HOLY HUNKS

Studies have shown that women are up to 45 percent more likely to read the Bible than men. And no wonder! "With the exception of Delilah and Jezebel, the hot men in the Bible outnumber the hot women 10 to 1," says Biblologist Judith Stanley, author of the renowned book *Guide to Holy Hotties*. "By reading between the lines, it's become clear who was sexy and attractive and who was fat and ugly (and boy was Mary a dog)!" For those who are planning on purchasing a Nude Bible of their own, Stanley shares her list of the most handsome hunks in the Good Book exclusively with *WWN* readers:

1. Jesus. "Jesus was the ultimate hunk," says Stanley. "God knew no one wants to worship an ugly savior. That's why He made Jesus in the image of men He saw on the cover of romance novels. The heaving chest; long, flowing locks like Fabio's; dark features and a square chin attracted hordes of formerly pagan women."

2. Adam. When God created Adam, He had no idea how sexy the first man should be to make a female want to sleep with him. So God gave Adam such a huge dose of testosterone that when Eve finally came along she would have been *very* pleased, except she had no basis for comparison.

3. Mathew, Mark, Luke, and John. "Jesus was no fool," says Stanley. "He knew people, especially women, weren't going to commit their lives to hideous men with beer bellies and warts, so he picked only the most attractive men with the most sex appeal. Mark especially wowed the ladies with his chiseled features and six-pack abs, and was constantly walking around toga-less. Luke was a physician. Everyone knows chicks dig doctors. And let's not forget Matthew was also called 'Levi,' because he was the first man with a great ass in jeans."

4. Noah. Noah wasn't the greatest to look at, but he had a big boat and gals really go nuts for a guy with a yacht. Also, he was constantly going on about how much he loved animals, showing that he wasn't afraid to display his feminine side—a real turn-on for the ladies.

5. Moses. "Oh the things Moses could get away with!" says Stanley. "Do you honestly think he could get the Israelites to give up their nice, cozy homes to wander around in the desert for 40 years unless he had animal magnetism out the wazoo? Of course not."

6. Satan. "For some reason, there are tons of women who like a guy who's gone wrong," says Stanley. "They're the nurturing kind who feel they can 'help' him. Also, it didn't hurt that he had red, glowing eyes that made biblical women melt under his steady, manly gaze."

7. Angel Gabriel. Gabriel was God's angel messenger who flew on golden wings. "What God didn't realize was that Gabriel liked to jet off to Sodom and Gomorrah for weekends to enjoy a couple days of debauchery. The loose women of S&G adored him. But the party was over when God got fed up with their shenanigans and smote the place."

8. Job. "Because Job was a kind, sensitive man who was made to suffer many, many hardships, he got the sympathy vote from the women," says Stanley. "Lots of times, he acted more upset than he was just to keep the ladies around. He was something of a drama queen."

Girl finds message from God in a tomato!

DUBLIN, Ireland — A 14-year-old girl sliced open a tomato — and found a handwritten message from God!

Schoolgirl Maggie Sterling showed British reporters a two-sided note allegedly found inside a tomato that she bought in Northern Ireland.

On one side were the words "There is only one God." On the other side: "Jesus is the messenger."

Christians from all over the world have journeyed to Ireland to see the mysterious tomato, which has been encased in plastic to preserve it.

JULY 9, 2002

APE STARTS NEW RELIGION!

WORSHIPERS are flocking to services led by one of the world's newest religious gurus — a 250-pound ape!

"Lao-Loc is one of God's holiest emissaries," said Bongyi Kawanamat, spokesman for the new Church of Light and Freedom in Bangkok, Thailand. "We believe he was sent here to spread the wonderful news of salvation through meditation and good works."

Kawanamat said Lao-Loc founded the church about a year ago. "I personally witnessed the great miracle," he said.

"One day, for no reason, I felt drawn to visit the zoo where Lao-Loc was a prisoner. As I gazed at him in his cage, our eyes met and I felt a great sense of peace and wonderment. Then a bright light suddenly appeared over his cage!

"I knew this was a sign from Heaven itself," he continued. "So I arranged to pay Lao-Loc's ransom to the zoo, and he was released to fulfill his great destiny."

Members of the Church of Light and Freedom built Lao-Loc an altar at which he presides over daily services. Worshipers bring a daily offering of bananas and grubs, then spend several hours a day meditating before the holy ape.

"He has taught us patience and self-examination," says a young woman who joined the church soon after it began.

"Sometimes he rises from the altar, beats his chest and calls out to Heaven with a thunderous roar. That is when our prayers become even stronger, for at that moment Lao-Loc has fallen under the watchful gaze of God."

NEW HOPE FOR THE DEAD

Monk brings corpses back to life

...with the power of prayer!

LINJUAN, China — Beloved Buddhist monk Tsii Qi can do what no man has ever done before — he can raise the dead and return them to the world of the living!

Witnesses in this remote mountain village say saintly Tsii has resurrected at least 14 people in the past four years, using ancient chants and prayers discovered in the ruins of an abandoned monastery in nearby Tibet.

"The Blessed Buddha has given Brother Tsii power over life and death itself, and I have seen the power at work with my own eyes," said awestruck village elder Yeh Hung-tien.

"With nothing but the healing hand of prayer, he brought my beautiful sister Mei — a nun — back from the grave more than a week after she died of pneumonia at the monastery.

"She has been back two years now, carrying on her work, and is as healthy as if she'd never been dead."

The remarkable monk acquired his mind-boggling powers after discovering a sacred, centuries-old manuscript baring the secret of eternal life during an expedition to Tibet in the summer of 1989.

"Brother Tsii found the document in a crumbling Vajrayana monastery," said journalist Juang Cho-yu, who's written numerous stories on Tsii's mystical powers. "The manuscript was so old it nearly fell apart in the monk's hands,

but he taped it back together and returned with it to Linjuan.

"It wasn't until after months of study, however, that he discovered he not only held in his hands the power of scotch tape, but the power of life and death as well."

In the spring of 1990, stoic Tsii used prayers and incanta-

By JOE BERGER

Staff writer

tions drawn from the 5th-century manuscript to restore the life of a Buddhist scholar from the nearby village of Piangja.

"Brother Tsii prayed and chanted over the man for nearly four hours, rubbing his body with an herbal ointment described in the yellowed manuscript," Juang told fellow reporters.

"And by the time his prayers were complete, the dead man was back on his feet, appearing in the pink of health.

"And he is still alive today — still fit and healthy."

Since then, the adored holy man has brought 13 others back from the grave without a single failure.

"He has received thousands of requests from around the world from the grief-stricken to restore the lives of their loved ones, but Tsii is convinced

he must not use his powers indiscriminately," Juang said.

"He brings back only the worthy, only those he believes the Buddha has approved for resurrection."

For instance, he has refused to bring back both Steve Guttenberg's career and former U.S. president Gerald Ford.

"It was one thing to do four Police Academy movies, but *Cocoon: The Return* and that terrible sequel to *Three Men and a Baby*....Brother Steve was just asking for it, I'm afraid," Tsii is rumored to have said.

"And as for President Ford, he has not yet passed on...I don't think."

"I don't want to interfere with the normal cycle of death," said somber Tsii. "When you have the power of life and death over all the citizens of the Earth, you must use that power very cautiously."

MYSTICAL monk Tsii Qi is blessed with the power to raise the dead.

WWN EXCLUSIVE DATELINE: AUGUST 26, 2003

MIRACLE CARP SAYS THE END IS NEAR!

No Ho-Ho this year . . .

SANTA FOUND FROZEN IN CHUNK OF ICE!

WORLD BIGWIGS CANCEL CHRISTMAS

How to tell your kids the bad news!

By FRED KENNEDY

THE United Nations hurriedly canceled Christmas in a secret session at the agency's headquarters in New York just days after U.S. researchers found Santa Claus' stiff, lifeless body frozen in an 11-ton chunk of ice on November 20.

It's unknown at this point whether foul play was involved in the death of the veritable spirit of the holiday season. But experts who have examined the thawed body, which appears to have been dead for at least four months, say the absence of bruises or injuries other than a sprained left ankle suggest that the fat man might have slipped on ice, and after falling, couldn't get up.

Under conditions within spitting distance of the North Pole, it wouldn't have taken long for Claus to become encased in ice.

Though shocking to everyone, children, obviously, are going to be hardest hit.

As one psychologist put it, "Telling a child that Santa Claus is dead will be traumatic.

"And there's the added difficulty of explaining why he won't be getting any toys on Christmas day. Of course, you could go buy them yourself and tell your kids Santa brought them — but that would be lying."

President Bush and his lame-duck Secretary of State Colin Powell have experienced what aides are calling "a meeting of the minds" on the issue of Santa Claus' untimely demise.

They agree that the United

UNITED Nations (above) made shocking decision that will disappoint million of kids.

Nations — not the United States — should break the news to parents and children worldwide.

They also are said to be furious that even though U.N. assembly members agreed to cancel Christmas during an unprecedented secret session on November 23, they have yet to make the announcement so people can prepare.

"This isn't a department store Santa we can replace with just any old fatso from a temp agency, this is the real Santa Claus," U.S. ambassador to the U.N. John Danforth told aides.

"I'd make the announcement myself just to get it over with, but it's like I told the General Assembly: After all the B.S. the President gave as excuses for invading Iraq, U.S. credibility is shot."

The discovery of Santa's body in the block of ice stunned a team of 14 U.S. researchers who were monitoring the hunting patterns of polar bears when they stumbled on the no-longer-jolly old elf.

"The ice was crystal clear and you didn't have to strain to see a bearded man in a red suit with a wide black belt right in the middle of it," says Dr.

Brenda Jenkins-Cole.

The block of ice was sliced free from the frozen ground with chain saws and airlifted to an undisclosed facility in Canada.

The body was thawed, but attempts to revive Santa with electrical shocks and experimental drugs "didn't work," a U.S. State Department source familiar with the operation says.

"Santa's death, though interesting in itself, is water under the bridge," says psychologist Dr. Marcia Kenmore, of Minneapolis, Minn.

"We've got 50 million small children to worry about breaking the news to in the United States alone."

Dealing with the kids "is going to be tough," she continues. "I suggest saying something like, 'Billy, Santa Claus is in Heaven now, so he won't be bringing you any toys ever again.'

"It's likely that the child will start crying or go into mild shock, but don't worry — you need to let him grieve. Once he's calmed down, distract him by asking to see his 'wish list' and then taking him to a toy shop to see how much of the stuff you can afford. Sure, kids love Santa, but let's face it — they're greedy devils.

"Once they come face to face with all the junk they're hoping to get for Christmas, they'll forget all about the fat man."

SURPRISING BIB PROP

Your preacher doesn't

JESUS will not return to Earth for another 1,000 years, according to the scriptures.

By VINCENZO SARDI/*Weekly World News*

It's O.K. to covet your neighbor's wife!

Holy Bible

ROME — A turncoat Vatican librarian has released a collection of sacred scriptures that were locked away in a secret vault for more than 1,600 years — because the prophecies they contain are so shocking they would revolutionize Christianity!

"The Pope doesn't want you to hear these prophecies and neither does your local preacher," declared Brother Emilio Vasso, a former assistant librarian at the Vatican.

"These are teachings that do not seem to 'fit in' with conventional theological views — and yet they are teachings that our Lord urgently wants us all to hear."

Brother Emilio claims that the parchments include more than 500 lines of biblical verse that were excised by the early Christian patriarchs around 310 A.D. In centuries past, to even speak of them meant being burned at the stake as a heretic, he asserts.

Brother Emilio, who recently published copies of the texts in pamphlet form through an underground Italian press, is himself facing possible excommunication and theft charges. In a curious statement, the Vatican has denied the authenticity of the so-called Lost Prophecies, while simultaneously demanding their "immediate return."

Here are some of the astounding teachings found in the Lost Prophecies:

✚ **IT'S O.K. TO COVET YOUR NEIGHBOR'S WIFE** — The lost scriptures include an exception to the 10th Commandment. The passage, apparently edited out by early Christian fathers fearful of encouraging wife-swapping, states: "Thou shall not covet thy neighbor's wife unless you in turn are willing to share thine own wife with him."

✚ **YOU CAN ENTER THE KINGDOM OF HEAVEN, NO MATTER HOW WICKED YOU ARE** — A passage in the Lost Prophecies says that as long as you love God with all your heart, you'll be forgiven for your sins and allowed to spend eternity at the Lord's side — even if you've spent your whole life lying, cheating and stealing from your neighbors.

✚ **JESUS WILL NOT RETURN TO EARTH FOR ANOTHER 1,000 YEARS** — Contrary to the teachings of many fiery evangelical preachers, the Second Coming is not around the corner. Rather, the Messiah will come back 3,000 years after His resurrection, "after mankind has built cities among the stars," according to the prophecies.

✚ **CHRIST WILL COME BACK AS A JOCKEY** — The Lost Prophecies state that when Jesus does return, it will be as a 5-foot-tall jockey whose victories astound the masses.

This echoes a biblical prophecy, "See your king comes to you, righteous and having salvation, gentle

...LE ...HECIES

...want you to read

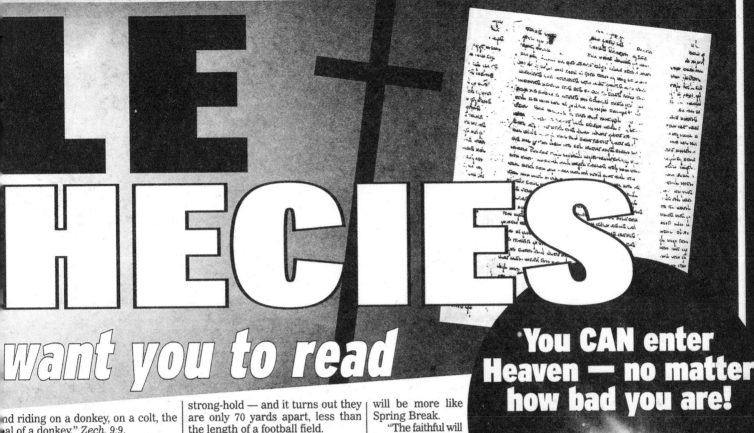

...nd riding on a donkey, on a colt, the ...al of a donkey," *Zech. 9:9.*

✝ **SAYING 5 SIMPLE WORDS WILL MAKE YOU RICH** — ...urprisingly, the prophecies state ...at simply by bowing down and ...ttering the words "Lord, I truly need ...oney," you can trigger a shower of ...ealth from the Almighty.

✝ **THE NUMBER 715, NOT 666, WILL TURN OUT TO BE THE ...UMBER OF THE BEAST** — In ...irect contradiction to the Book of ...evelation, the Lost Prophecies warn ...at the Antichrist, Satan's earthly ...ncarnation, will use 715 as a lucky ...umber. "The prophecies indicate ...at this will be an address or hotel ...uite," Brother Emilio says.

✝ **AN L.A. RADIO STATION WILL ...OPEN UP DIRECT COMMUNI- ...ATION WITH GOD** — "Men of the ...reatest city of the new world, ...ho have learned the art of ...peaking through the air" will ...ontact the Lord through a ...uke, the parchments ...tate. The morning show ...ill become one of the ...ighest rated ever, the ...rophecies indicate.

✝ **THE EXACT LOCA- ...TION OF HEAVEN ...ND HELL WILL BE ...EVEALED** — Scien- ...ists will discover the ...hysical locations of both ...od's home and Satan's

strong-hold — and it turns out they are only 70 yards apart, less than the length of a football field.

✝ **THE WORLD IS NOT COMING TO AN END** — Contrary to popular belief, history isn't grinding to a halt. The Lost Prophecies state that six signs will herald the end of the world — and none of them are likely to occur in the near future. The six include "the destruction of man's largest city on Mars," and other events that experts say won't be possible for hundreds of years.

✝ **ALL MANKIND WILL STOP WORKING AND PARTY 24 HOURS A DAY** — Despite the grim descriptions of the End Times found in the Book of Revelation, the Lost Prophecies make clear that the final days before Judgment Day

will be more like Spring Break.

"The faithful will forgo their labor and rejoice, while the sinners exhaust themselves with drinking, dancing and fornication," according to the prophecies.

You CAN enter Heaven — no matter how bad you are!

How you can speak directly to God!

Check out these revelations from other holy books

In recent decades, scholars have unearthed other ancient documents that cast light on the world's religions, often exposing misconceptions followers have held for centuries. Here are just a few examples:

● **IT'S O.K. FOR HINDUS TO EAT BEEF** — Today, many Hindus believe that eating "sacred" cows is a mortal sin, but ancient Sanskrit texts uncovered by Indian researchers back in 1972 reveal that early Hindu priests regularly feasted on cattle.

● **MUSLIMS DON'T NEED TO FACE MECCA TO PRAY** — According to the so-called *Lost Book of the Koran*, found by archaeologists in 1983, millions of Arabs and other believers in Islam have got it wrong. Mohammed said praying toward any major city will work just as well as the holy city of...

MUSLIMS can pray any way they like.

HINDUS can eat beef.

Mecca, since "Allah is in all places."

● **JEWISH BOYS DO NOT HAVE TO BE CIRCUMCISED** — Generations of Hebrews have undergone this painful procedure needlessly, if the Dead Sea scrolls are right. Writings found in these parchments, discovered in 1945, state that the tip of the penis should be removed only if there is infection or it becomes hopelessly stuck...

ONLY in *Weekly World News*

EDGAR CAYCE REBORN AS PSYCHIC FLY

The 'Sleeping Prophet' is back — and his predictions are more accurate than ever

By MIGUEL FIGUEROA/*Weekly World News*

MADRID — Famed psychic Edgar Cayce has been reincarnated as a common housefly — and is issuing a stern warning: "The end of the world is near!"

Incredibly, the fly's face is a dead ringer for Cayce, America's own "Sleeping Prophet," who died 57 years ago in 1945.

"When you have a fly with a human head and a face that clearly is identical to Edgar Cayce's and the fly is heard spouting predictions, I don't think it's much of a stretch to say the fly is a reincarnation of the psychic," said paranormal expert Luis Morales. "In fact, it would be more unbelievable if the fly were not a reincarnation of Cayce.

"And since this fly logically is Cayce, we should treat its predictions with great respect," Morales said.

At least 39 eyewitnesses in 11 different government offices — including the Assistant Secretary of Defense — say they've seen and heard the buzzing prophet of doom.

"It looks like a fly with a man's face. And it isn't a bit afraid of people," shaken Department of Agriculture aide Alonso Hernandez, who took the only known photograph of the bizarre bug, told a Madrid newspaper. "It wants to communicate with us. It speaks in a high-pitched, squeaky voice.

"I heard it speak with my own ears. It said: 'The end of the world is near.' It scared me."

Religious leaders have hesitated to comment on the amazing fly and its startling message. But one official inside the Vatican confirmed, "The fly's predictions are being studied at the highest level."

Efforts to catch the chatty bug have failed. Once it was nearly swatted by a secretary who had a head cold and could not hear it speaking to her.

Some of the fly's other predictions:
- "A swarm of heroic flies saves a bus full of schoolchildren from certain death by pressing down the brake after the driver passes out from a heart attack."
- "A bright light will come from the sky, eliminating darkness from Earth for three years straight."
- "Water discovered below the ocean floor will be found to cure deadly disease."

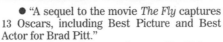
'A fire at a flyswatter factory destroys $1.4 million worth of inventory.'

'A computer glitch will erase the debt of every American man, woman and child.'

- "A sequel to the movie *The Fly* captures 13 Oscars, including Best Picture and Best Actor for Brad Pitt."
- "A visitor from another world will have hypnotic powers over the women of Earth — and force them to turn against their mates."
- "An explosion at a sugar plant in Mexico injured no one — but leads to the largest gathering of flies in the history of the world."
- "A seed will be planted that will grow enough food to feed the entire world."
- "An epidemic of love and happiness will sweep the planet, bringing good cheer everywhere — including the war-torn Middle East."
- "A college student will discover a way to communicate with beings from other galaxies — but only on his laptop computer."
- "A diet pill will allow you to eat whatever you like — while shedding all the weight you want."
- "A storm will

WWN EXTRA

When *WWN*'s prophecy bureau tried to reach the Edgar Cayce Psychic Fly for comment three years after this story ran, to see why none of its prophecies have yet to come true, they were informed that it had died tragically in a electrical accident.

"He flew right into a halogen lamp and burned to death," said an administration official. "Poor little guy didn't even see it coming. Kinda ironic, when you think about it."

'A one-eyed child teaches mankind to see the future through a toilet paper roll.'

rage for days and days over America's southern states — raining flakes of pure gold and making millions of residents filthy rich."
- "The common housefly will be named the 'Official Insect of the United States.' Six states even declare the fly their state bird."
- "A beloved American President will return after many years in the grave — and lead America into its greatest era of peace and prosperity ever."
- "An 83-year-old grandmother will find the actual Fountain of Youth while gardening in her backyard in Scottsdale, Ariz."
- "The development of inexpensive flying cars fueled by the sun will render Earth-bound vehicles, roads and highways obsolete."

'From the great ocean will come a wave that will drown every spider in the world.'

NOSTRADUMBAS

Found! Wacky predictions of Nostradamus' idiot brother

By JON ZAIRE
In Paris

FAMED seer Nostradamus had a pea-brained idiot of a brother who almost single-handedly destroyed the rule of French King Francis I with his crackpot predictions and bad advice, all couched in silly sing-song rhymes that sound like something, well, a moron dreamed up!

Nostradumbas, as the French press is calling Maurice de Nostradame:

● Persuaded Francis to embark on not just one or two, but FOUR un-winnable wars against King Charles V of Spain: "There is a king in Spain, his reign is on the wane, if Francis goes in, Charles will pretend to win, but won't!"

● Insisted that the discovery of a race of "subhuman creatures who love people" would revolutionize the French economy by providing an inexhaustible source of cheap labor from the New World: "The Canadians are stupid and will work for a pittance, and when they get old, we'll bid them good riddance — and they won't know the difference!"

● Prophesied that Francis' son, future King of France Henry II, would change his last name to Ford and develop an assembly line on which to mass-produce mechanical horses to pull carriages: "Horses from metal, made by a Ford, but wait — it's really Henry, our Lord!"

IT RUNS IN THE FAMILY: Maurice de Nostradame, brother of legendary psychic Nostradamus, had a unique take on what the future held for us — rooted more in humor and irony than in psychic powers.

"And those are just the predictions that sound half-way reasonable," says Jean-Jacques Pretet, a University of Paris historian and leading authority on Maurice. The lesser-known seer was born two years after big brother Nostradamus in 1505.

"What's really remarkable is that Maurice had no particular talent for prognostication, but he was still able to seize on what Nostradamus was doing and figure out how to make a good living at it.

"He might not have been psychic, and he certainly wasn't exactly struggling under the weight of a triple-digit IQ, but he had an instinct for marketing and self-promotion.

"He repackaged and sold King Francis the same load of manure over and over again."

Since the 16th century, the writings of Michel de Nostradame — Nostradamus — have fascinated the world. True believers are convinced that he predicted many global events, including World War I and II and America's rise to prominence on the international political stage.

Maurice, on the other hand, had been largely unknown outside academic circles until Pretet wrote a magazine article bringing some of his so-called predictions to light.

"Before his death in 1544, Maurice offered up hundreds of predictions in his trademark sing-song style that seemingly mocked Nostradamus' far more serious and challenging quatrains," says the historian, whose lighthearted book, *Maurice de Nostradame — The OTHER Nostradamus*, is slated for an August release.

"My personal favorite involved what obviously was a spur-of-the-moment prediction involving a forthcoming 'gas attack' that Francis I would suffer in Maurice's presence.

"'From troubled bowels vile gasses shall smoke and hiss. Was it me? No. Was it her? No. It was Francisssssssssssssssssss!'"

SILLY SEER'S PEA-BRAINED PROPHECIES

for the world today!

HERE are a few of Maurice de Nostradame's nutty predictions for modern times, translated, interpreted and paraphrased for clarity:

● After making the world safe for democracy by defeating "Federation of Evil" allies Italy, Spain and the United States in 1938, beloved cartoon artist and top Nazi Adolf Hitler will reveal himself to be the New Messiah — and rise up into Heaven alive.

Popular TV evangelist Osama Bin Laden's dreams of turning the world into a gigantic mosque where everybody worships Allah will be shattered by a father and son terrorist team, George Bush and George Bush. They, said Maurice, will incinerate Bin Laden with a flamethrower as he slips out of his elegant Washington love nest on the back of what appears to be a cross-eyed goat.

● The demolition of New York City's Twin Towers to make way for even taller "triple towers" should have been announced "well in advance," predicted Maurice, "so people in the 'New Land' would not live in fear thinking they were under attack."

● President Hillary Clinton not only will become America's first lady president, she'll become one of the oldest American women in history to get pregnant and give birth to twins. "Not even I," Maurice scribbled in a footnote to the prediction, "can name the father of this child. But I know it isn't the one named Bill."

● Doctors will rue the day they "put themselves out of business" by finally admitting that cancer, heart disease and other killer illnesses can be cured with an ordinary table spice. "Better to keep these things secret," he counseled, "for your own good."

THE PROPHETS GO HEAD-TO-HEAD

Weekly World News strives to provide you with the most startling insights from the world's foremost fortunetellers. But predicting the future is an art, not a science, and even the most renowned prognosticators don't always get it right. (For example, the world didn't end in 2000 or 2001, as many predicted.) So how'd the big guys do? Use *WWN*'s handy guide to the prophets to figure out who you should trust.

PROPHET	MICHEL DE NOSTRADAME	EDGAR CAYCE	P'LOD THE ALIEN	VANESSA SHROPSHIRE, *WWN* Admin. Asst.
NICKNAME	Nostradamus	The Sleeping Prophet	P, 'Lod	Cupcake, Nessie, V-Shrop (preferred)
ASTROLOGICAL SIGN	Sagittarius	Pisces; formerly a Gemini, Scorpio, Leo, Libra, and twice an Aries	Phlegmarius and Analius	Capricorn, according to *People* magazine, Aquarius, according to *TV Guide*
METHOD OF PROPHESIZING	Flame- and/or water-gazing	Entering a sleep-like state	Lobe rubbing	Reading the clumps of powdered creamer floating in a coffee cup
MOST FAMOUS PREDICTIONS	The French Revolution, the rise of Hitler, the atom bomb, possibly the September 11, 2001, terrorist attacks	Castor oil cures everything, U2's Bono is the incarnation of Jesus Christ	Presidential victories of Ronald Reagan, George Bush I and II, and Bill Clinton; Arnold Schwarzenegger's gubernatorial victory	When the copy machine will run out of paper, when a computer is about to crash, when the boss is in a bad mood, and that the new girl is a kind of a ho
MOST FAMOUS MISPREDICTION	Brad Pitt and Jennifer Aniston will have a long and happy marriage	Scientists will discover a death ray from Atlantis in 1958	*The Golden Girls* will sweep the 1989 Emmys	Stuart from IT is totally gay*
PERCENTAGE OF ACCURACY	56%	64%	96%	99–100% *still denies this is a misprediction even though Stuart has been married for three years

SUICIDE BOMBER: 'THERE ARE NO VIRGINS IN HEAVEN'

By CYD TEDDER
Correspondent

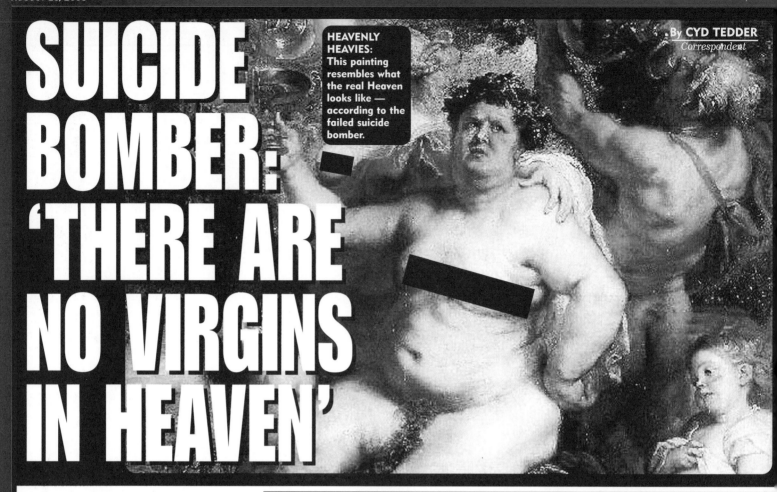

HEAVENLY HEAVIES: This painting resembles what the real Heaven looks like — according to the failed suicide bomber.

— THE WOMEN ARE FAT & THE PLACE IS A DUMP!
...near-death experience reveals!

A FAILED suicide bomber is down in the dumps because the 72 beautiful virgins he was promised in paradise turned out to be a bunch of fat, naked women who wouldn't leave him alone!

Crestfallen Mustafa Muhammad, 30, lost an arm and was blinded when the dynamite he had planned to detonate on a crowded bus in Jerusalem exploded in his kitchen in the wee hours of August 2.

According to doctors, the would-be terrorist died during surgery and remained dead for 5 minutes before they managed to revive him.

During that time he claims to have visited "martyrs' paradise" — the place that every starry-eyed terrorist in the Middle East dreams of going when he dies.

But "terror Heaven" wasn't what it's cracked up to be. And Muhammad says it left him "depressed, disillusioned and disenchanted with the whole terror concept — now and forever."

"Seventy-two sexy virgins? Fine wines? Satin sheets? All I got was a cold cup of muddy coffee and a bunch of overweight, naked women who smelled like goat. And they chased me around like dogs in heat the whole time I was there," the one-time martyr-wanna-be fumed to reporters in an interview from his hospital bed in Jerusalem.

"It's like they hadn't seen a man in 100 years, or something.

"There was milk — but it was curdled and sour. There was honey — but it was crawling with vermin and bugs.

"There were no streets of gold, just garbage-strewn alleyways. There were grand houses — but they were devastated by bombs.

"The paradise I had been promised was a garbage dump suspended between the edge of the universe and infinite nothingness — a place as unappealing as camel dung plopped in a sea of hot desert sand."

Muhammad's description of "paradise" as little more than a filthy ghetto stands in sharp contrast to the rosy picture painted by terror kingpins who promise gullible young men an eternity of pleasure in exchange for their martyrdom on earth.

Because most terrorists who die actually stay dead, they are unable to report the truth about conditions on "the other side." That gives recruiters free reign to describe them in lavish and compelling detail.

For men who've spent their lives gazing wistfully upon women who hide their bodies and faces behind thick burqas, scarves and veils, the promise of 72 scantily clad virgins is enough to make all but the strongest strap on the dynamite, snatch up a handful of blasting caps and sprint to the nearest bus depot, Western analysts agree.

"I never would have considered going through with a suicide bombing if I hadn't believed I would be able to enjoy all the luxuries I've never had on earth," said Muhammad.

"But everything I was told about Heaven was a dirty lie. Even the sky was overcast and gray — and the air was thick with the stench of the sewers.

"I didn't see God. I didn't see the great martyrs who had gone ahead before me. I did see unhappy people gnashing their teeth and tearing their hair and crying out to no one in particular, 'Where did we go wrong?'

"If I never go back," he added, "it will be too soon."

On this side of the Atlantic, a Muslim cleric in Miami says there may be a good reason "paradise" wasn't to Muhammad's liking.

"Muslims are peace-loving people and our Heaven is reserved for true, kind and faithful believers," he explains. "I think any rational person would realize that terrorists such as Mr. Muhammad don't go to paradise.

"They go to Hell."

Asked for comment, Muhammad said: "I don't want to talk about it. All it know is I don't want to be a suicide bomber no more."

BUDDHA'S FOOTPRINT FOUND — AND IT'S GUARDED BY A FROG!

KOH-CHANG, Thailand — Faithful pilgrims are flocking by the thousands to the site of a giant puddle — because they say it is actually a sacred footprint left by the holy foot of Buddha!

The puddle was discovered at the top of the Had Sai waterfall and is apparently being guarded by a frog.

The throngs of buddhist believers are arriving day and night to pray on this hallowed ground, and many have left incense, flowers, and candles by the puddle's edge.

Visitors claim the water in the puddle can be used as a balm to cure illness and bring about good fortune.

Other enterprising folks have been asking the frog to reveal winning lottery numbers. In fact, the poor frog reportedly came close to death, because so many people were rubbing talcum powder on its slimy skin in hopes of catching a glimpse of the winning numbers.

COULD Buddha's frog guardian know the winning lotto numbers?

A spokesman for the national parks commission says he is worried about the natural setting being damaged.

"Today I ordered my officers to control the area, but people now think this is a holy place and we are powerless to stop them coming here," says the spokesman.

BUDDHA is revered by millions of people — and apparently frogs too.

MILLION IMAM MARCH!
— Clerics Rally in Washington to Demand AC in Middle East!

WASHINGTON, DC – The "Million Imam March," which organizers say was conceived of in the wake of the U.S. declaration of victory in the Iraq War, is being hailed as a huge success, though DC police put the actual number of participants closer to 47,650. Islamic religious leaders from around the globe congregated in the U.S. capital for a weekend of seminars and panel discussions on the topic of wealthy western nations' responsibility to provide air conditioning for mosques across the Middle East, especially in Afghanistan and Iraq. The gathering culminated in a peaceful march from the plaza to the concrete "protest pens" across the street from the White House.

Spirited chants could be heard from the marchers, including many refrains of, "What do we want?" "Central air!" "When do we want it?" "Before Allah the Father brings the faithful to paradise for their eternal reward!"

According to one of the protest's organizers, Mohammed al-Haruf, from the Central Mosque in Praise of the One True God, in Westvale, Minnesota, "We believe it is the responsibility of [the western Christian] nations to improve the quality of life in the countries they have invaded in the name of democracy."

"Show me one democratic nation," al-Haruf continued, "that doesn't at least have window-mounted AC units in its homes, churches and municipal institutions! Even for a nation of infidels, the United States has behaved barbarically in the course of its recent activities, and we hope to focus the attention of the international community on this pressing issue."

Reached at his Crawford, Texas, ranch for comment, the vacationing President George W. Bush said, "Well, heh, if they think it's so darned hot, maybe they should move somewhere else." After a moment's consideration, the President added, "Just not here, of course."

IT'S A MIRACLE!
— U.S. Soldiers at Iraqi Detention Facility Discover Mashed-Up Pages from the Koran Make Wrinkles Disappear!

WEEPING VIRGIN MARY STATUE RUINING CHURCH — WITH TEARS

'...she's caused so much flood damage, she'll have to go' says pastor

THIS statue of the Madonna cries tears by the gallon, which is ruining the church where it's displayed.

CAPE TOWN, South Africa — A statue of the Virgin Mary that weeps real tears is causing havoc for the small church where it's displayed — because the figure is gushing like a waterworks and won't stop!

"I've had it," sputters the church's janitor, furiously mopping the floor around the icon in a rare moment of peace. "All I do now is clean up after this thing — not to mention the mold growing everywhere from all the dampness, and the mud getting tracked in. And if I'm not mopping, I'm emptying the bucket underneath her.

By KATE McCLARE
Weekly World News

"I love the Blessed Virgin as much as anyone," he says, making the sign of the cross over his sweat-soaked shirt, "but this has got to stop."

Weekly World News has agreed not to give the specific location of the so-called Bawling Madonna at the request of the church. Chaos has reigned at the facility since the holy howler began overflowing four months ago. Pilgrims from around the world are flocking here by the thousands, worshiping the sobbing statue and seeking its intercession in everything from disease to marital problems.

"It's been a nightmare," says the pastor. "We had a wedding the other day, and the floor was so slick, the bride took a nasty spill. Half her bridal party went down with her.

"The floor boards in the church are warping, there's a terrible mildew smell, and the ceiling's coming down in the church basement. Father Stan got a mild concussion from a chunk of plaster that fell on him while he was calling bingo the other night.

"And worst of all, our insurance company won't pay for any of the repairs. They say it's an act of God, so it's not covered."

Noted religious scholar the Rev. Rex Moore says he's "flabbergasted" by the church's complaints about the Bawling Madonna. "They have a bona fide miracle here, and they don't realize it. This could be one of the most significant religious events since visions of the Virgin Mary appeared to a young peasant girl at Lourdes in the 19th century."

Rev. Moore traveled to Cape Town with a team of scientists, who found no evidence of man-made trickery. The plaster statue doesn't appear to have been tampered with, and isn't hooked up to any water source.

"There is no scientific explanation for this that I can think of," says one of the scientists, who subjected the Bawling Madonna to X-rays, chemical analysis and other tests. "It's beginning to look like God's at work here."

Local church leaders are confounded as to what the Bawling Madonna is trying to accomplish. "All she does is cry — by the gallon," says the pastor. "We're not sure what she's crying about, but whatever it is, she just needs to get over it."

REV. Rex Moore

OUTSIDE the Cape Town church where the Bawling Madonna is causing serious problems.

MARY'S NOT THE ONLY CRYING IDOL!

THE PHENOMENON of weeping idols is not limited to statues of the Virgin Mary. 1) "Christ of the Tears," weeping and bleeding statue — Cochabamba, Bolivia. 2) "Padre Pio," blood-weeping statue — Messina, Sicily. 3) "The Crying King," tear-weeping statue — Duerne, Netherlands. 4) "American Idol, Kelly Clarkson," weeping contest winner — Los Angeles, California.

VATICAN EXPERTS CONFIRM:
BLEEDING STATUE OF MOTHER TERESA HAS PMS!

By VINCENZO SARDI

BLOOD that miraculously appears on the robes of Mother Teresa's statue once a month is human, experts say.

A STATUE of Mother Teresa that miraculously bleeds once a month also gets cranky and irritable around the same time — and Vatican investigators have concluded that the spirit of the saintly nun suffers from PMS!

"Scientific tests have confirmed that the fluid is consistent with human menstrual blood," reveals Father Luigi Sicilia, a Jesuit priest leading the panel.

"Those who knew Mother Teresa in her younger days say she suffered from terrible mood swings during her time of the month. While normally she was serene and compassionate, with the patience of Job, whenever her 'Aunt from out of town' visited, she would, in the words of one sister we interviewed, turn into 'an irrational, raving bitch on wheels.'

"It seems that the PMS Mother Teresa experienced during much of her life has followed her into the afterlife."

The experts base their conclusions on extensive tests of the 4-foot-tall stone likeness, which sits on the grounds of St. Mary's High School in Calcutta, where Mother Teresa taught from 1931 to 1948, as well as videotapes, photographs and the testimony of 410 eyewitnesses.

For three days each month, always beginning the 21st, the statue bleeds — not from the eyes, as has been observed in sculptures of Jesus — but from what one Indian newspaper delicately refers to as "the bikini area."

During those spells:

● The lame, blind and sick who flock to the shrine to pray for miracle cures and normally are healed receive no relief — and often leave worse off.

● The statue's usually kindly face becomes distorted, looking depressed one minute and angry the next. "She becomes especially aggravated when someone lingers at her feet for more than two minutes or fails to leave a donation in the collection box," Father Sicilia says.

● A young man who knelt before the statue to pray for a cure for his acne fled in terror after he heard the statue snap, "Get lost — come back when you have a real problem."

● A prostitute was whacked in the back of the head by a stone hand as she bowed before the statue, begging for forgiveness.

Mother Teresa, born Agnes Gonxha Bojaxhiu in Skopje, Macedonia, in 1910, founded The Missionaries of Charity, an order dedicated to caring for the poorest of the poor in Calcutta. Since her death on Sept. 5, 1997, Pope John Paul II has put the revered figure on the fast track for sainthood. He has already beatified her, the first step of the process.

The investigators predict their findings will expedite matters.

After the blood stops, she gets grumpy

ARE YOU KIDDING?

PMS is cited as a factor in three out of four homicides committed by women, according to FBI statistics.

"On the road to canonization, the biggest obstacle is establishing miracles attributable to the intended saint," notes Father Sicilia. "In this case, we have evidence of a bona fide miracle."

'MAKE HOWARD STERN A SAINT' ...urges priest!

By
BARRY DUTTER
Weekly World News

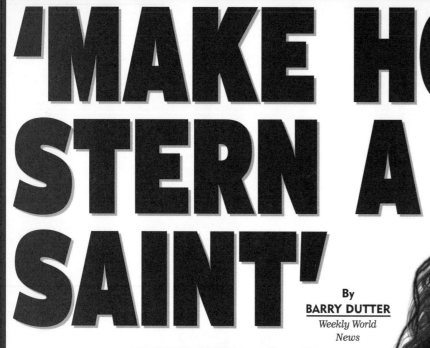

'He is accepting of gays, midgets, stutterers and others who are shunned by society'
— Father Tugman

MANHATTAN — Over the years, many great men have been chosen for sainthood: Thomas Aquinas — Francis of Assissi — and now, if one priest has his way, radio shock-jock Howard Stern!

Most men are awarded sainthood after they die, but Father Nicholas Tugman feels Stern should be the first to be elevated while he is still living.

And to make this nomination even more controversial, Stern is Jewish, or, as he claims on his radio show, at least half-Jewish.

But as Father Tugman points out, "Jesus Christ himself was a Jewish man, so it's not unthinkable."

How did this out-of-left-field nomination come about?

"I first had the idea after I saw an article in the *Weekly World News*," Father Tugman explains. "There was a story there about a priest who thought Howard Stern was possessed by Satan and was trying to exorcise him thru his radio." (*Weekly World News* Nov. 26, 2002)

"I had never heard the Stern show before," Father Tugman continues, "but I thought I should give it a listen, to see if I should join that other priest in his crusade. What I found was that, in fact, the opposite was true. Howard Stern is no devil."

Father Tugman calls Stern a true humanitarian. "He is very tolerant of other people. He is accepting of gays, midgets, stutterers and others who are shunned by society, just like Jesus was. He takes in those who would be deemed 'freaks' by others, and gives them a home in his radio family."

Father Tugman even defends Stern's bad-boy behavior.

"Howard Stern seemingly engages in sinful activities on his radio show. But if you pay close attention, Howard himself never commits any of those sins himself. His show is like a staging area where people come in, and Howard exposes them to temptation.

"He tests people, and those who succumb are buying themselves a one-way ticket to Hell.

"He may encourage people to get naked, to gamble, and to engage in lewd behavior, but he doesn't force anyone to do anything. People are free to make their own choices.

"Those that resist temptation will go to heaven. Those who do not are doomed for all eternity. So Howard Stern is really doing the Lord's work."

Father Tugman knows that it will be an uphill battle convincing his superiors that Stern is worthy of sainthood, but he feels the effort will be worth it.

"Deep down, Stern is a good man with a good heart. I'd like to meet him.

"I just need to find proof that Stern has performed three miracles. Once I do that, the rest will be easy."

A spokesman for the Catholic Church says the chances of there ever being a Saint Howard look pretty unlikely. "Howard Stern has no more chance of becoming a saint than the Pope has of becoming a Hell's Angel."

FATHER TUGMAN

DALAI LAMA LOSES COOL OVER BRATTY 6-YEAR-OLD DURING KIDS' MOVIE

By DAVID TOLSEY

"GO AWAY kid, you're bothering me." Who would've thought those words would come out of the mouth of the Dalai Lama? But according to sources, they most certainly did . . . and more.

The Dalai Lama was reportedly in New York City recently when he and his entourage decided to catch the matinee showing of *Shark Tale*. Apparently, it was there that His Holiness encountered the kid from Hell, 6-year-old Tommy Modine.

"That little kid kept kicking His Holiness's seat during the trailers," says a spokesperson for the Dalai Lama. "We could see he was getting increasingly annoyed with the kid. I mean, who wouldn't?"

When the exiled Tibetan spiritual leader went to the snack bar, Tommy Modine followed close behind, continuously tugging at his robe. It was then that the Dalai Lama snapped and told the boy to "go play in traffic!"

"I saw the whole thing," says moviegoer Scott Trufant. "That kid had it coming to him. I don't think any differently of the Dalai Lama since he lost his cool. Heck, Gandhi would've taken a swing at the little brat."

POPE WANTS MEL GIBSON AS SUCCESSOR

By VINCENZO SARDI
Correspondent

Ailing pontiff feels bold change is necessary to save the church!

POPE MEL? By this time next year, actor/director Gibson could be wearing a new hat, Vatican insiders claim.

POPE JOHN PAUL II is reportedly poised to announce his handpicked successor: Hollywood hunk Mel Gibson!

The devoutly religious *The Passion of the Christ* director has the charisma, commitment and strength of character needed to steer the Catholic Church through its current crisis and "lead it into the 21st century," the ailing 83-year-old pontiff is said to have told a small group of cardinals on March 21.

"His Holiness is not impressed with the caliber of those who would normally be in line to succeed him," reveals a high-ranking Vatican insider.

"He considers them weak and is angered at how they've let scandal destroy the good name of the church.

"In his view, Mel — a robustly heterosexual father of six and a quintessential man's man — is exactly what's needed to restore the image of the priesthood.

"The pope believes that under Mel, archbishops wouldn't dare to protect pedophile priests. They'd be too terrified that the 'Road Warrior' would whale the tar out of them."

Until he came out with the *The Passion*, few people were aware of the star's deep religious faith. In all the publicity surrounding the film, it came out that Gibson favors a highly orthodox brand of Catholicism and attends one of the few churches that still says mass in Latin.

"His thinking is right in line with the pope's" says the insider.

The hit Bible flick has helped to reverse the fortune of the church, which had taken a beating over the past few years due to child-sex scandals.

"The church was hemorrhaging parishioners," the insider says. "Mel turned that around. Attendance is up; donations are up.

"The pope is impressed and grateful. He calls Gibson 'Miracle Mel.' He told us, 'Miracle Mel is a lethal weapon against Satan.' "

The revered spiritual leader is reportedly set to formally announce his bold selection in two months. Officially, a new pope is elected by cardinals — and rumors are already flying of a "Stop Mel" campaign brewing among jealous church officials who feel they've been passed over.

"But practically speaking, when a popular pope makes his wishes so explicit, it will be hard to overrule him without igniting an uprising by lay people," says The Rev. Fredo Bianchi, an expert on ecclesiastical law.

He adds that there's no rule requiring a new pope to have formal religious training. "John Paul II could ordain Mel right now and he'll be a priest."

Would one of the most powerful men in Hollywood leave his glamorous world behind to shoulder such a burden?

Quite possibly, industry insiders say. "At 48, with his looks fading fast, Mel's only future in motion pictures is in character parts or behind the camera," explains entertainment writer Jill Workburn of Los Angeles. "He might see this as a challenge, just as Arnold took the bold step of running for governor."

The pontiff reportedly plans to make the actor/director an offer he can't refuse — sweetening the deal by giving Mel dispensation to enter the priesthood although married, much like Anglican priests who jump ship to Catholicism.

Reveals the Vatican insider: "He's drafted a letter that tells Mel flat-out, 'The Holy Mother Church needs you, my son — only you can save her.'

"I expect Mel will be very humbled by such an offer and he'll accept."

AFRICAN TRIBE WORSHIPS SALMA HAYEK'S BREASTS!

By MARK MILLER

THE MANDINKA tribe of Gambia, Africa, adheres to a religious practice completely unique to its people — they worship actress Salma Hayek's breasts!

While most primitive societies tend to pray to animal or ancestral spirits, or to stars and planets as the Mandinkans once did, that all changed in 1995.

Mandinkan farmer Danjuma Kianga remembers, through an interpreter, the moment it happened.

"As a special treat, Chief

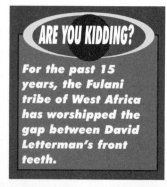

ARE YOU KIDDING?

For the past 15 years, the Fulani tribe of West Africa has worshipped the gap between David Letterman's front teeth.

Tuamanguluka arranged for a movie to be shown here for the first time ever. The movie was *Desperado*, starring the blessed Salma Hayek as Carolina, a beautiful woman who works for the local drug lord."

When Hayek first appeared on screen, the Mandinkans were blown away by the sight of the 36C-25-37 actress. "Everyone gasped — men, women, and children," recalls Kianga. "Salma was breathtakingly exquisite. She gave off a force, a light, an energy that came right through the screen and entered our very souls."

After that screening, all any of the Mandinkans could talk about was Salma Hayek — her looks, her spirit, her energy.

In the years since, the tribe has arranged screenings of every one of her films including, *From Dusk 'Til Dawn, Fools Rush In, Dogma, Wild Wild West, Traffic, Spy Kids: 3D, Once Upon a Time in Mexico,* and, especially, *Frida,* which was nominated for six Oscars including best actress for Hayek.

The Mandinkans found themselves especially affected by the sight of Hayek's breasts, which are often on full display in her movies.

"Salma's chest globes are magnificent forces of nature," gushes Kianga. "They are large and firm and perfectly formed. Whenever they appear on screen, it is almost as though they are calling to us: 'We're here. We're here for you. Take power from us. Let us be your energy force. Close your eyes and let us engulf you.' "

Around their necks, the Mandinkans wear stone and wood amulets fashioned as miniature replicas of Hayek's awe-inspiring milk wagons. Before undertaking any strenuous or dangerous task, going on any hunting expedition, or praying for anything, they lick Hayek's breasts one hundred times for luck.

One of the villages has even constructed a giant 37-foot high scale replica of Hayek's sweater puppets. The breasts themselves are formed of rare black obsidian stone, and the nipples are solid gold.

Villagers form a large circle around the statue, hold hands, and dance themselves into a frenzy while chanting the following:
*Oh glorious funbags of Salma,
Fertilize our fields, protect us, and bring us luck.
Especially we ask for sexual potency from the
Life-changing, awe-inspiring twin peaks of Salma.
Suckle us with your magical orbs,
Squeeze our faces between those luscious flesh mounds,
Our strength, hope and joy derive from the wondrous bazongas of Hayek!*

Gahiji Ngozi, a 22-year-old craftsman, speaks for the entire Mandinkan tribe when he says,

"Worshipping Salma Hayek's breasts has added meaning, direction and wonder to my life."

SALMA HAYEK's jewel-like ta-tas are definitely worship-worthy.

TWO OF JESUS' APOSTLES WERE WOMEN!

THIS ISN'T JUDAS – IT'S JUDITH!

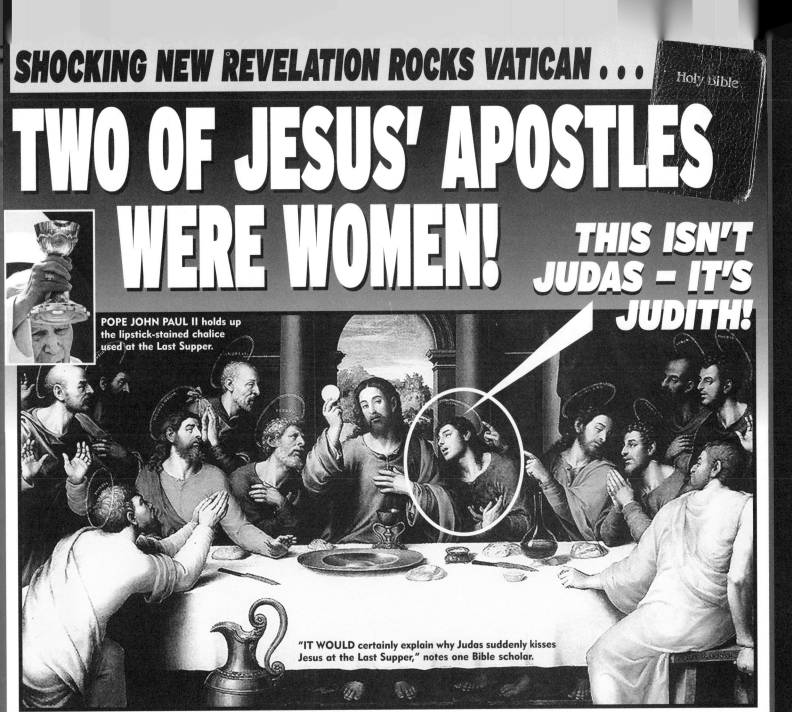

POPE JOHN PAUL II holds up the lipstick-stained chalice used at the Last Supper.

"IT WOULD certainly explain why Judas suddenly kisses Jesus at the Last Supper," notes one Bible scholar.

By MIKE FOSTER/*Weekly World News*

FYFE, Scotland — In paintings of the Last Supper, all of Christ's followers are depicted as men, but startling new evidence has emerged proving that two of the Apostles were sassy, full-bodied gals!

And the forgotten 13th disciple, named Joanna, didn't just tag along with the boys to do their laundry and wash their dishes — she played a critical role in getting Christianity off the ground, experts say.

The mind-blowing revelation may finally help to solve some of the most intriguing Bible mysteries of all time,

such as the puzzling discovery of lipstick on the Holy Grail, the chalice used at the Last Supper.

And it has led to speculation that other of the Apostles may have belonged to the fairer sex as well — including turncoat disciple Judas, who, experts now suspect, was really a woman named Judith.

"It would certainly explain why Judas suddenly kisses Jesus at the Last Supper,"

notes one Bible scholar.

"Judas' was Our Lord's most devoted follower one minute and His betrayer the next. Her impulsive decision to turn Jesus in suggests a scorned woman acting out of jealousy and rage.

"Or perhaps it was simply her time of the month."

But while the notion that Judas was really Judith remains controversial, research- ers are now quite certain that Joanna was a lady Apostle.

The wife of a prominent courtier to King Herod, Joanna changed her name to Junia when she became a follower of Christ, says Richard Bauckham, professor of New

Testament Studies at St. Andrews University.

The Bible makes the importance of this figure quite clear. In St. Paul's letter to the Romans, he describes Junia as "prominent among the Apostles."

The feisty den-mom disciple witnessed the crucifixion and was also on hand for Christ's miraculous resurrection.

But in the Middle Ages, when the Bible was being translated, scholars altered her name to the masculine form, Junias — either by mistake or to impose their own sexist views — and her role was largely forgotten.

"The medieval church was male-dominated and they wanted it to stay that way, but whether someone was cooking the books to make it appear that the Apostles were all men is not yet certain," Robert Bartlett, a professor of medieval history at St. Andrews, said in an interview.

A source inside the Vatican says Pope John Paul II is stunned by the possibility of a female Apostle.

"This could lead to some big changes in the role that women play in the Catholic church," the source predicts.

Feminists are reportedly ecstatic over the shocking revelation.

THE LORD GIVETH — AND THE LORD TAKETH AWAY...

EAT ALL YOU WANT IN HEAVEN — AND NEVER GET FAT!

By **BRETT ANNISTON**/*Correspondent*

Heaven is not only filled with adorable angels, but chock full of culinary delights, too!

GET READY to sink your teeth into some good news about Heaven: Once there you can eat as much junk food as you like and never gain an ounce!

Eleven overweight people who visited Heaven after they "died" in surgery or in accidents, and then were revived by doctors, say God's radiant kingdom is indeed a cheeseburger lover's paradise.

"Everyone loves burgers, shakes and fries in Heaven," says 390-pound Esther Smoyke, a 54-year-old Tampa, Fla., woman who was clinically dead for six minutes after her heart stopped in the middle of stomach-stapling surgery.

"Even the angels love their fries — they drown them in ketchup."

The intriguing cases, in Florida, Georgia and South Carolina, were compiled by medical researcher Dr. Herbert Greenward, who has long been interested in so-called near-death experiences (NDEs).

"The obese suffer cardiac arrest in far greater numbers than the general population, which I felt made them excellent subjects for an NDE study," he explains.

"These findings are wonderful news for overweight people — many of whom fear that in Heaven, they'd be forbidden from committing the sin of gluttony or unable to even taste food.

"Apparently, the opposite is true. Indulging in the feast provided by the Lord is encouraged and food tastes even better in Heaven than it does on Earth."

Some of the other cases cited by Dr. Greenward:

● A South Carolina man weighing 420 pounds was revived with mouth-to-mouth resuscitation after drowning at Myrtle Beach. The "beached whale" later told doctors that while in Heaven he wolfed down three huge chocolate milk shakes, two king-size bags of M&Ms and a large order of fries. "Everyone around me was eating like there was no tomorrow too," he told Dr. Greenward.

● A 350-pound mother of three briefly visited Heaven after choking on a ham sandwich. An angel told her it was "not her time" and her family needed her back on Earth. But before sending the woman back, he invited her to snack on her favorite junk food: Pizza with all the toppings.

"I told him I really shouldn't because I'm trying to cut down," she told Dr. Greenward. "He said not to worry because I wouldn't gain any weight."

● A 260-pound Georgia man, who was revived by EMS workers after an auto accident, says that in Heaven he ate three buckets of fried chicken within five minutes and they were the best he'd ever tasted. "The service was also great," he told the researcher. "The angels didn't screw up my order like always happens at the drive-thru."

Not everyone is so lucky. Dr. Greenward says that of the 16 cases in his study, five of the obese people found themselves in Hell.

"That situation couldn't be more different," the researcher reveals. "Subjects told me that in Hell there's plenty of food, all right — sumptuous gourmet meals. The problem is it's just out reach of all these millions of naked fat people, who are chained to boulders and struggle to reach it for all eternity."

TORNADO IN JAR BLOWS DOWN TRAILER PARK!

NOBODY was injured but three mobile homes were damaged, one extensively, when the "tornado in a jar" a 12-year-old schoolboy made with water, laundry detergent and white vinegar in a science class escaped its container in High Springs, Fla., police and firefighters report.

Teenager hacks into Heaven

'AFTERWORLD IS LIKE AMERICA ONLINE – BUT WITH DEAD PEOPLE'

By **DERRIK J. LANG**
Correspondent

SONNY Mullenhaal has been to Heaven and back — on his computer!

Mullenhaal, a self-proclaimed hacker who once defaced his high school's Web site with profanity, claims he accessed Heaven while using his laptop at a local Starbucks.

The curious adolescent, who didn't believe in God before the experience, spent five hours and drank six lattes while attempting to hack the heavily encrypted Heaven.

"Hacking into Heaven was hell," says Mullenhaal. "Heaven is not just a Web site. It's like this whole separate Internet. Like America Online but with dead people."

Once he logged into Heaven, Mullenhaal's laptop began glowing and emitting angelic harmonies. After squinting his eyes, he could see Heaven looked like a chat room with several other users logged on, including Gandhi and Mullenhaal's dead grandmother, Sophia. Mullenhaal wasn't able to contact either. However, St. Peter, keeper of the Pearly Gates and Heaven's apparent Web master, instant-messaged the 16-year-old.

Here's the exclusive transcript of the conversation:

SaintPeter01: Who the Heaven is this?

AzzKicka83: I am the Azz Kicka!!!!!

SaintPeter01: That's a pretty stupid name. Is this Satan?

AzzKicka83: Nope. screw you, meatball.

SaintPeter01: Do you know where you are right now, Sonny?

AzzKicka83: starbuckz. how did you know my name???

SaintPeter01: God just told me. And I Googled you.

AzzKicka83: For real?

SaintPeter01: For real. God says at the rate you're going, this is as close as you're ever going to get to Heaven.

AzzKicka83: why????

SaintPeter01: Hackers don't go to Heaven, Sonny. They go to hell.

At that point, Mullenhaal's

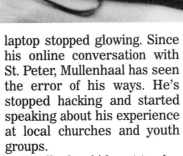

ST. PETER is not only keeper of the Pearly Gates, but also Heaven's Webmaster.

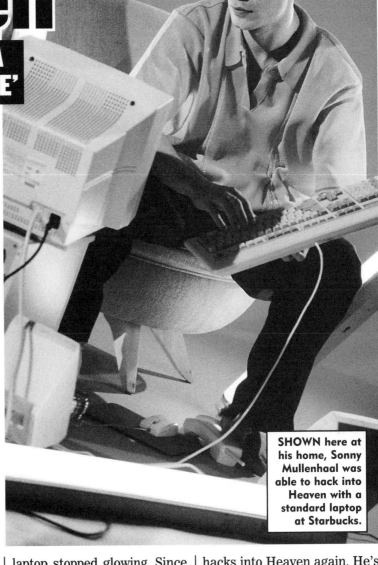

SHOWN here at his home, Sonny Mullenhaal was able to hack into Heaven with a standard laptop at Starbucks.

laptop stopped glowing. Since his online conversation with St. Peter, Mullenhaal has seen the error of his ways. He's stopped hacking and started speaking about his experience at local churches and youth groups.

"I tell other kids not to play games or download porn," says Mullenhaal. "We should only use computers to study God's word and download free music."

Mullenhaal hopes the next conversation he has with St. Peter is more pleasant. The teen will be dead before he hacks into Heaven again. He's logged off for good but keeping his computer as a "souvenir of the experience."

Sgt. Jefferson Brown, the police officer who gave Mullenhaal 13 hours of community service for hacking his high school's Web site last March, says he won't punish Mullenhaal for hacking Heaven.

"I think the experience taught him a good lesson," says Brown. "Besides, Heaven isn't really in my jurisdiction."

BIBLE'S 4 HORSEMEN ASK FOR DIRECTIONS IN PARIS

Book of Revelation's bad guys didn't know where the hell they were going, say cops!

Four Horsemen of the Apocalypse appeared in France looking for directions to Rome, say cops.

PARIS — A funny thing happened on the way to Doomsday — the Four Horsemen of the Apocalypse got lost and had to ask for directions!

That is the wild story of a French police officer who claims that one of the fearsome riders trotted up to him on the roadside and sheepishly asked, "Do you know the way to Rome?"

"It was the one on a red horse, holding a broadsword. I guess that must be the Second Horseman, the War guy," highway patrolman Michel Clenard told a Paris newspaper.

By MICHAEL FORSYTH
Weekly World News

"I was totally taken aback. I mean, these guys are supposed to be determining the fate of all mankind — but they seem to have no Earthly idea where they're going. And I didn't know whether to point them in the right direction or send them on a wild goose chase."

According to prophecies in the Holy Bible, a warning sign that the end of the world is near will be the arrival of four mysterious horsemen, representing the major calamities that will plague man in the last days — war, famine, pestilence and death (Rev. 6:2-8).

The uncanny encounter took place 13 miles outside Paris on the highway from Dijon. Officer Clenard was assisting a female motorist whose auto had broken down on the side of the road, when he first spotted the hooded horsemen and their giant steeds.

"They had stopped on the other side of the road and they were arguing over their map about which way to go," said Officer Clenard. "I was concerned because cars were whizzing by really fast and the horses seemed like they were getting anxious."

Officer Clenard said eventually one of the horsemen was sent over to his patrol car.

"The guy seemed reluctant and when he got close enough for me to recognize him from illustrations in my Bible, I understood why," he said. "The guys are supposed to be these big, bad harbingers of doom — asking for help must have been humiliating."

Officer Clenard said the Second Horseman spoke in an antiquated form of French.

"I advised him to keep his sword sheathed and I gave him directions, but I'm not sure he got them right," the cop said. "When the riders took off, two of them headed the wrong way!"

HELL REALLY IS FREEZING OVER!

By RYAN HINSON/*Weekly World News*

ROME — Temperatures in Hell are dropping like a lead balloon — and unless something is done, Satan and his unholy host of demons will freeze their tails off this winter!

That's the alarming conclusion of an Italian scientist who says that a probe dipped into Lucifer's domain has recorded a temperature of 406 degrees, the lowest in 520 years.

"That may sound quite toasty to the average person, but you've got to understand the normal temperature in Hell is about 10,800 degrees Fahrenheit — hotter than the surface of the sun," declares physicist Dr. Antonio Franzini, who conducted the test.

"What's more, if the temperature keeps dropping at the current rate, by next January, it will be minus 465.67 degrees in Hell. That's six degrees below absolute zero.

"Demons simply are not equipped to tolerate those kinds of bitter temperatures."

Dr. Franzini made the measurement by lowering a probe into Satan's Well, an old stone well near Florence traditionally believed to be one of the nine entrances to Hell.

"Leonardo da Vinci used this method in 1581 to record the temperature in Hell and at that time he got a reading of 11,025 degrees," says Dr. Franzini.

"Over the centuries when other scientists have taken measurements, the temperature has fluctuated.

"But over the last two years, there's been a steady cooling trend. It's frightening."

Dr. Franzini, who thinks the hole in the ozone layer is to blame, has a warning for man.

He says, "When the cold becomes unbearable for Satan's demons, they may head en masse for warmer parts — such as the surface of the Earth!"

Temperatures in Satan's domain are at their lowest ever, says scientist

DR. Antonio Franzini

COMPUTER creation of what Hell would look like frozen over.

THE COOLER weather in Hell just might take the "tan" right off Satan, says scientist.

6 IDIOTS FORMING NATIONAL UNION

Extraordinary Exclusives on Politics and International Affairs

Although the *Weekly World News* has never backed down from reporting difficult, offensive, or just plain disgusting stories, for the first several years of its existence there was one subject too repulsive even for us to touch: politics. But in the late 1980s, our reporters put on the latex gloves, strapped on their gas masks, and started covering American politics and foreign affairs with *WWN*'s unique brand of kick-ass, take-no-prisoners journalism.

Most newspapers—whether liberal, conservative, or alien in their editorial bias—just don't report on the political stories that really matter: George W. Bush trying to sell Hawaii to pay for the war on

terror, for instance, or the 14 aliens masquerading as U.S. senators. Instead, it's fallen to *WWN* to insure the public hears about such stories as Saddam Hussein and Osama bin Laden's torrid, "bilateral" romance and the countless other stories that "slip through" the fingers of the mainstream media.

By exposing the mind-boggling secrets and underhanded shenanigans that world leaders try so desperately to conceal, *WWN* has not just protected the public trust, it has repeatedly changed the course of human history. "*Weekly World News* has put government officials everywhere on notice that they can't get away with what they used to," says one political insider. "Let's just say, if *WWN* was around in 1945, the public would have never allowed Truman to use alien technology to end World War II."

Public officials have to use more discretion in their personal lives, too. If Hillary Clinton has a steamy love affair with an E.T. or Donald Rumsfeld is sleeping with a G.I. Joe doll, you can bet that *WWN* will be there, covering the story from beginning to end.

The newspaper's unceasing quest for the truth has been fraught with danger, however, and, on occasion, marred by tragedy. In 1989, agents of Cuban dictator Fidel Castro—angered over *WWN*'s report that he had a secret hunger for Roseanne Barr and Big Macs—burst into the paper's Havana bureau and dragged away two hapless reporters. They were never heard from again.

And in 2004, a correspondent who had slipped into North Korea to report on Kim Jong Il's decree that all citizens perform the hokey pokey or be executed on the spot was taken into custody and had to be freed from his barbaric jail cell by Bat Boy, who bit his way through seven concrete barriers and countless yards of barbed wire, killing 37 armed guards en route.

The risks have been great, but the service *WWN* provides to its readers is worth it. For example, many credit the *Weekly World News* with ending Soviet Communism. "Communism requires a closed and secret society, and it simply proved impossible to operate with the *Weekly World News* continually infiltrating the government," Vladimir Putin has been quoted as saying. "Finally, Communist leaders just had to throw in the towel and say, 'you win.'"

ABE WAS

Lincoln actually

HISTORIC photo shows America's 16th President in a very feminine position — sitting with her legs crossed.

By MIKE FOSTER / *Weekly World News*

LEXINGTON, Ky. — Abraham Lincoln was a woman — and the discovery of a secret cache of 43 photographs shot by famed Lincoln photographer Matthew Brady proves it!

That's the word from maverick historian Jessica Durbeen, who presents an overwhelming mountain of evidence — including the Brady photos that were found in the basement of the White House — to bolster her claim that Honest Abe was not the man she pretended to be.

"Although President Lincoln was known as 'Honest Abe,' it turns out she fibbed about one thing to the

"BABE" Lincoln allowed a trusted photographer to take this picture of her in a housedress.

Was assassin John Wilkes Booth Abe's lover?

As shocking as it may seem, historical evidence now says that Abraham Lincoln may have been slain as the result of a lover's quarrel with the man she loved!

According to details pieced together by historian Jessica Durbeen, assassin John Wilkes Booth and Honest Abe were illicit lovers and it was Booth's experience as an actor that enabled "Lady Lincoln" to artfully use makeup, costumes and body language to pose as a man!

The two met at Lincoln's second inauguration, which Booth attended with then-girlfriend Lucy Hale, whose father, John Hale, the cross-dressing President had appointed as ambassador to Spain. "The attraction was immediate," Durbeen said. "Booth dumped Lucy and began a torrid,

secret affair with President Lincoln. He also used his acting experience to coach her on how to look and act more manly and perfect her disguises."

The two had a falling-out after a series of spats in which Abe refused to leave Mary Todd for Booth. Enraged, the spurned lover took his final revenge at Ford's Theater on April 14, 1865 — shooting the President dead.

A BABE!

AUTHOR Jessica Durbeen.

America's first LADY prez

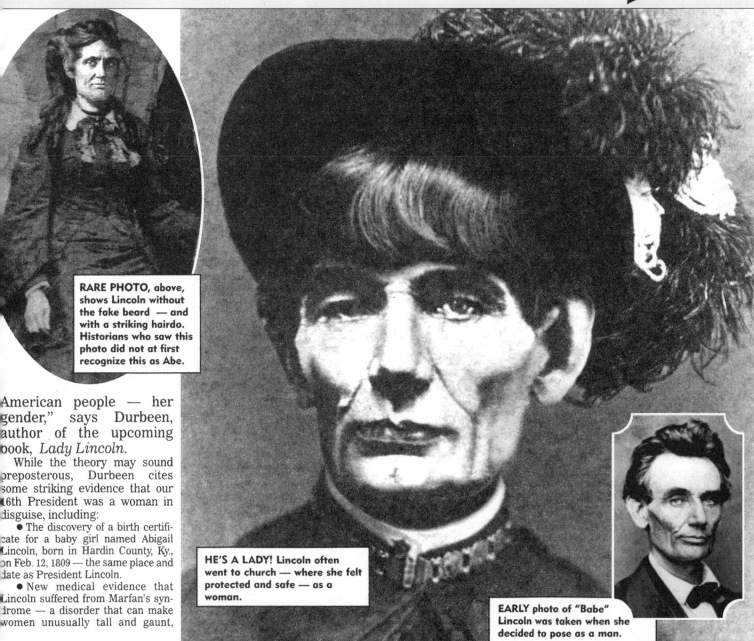

RARE PHOTO, above, shows Lincoln without the fake beard — and with a striking hairdo. Historians who saw this photo did not at first recognize this as Abe.

American people — her gender," says Durbeen, author of the upcoming book, *Lady Lincoln*.

While the theory may sound preposterous, Durbeen cites some striking evidence that our 16th President was a woman in disguise, including:

● The discovery of a birth certificate for a baby girl named Abigail Lincoln, born in Hardin County, Ky., on Feb. 12, 1809 — the same place and date as President Lincoln.

● New medical evidence that Lincoln suffered from Marfan's syndrome — a disorder that can make women unusually tall and gaunt,

HE'S A LADY! Lincoln often went to church — where she felt protected and safe — as a woman.

EARLY photo of "Babe" Lincoln was taken when she decided to pose as a man.

BABE-raham Lincoln fooled them all!

> **LINCOLN** is shown here in a simple but dignified outfit befitting her high station.

with long, gangling limbs and big hands.

● A jar of glue used by actors to apply fake beards, found among Lincoln's personal effects at the Smithsonian Museum — along with a dozen sanitary napkins.

● A long-missing page from the diary of John Wilkes Booth, in which the presidential assassin rails against "the White House lover who spurned me." (See: "Was assassin John Wilkes Booth Abe's lover?" on page 6.)

● The fact that autopsy photos taken of Lincoln's nude body were suspiciously burned.

Durbeen says she embarked upon her investigation after happening upon a tattered old Confederate pamphlet that charged that the Yankee leader was really female.

"At first, I thought it was just wartime propaganda, but then I took a closer look at a photo of Lincoln and realized the beard does look bogus," the Lexington historian says.

"Then I learned through a White House source that a cache of Matthew Brady photos actually showing Lincoln as a woman had been discovered — and until now, suppressed — when Bill and Hillary Clinton were moving from the White House."

Durbeen believes that Marfan's syndrome stretched young Abigail Lincoln to her eye-popping height of 6-foot-4 and gave her a mannish physique.

"Between that and Abigail's tomboy nature, it was perhaps inevitable that she would come to dress as a boy and in time insist upon being called 'Abe,'" Durbeen says.

"Passing herself off as a young man, she went on to work in 'macho' jobs such as rail-splitter and surveyor — even enlisting as a volunteer in the Black Hawk Indian War."

Only a handful of President Lincoln's closest aides — and Brady himself — ever knew her astonishing secret, Durbeen believes.

She also argues that Lincoln was the mother, not the father, of six children and that homely First Lady Mary Todd Lincoln was a man posing as a woman.

"Take a look at a photo of Mary Todd Lincoln and you'll be convinced," Durbeen says.

Despite the shroud of secrecy, Confederate spies learned the President was a she. "The South briefly tried to use it for propaganda, but no one believed it," says Durbeen.

IF THEY ONLY KNEW: Lincoln often wore a top hat to hide her long locks — as shown in this battlefield photo.

> ### 'Lincoln was the mother, not the father, of six children'
> — *Author Jessica Durbeen*

FIRST LADY SHOWING HER TRUE COLORS

Hillary Clinton wants to paint the White House BLUE!

THE FIRST LADY wants to leave her mark on the White House.

WASHINGTON — First Lady Hillary Rodham Clinton is plowing ahead with plans to change the color of the White House for the first time in history — by painting it blue!

The scheme might sound like a joke, but insiders insist it's all too true.

By MARIKA MILLER
Correspondent

According to those sources, Mrs. Clinton believes that the change of color will set a new tone for President Bill Clinton's administration, which remains under fire from reporters who want hard answers about the President's involvement in the Whitewater real estate scandal and nagging concerns about his alleged womanizing.

"Mrs. Clinton is intent on creating a diversion to take the heat off the President and painting the White House blue certainly seems to fit the bill," said one source with close ties to the Oval Office.

"Not so apparent, but equally important, is what the First Lady herself has to gain from it. If she can change the color of the White House — which is the oldest public building in Washington and has been home to every president since John Adams in 1800 — she can do any-

thing. And if the public believes she can do anything, her chances of becoming America's first woman president in the year 2000 will increase dramatically.

"That possibility has factored heavily in her decision to make an issue of the color of the White House. And because she knows that her plans will be thwarted if she makes them public prematurely, she intends to put the project in motion behind the scenes. By the time the media and public find out, it will be too late to do anything about it. The White House will be blue. Mrs. Clinton will take the credit. And when the furor dies down, she will be remembered as the woman who changed one of the most important and revered symbols in our nation's history."

Mrs. Clinton bristled but

managed to maintain her silence when queried about the allegations. Not surprisingly, White House spokesmen followed her lead, declining to comment on the report in any form whatsoever.

"Official silence is expected but it's an odds-on bet that the White House will soon be known as the Blue House," said the source. "The only thing holding Mrs. Clinton back at this point is the choice of shade. From what I understand, she is torn between royal blue and sky blue. When she decides, painters will show up at 1600 Pennsylvania Avenue with brushes, ladders and scaffolds and start painting."

President Clinton's response to the plan is not known. In fact, he might not even know about it, sources say. "Mr. Clinton gives his wife a free reign so it's doubtful that he will stand in her way," one insider said.

WWN EXTRA

LAURA BUSH WANTS TO PAINT THE WHITE HOUSE RED!

WASHINGTON – Uh oh, here we go again! Now, Beltway insiders say, First Lady Laura Bush is secretly plotting to paint the White House fire-engine red. This, despite the fact that Hillary Clinton's scheme to paint the President's residence blue roughly a decade earlier went down in flames.

First Lady Bush considers the elections of 2000 and 2004 to have given her a crimson mandate. And though she is well aware of the "Blue House" scandal, Bush prefers to think back a little further, when First Lady Jacqueline Kennedy redecorated the interior of the austere structure and was praised for her fashion-forward taste.

There is no indication that the First Lady's choice of red has anything to do with that color's obvious association with the Republican Party, and friends of Mrs. Bush say she would never involve herself in anything political.

The coincidence, however, is not lost on the President's staff. A senior administration official noted that Karl Rove hasn't been this elated since the infamous Howard Dean scream during the 2004 presidential campaign. "[Karl's] just beside himself these days. He keeps screeching 'Wee-haaa!' and offering to take us all out to paint the town red, too, once the 'Red House' becomes a reality."

World's Hottest GOSSIP

Edited by Joe Berger and Cindy O'Neil

Commie boss WAS crazy over Vanna, but now . . .

FIDEL CASTRO IS MADLY ♡ IN LOVE WITH ROSEANNE

Lovelorn **Fidel Castro** has washed his hands of svelte **Vanna White** — and has fallen head over heels in love with roly-poly **Roseanne Barr**!

Although the tough-talking tyrant used to be cuckoo for the letter-perfect game show hostess, he has now installed a fancy new satellite dish outside his Havana home to make sure he never misses a minute of the waddling comic's hit show *Roseanne*. And he tapes every episode so he can watch rotund Rosie strut her stuff over and over again — often into the wee hours of the morning.

"Fidel is mooning around like a schoolboy with his first crush," said a former Castro confidante recently exiled to Mexico City.

"He calls Roseanne his great big bundle of love, and he watches her show until he's so bleary-eyed he can barely see. He slaps his knee and roars with laughter very time she opens her mouth.

. . . & wants to marry her!

"He told me he dreams of the day he can hold the lady in his arms — and he said he may someday marry her."

CASTRO SMUGGLING BIG MACS INTO CUBA

CASTRO'S a true fanatic — for fast food, say his ex-cronies. Word has it that the Commie bigwig's gone nuts, ever since docs cut him off from his cigars several years ago.

— for himself!

By JOE BERGER

Kooky Cuban kingpin Fidel Castro swears he'd rather eat grass than let McDonald's invade his island empire. But behind closed doors, the wily windbag gulps down Chicken McNuggets like popcorn and bolts down Big Macs by the bushel!

Fidel bans American fast-food joints — and then secretly pigs out on burgers & fries!

"Fidel is so wild about McDonald's stuff he has it smuggled in at least three times a week — and he's usually waiting with a bib around his neck when it arrives," former Castro confidant Carlos Gomez told a reporter.

"His staff says he'll wake up in the middle of the night screaming for someone to bring him a tray of Big Macs.

"And I've seen him watching TV in his den, popping those McNuggets in his mouth hour after hour like a kid eating candy. It's really a sight, him sitting in an elegant room in his silk pajamas with a mountain of McDonald's cartons at his feet."

A Castro henchman recently scoffed at the notion that Cuba should embrace the Golden Arches like their Commie pals in Russia.

"We'll eat grass if necessary to defend our revolution," sneered Ambassador Elises Estrada Lescaille. But while most Cubans are forced to suffer their Big Mac attacks in silence, their burger-chomping chief has become a ranting, raving junk-food junkie.

"Fidel doesn't want just Big Macs and McNuggets, he wants it all — McDLTs, Quarter Pounders, fries, McMuffins, everything," said former sidekick Carlos, who recently fled to Mexico.

"And he throws a fit when he can't get what he wants. He's fired at least three chefs because he ordered them to make hamburgers just like McDonald's and they never got it right.

"He was so furious, those poor guys are probably in prison right now — all because their cooking skills didn't include Big Macs."

Gomez says the dingbat dictator got hooked on hamburgers several years ago when doctors insisted he give up cigars.

"Without his cigars, he just kind of went crazy," his former adviser recalled. "He got a giant satellite dish and started watching American TV until he was glassy-eyed.

"He saw all those commercials for McDonald's and started having his burgers airlifted in at night. It was just like a dope smuggler bringing in cocaine.

"The rest of the people may have to eat grass to keep the revolution going, but Fidel's going to have his Big Macs or bust."

WWN EXTRA
DICTATOR LOVE

Besides pining over **Roseanne**, Fidel Castro has also fallen madly in lust with **Vanna White** and **Phyllis Diller**—not to mention his fling with hairy-legged **Saddam Hussein**. And, of course, *WWN* has been there to report on Fidel's bilateral affairs the whole time.

But Castro is not the world's first, or only, tyrannical dictator who has been afflicted by a drooling, schoolboy crush on an unexpected lady. For instance, **Adolf Hitler** dreamed of getting it on with **Uta Hellick**, a brassy, blonde dwarf he met at a Berlin carnival in 1916. North Korean nitwit **King Jong II** is over the moon for former First Lady **Barbara Bush**, ever since he saw her guest-appearance on ABC's *Desperate Housewives*. And Libyan leader **Moammar Khadafi** has a hankering for hanky-panky with **Helen the Bigfoot hooker**, but Helen vows she'll rip him limb from limb if he ever lays a hand on her hairy bod. "I have my reputation to think of," she insists, no doubt referring to her well-publicized preference for free-world leaders.

John F. Kennedy survived 1963 assassination attempt —

JFK MEETS JACKIE

JACKIE Kennedy Onassis

A crippled and white-haired but very much alive President John F. Kennedy met with ex-wife Jackie for 25 minutes on September 24 in what some observers are calling "the most astonishing family reunion ever!"

That's the word from author and top Kennedy expert Jackson Kelly, who quoted highly placed Washington insiders as having said that the former first couple embraced, kissed and chatted about old times on a secluded estate west of Richmond, Va., before bodyguards spotted and chased a photographer who attempt-

By NICK MANN

Special report

Historic

ed to capture them on film

Kelly declined to name the photographer and would neither confirm nor deny allegations that he was working for the CIA.

The expert did release a poignant series of photographs that show the wheelchair-bound Kennedy, now 76, and Jackie, 64, together for the first time since he survive

and now lives a secret life in hiding!

FOR THE FIRST TIME IN 30 YEARS

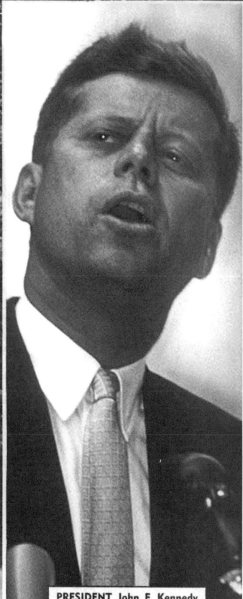

PRESIDENT John F. Kennedy, shown in 1962 photograph.

reunion lasts 25 minutes!

the attempt on his life in Dallas 30 years ago — on Nov. 22, 1963.

"It wasn't the return of Camelot — but it was close," said Kelly, whose provocative new book, *JFK Yesterday, Today and Tomorrow*, is slated for a Christmas release.

"When it comes to reunions, I just don't see how you could get any more dramatic than this."

Kelly's report on the historic meeting struck a raw nerve in Washington, where some of the most powerful men and women in government found themselves confronted with issues that they didn't particularly want to face.

First and foremost were questions about the former first couple's right to privacy 30 years after they left the White House and chose to shun the public spotlight.

For his part, Kelly dismissed the privacy issue "as a sidelight at best."

He cited a series of headline-making reports that have surfaced since August 1990, when European neurosurgeon Sonya Faron stunned the world with the revelation that JFK faked his death in Dallas in 1963 and has been in hiding ever since.

At the time, the doctor said Kennedy suffered massive head injuries but survived the assassination attempt.

Continued next page

World exclusive

1 BODYGUARD wheels a crippled JFK toward his ex-wife Jackie as a second bodyguard stands watch.

2 HISTORIC SHOT of former first couple as they embrace for the first time in 30 years.

3 JACKIE AND JFK engage in quiet conversation for approximately 25 minutes.

ABOVE: Artist's conception of John F. Kennedy as he looked in 1991.

4 INCREDIBLE REUNION is interrupted when a bodyguard spots the unidentified cameraman hidden in wooded area on the estate. One man shields Jackie as the other rushes toward the photographer. Sources said the meeting ended soon afterward, as the cameraman was able to escape with film intact.

photographs taken at Virginia ranch just days ago!

She went on to say that Kennedy fled the U.S. and moved to a secret location in Europe, where he remained conscious and aware, though crippled from the waist down, as late as 1990.

Dr. Faron also claimed that JFK secretly advised Presidents Nixon, Ford, Carter, Reagan and Bush.

Even more recently, Kelly quoted highly placed Washington insiders as having said that Kennedy consulted with President Bill Clinton during a two-hour meeting at Camp David on June 16.

"I'm not at liberty to say how I found out about the meeting between Jackie and JFK but when you get right down to it, the pictures speak for themselves," said Kelly, who reports that repeated attempts to get a comment from Jackie went unanswered.

"From what I understand, Kennedy contacted Jackie and arranged to meet her on a sprawling but secluded ranch owned by mutual friends on September 24.

"Jackie arrived at the ranch, which is located about 80 miles west of Richmond, a day early and spent the night," he continued.

"The next morning, Jackie took a walk with one of her bodyguards and waited for JFK beside a paved path. About 10 minutes later, yet another bodyguard wheeled JFK to the spot.

"For a few moments the couple stood in silence. Then Jackie hugged Kennedy and gave him a kiss."

Kelly said JFK and Jackie talked for about 25 minutes. He doesn't know exactly what was said.

But sources suggested that the couple discussed old times — including JFK's alleged affair with actress Marilyn Monroe and Jackie's marriage to Greek shipping magnate Aristotle Onassis — before one of the bodyguards spotted and chased the photographer, who apparently escaped on a motorbike.

"I've been told that Jackie and JFK agreed to meet again but I certainly can't confirm that," said Kelly.

JFK EXPERT
Jackson Kelly

CLOSEUP photo of JFK, taken September 24, 1993!

'For a few moments the couple stood in silence — then Jackie hugged Kennedy and gave him a kiss.'

3-BREASTED JOINS CLINTON AS HIS NEW INTERN!

NEW YORK — Former U.S. President Bill Clinton really has his hands full these days — his new intern is reportedly the famous three-breasted woman!

Sources close to the ex-president confirm that Kimberly Shariff, the eye-popping beauty whose tantalizing chest has made her a minor celebrity, is now "serving directly under" Clinton at his Harlem office.

"When Kimberly walked into the office and asked for a job a few days ago, Mr. Clinton was immediately impressed by her and he gave her the position — without even bothering to look at her resume," said an aide who asked to remain anonymous.

"He said, 'I've seen all I need to see. I can tell this young lady has a lot of potential.'"

Clinton has so far neither confirmed nor denied the story. Aides say that because of his skirt-chasing reputation earned during the Monica Lewinsky sex scandal, he's concerned about "how some folks might take it" if news that he's hired the well, well, well-endowed cutie as an intern leaked out.

But Kimberly herself confirms the report, saying that she's now helping to answer phones, file papers and "take care of whatever else pops up" in Clinton's office.

"Mr. Clinton has been so nice to me it's unbelievable — he treats me like I'm the only employee in the office," she told *Weekly World*

By VICKIE YORK
Weekly World News

News in an exclusive interview.

"I am so grateful that he's giving me a chance and he's been willing to overlook the fact that my only real job up until now has been as an exotic dancer."

Amazing Kimberly first made headlines when *Weekly World News* ran a profile on the curvy Cleveland stripper and her stupefying physique.

'This young lady has a lot of

GAL

PHOTOGRAPHER captured this shot as Kimberly Shariff discussed some of her attributes with former President Bill Clinton inside his Harlem office.

In a strange turn of events, she later married three-handed baseball star Mustafa Shariff, a centerfielder for a Santo Domingo team.

Most recently, the odd couple made the news again when Kimberly gave birth to a 6-pound baby girl name Trish. The tot is completely healthy and normal apart from having three legs, as *Weekly World News* reported in our Sept. 4, 2001 edition.

While it might sound like a marriage made in Heaven, the couple's romance has a been rocky one — punctuated by a divorce, a remarriage and numerous separations.

"Mustafa has always been jealous of all the attention I get from other men because of the 'extra stuff' I have up top," Kimberly reveals. "And now when I walk around carrying Trish, guys have been staring at me even more.

"I told him it probably was because the baby has three legs, but he was convinced it was because of the way my boobies got even bigger than before on account of my pregnancy. Either way, it drove Mustafa crazy and he'd rant and rave around the house."

The star-crossed lovebirds separated once again in October and in late November Kimberly moved to New York, seeking a job.

"I was looking for receptionist work, but I got doors slammed in my face because of the way I looked. They never said that's the reason, of course, but I knew," she says.

"Mr. Clinton is the first person to give me a break. He's a real prince."

But some Washington political strategists say that the crafty ex-president

potential,' says Bill

SURPRISED: Hillary Clinton says Bill will REALLY have his hands full with the three-breasted woman.

She's helping to answer phones, file papers & 'take care of whatever else pops up'

BILL Clinton and three-breasted beauty Kimberly mug for the camera.

(Continued)

may have an ulterior motive for hiring the three-bosomed bombshell.

"He knows this will drive Hillary crazy," says one Capitol Hill insider.

"He's still steaming over that incident in which his wife was allegedly caught cuddling with a space alien in a New York hotel room.

"Every minute he's alone in his office with that new girl, Hillary has got to be worried about what he's doing. After all, he's known for his 'hands on' management style."

In fact, Mrs. Clinton seems to be taking the new hire in stride.

According to one pal: "When Hillary heard the news she turned white as a sheet — and then laughed her head off. 'I thought he was a leg man,' she snapped. He's gonna have his hands full now.'"

"YOU'VE SEEN ENOUGH," says Bill, as he waves off the lucky photographer who caught him with Kimberly.

THREE BOOBS — and proud of 'em! Kimberly, shown in file photo taken earlier this year.

IDIOTS FORMING NATIONAL UNION

By
MICHAEL CHIRON
Correspondent

America's 50 million dummies to unite!

WONDERFUL news for America's idiots: Soon you'll be able to join your own organization, the National Union of Idiots (NUI), and finally get some clout in this country!

"Affirmative action, that's what this is all about," declares union organizer and self-declared idiot Wilson Baxtor. "For too long this minority group has been maligned and scorned by society. Soon, 50 million strong, we will be bigger and have more power than the National Rifle Association and the Teamsters combined."

To join the NUI, all applicants have to do is fail a number of simple tests.

One test is to screw up a simple fast-food order like "Two cheeseburgers, two medium fries and a banana shake."

Another is to prove you can drive like an idiot on a busy highway, and a third question reads: "Which country should the U.S. nuke: Iran, Syria or Andorra?"

If you choose Andorra, you're in.

Asked whether it wouldn't simply be easier to give prospective members an IQ test, Baxtor admits, "I never really thought of that."

Plus the bonehead bigwig insists there's more to being an idiot than simply having a substandard IQ. Despite their Ph.Ds, the rocket scientists who got feet mixed up with meters, causing a Mars-bound space probe to blow up, were "probably highly functional idiots," Baxtor says.

Baxtor bristles when he hears the term "idiot" used interchangeably with "cretin," "moron" and "retard," noting that each has a very distinct meaning — although when pressed, he could not explain the difference.

"Being an idiot is a mindset, it's a unique way of looking at the world," Baxtor maintains. "And unfortunately, it's a mindset that has been excluded from our society far too long."

The NUI will change all that, he vows, claiming that the organization already has 1,300 members nationwide — and that its ranks are swelling every day.

"We plan to take our place in govern-ment and demand equal opportunity for employment in federal agencies like the IRS, Immigration and the post office, as well as the armed services," says Baxtor, a 39-year-old D.C. resident whose day job is delivering newspapers by bicycle.

Like other giant labor organizations such as the AFL-CIO, the NUI intends to use its influence to affect major legislation on Capitol Hill. Among the items on its agenda:

● Funding the teaching of Latin to every schoolchild in the U.S. to "help improve relations with our neighbors in Latin America."

● Building a bridge to connect the United States to Europe, allowing "tourists who are afraid of flying to drive."

● Banning "third-hand smoking" in public.

● Declaring war on Ireland to "liber-ate the downtrodden leprechauns."

Some Washington insiders insist that no union is necessary because idiots are already over-represented in government.

"From what I've observed, at least 70 percent of federal employees are card-car-rying idiots and that goes right up to the Cabinet level," says a Capitol Hill source.

"This is a union without a purpose. It sounds like the organizers are, well, a bunch of idiots."

JOHN KERRY IS POSSESSED BY AL GORE

The chilling reason Kerry has such a droopy face — and zombie-like manner!

Alien's shocking revelation rocks the capital:

12 SENATORS ARE FROM OUTER SPACE!

"THEY look like ordinary humans, but they're not," says UFO expert Nathaniel Dean, below.

By NICK MANN

Special report

WASHINGTON — A space alien who stunned the world by revealing that five U.S. Senators were extraterrestrials in 1992 dropped another bombshell when he met with President Bill Clinton in the White House just days ago — and named seven more senators who hail from distant planets!

And far from denying the extraterrestrial's allegations, Senators Phil Gramm, Dennis DeConcini, John D. Rockefeller IV, Bennett Johnston, Howell Heflin, Christopher Dodd and William S. Cohen conceded that "the time is right to make our true identities known."

"Senators John Glenn, Orrin Hatch, Nancy Kassebaum, Sam Nunn and Alan Simpson came out of the alien closet two years ago and now we find that seven more senators are not from Earth," said author and UFO expert Nathaniel Dean, who identified the first group of space alien senators in a news conference that made international headlines in November 1992.

"The implications," he continued, "are almost beyond comprehension. For one thing, we now know that the des-tiny of the most powerful nation on Earth is being shaped and guided by entities who aren't even human.

"I'm not saying that this is bad, because it might very well be good.

"If the universe is inhabited by other creatures and civilizations, we need to know about them.

"We also need linkage.

"And if nothing else, these space alien legislators can serve as our links to a world that is even more advanced than our own."

Dean's report stunned political analysts and threatened to touch off a public panic that, as one CIA source put it, "could quickly get out of control."

White House spokesmen declined to comment, but sources privately confirmed that the President's meeting

'It's all true. We are space aliens. I'm amazed that it's taken you so long to find out.'

— Senator Phil Gramm

with the alien took place when the Secret Service escorted the creature into the White House at 4:36 a.m. on April 24.

They also suggested that the President will address the issue in an upcoming news conference, although they could not provide a time or date.

While analysts scrambled to gauge public reaction, the sen-

Turn page for MORE

THE ALIEN ELECTORATE
A Political, Cultural, and Economic Analysis

BOCA RATON — Not only did a significantly greater number of households respond to the newly automated 2000 national census (even when compared to the overall growth of the nation), but the list of possible ethnicities that respondents could claim to be was refined, exponentially multiplying the U.S. government's ability to analyze the population — including the aliens living among us. Here's the newly mined E.T. gristle WWN demographers chewed over.

The list of categories in 2000 worked like this: If you didn't check the boxes for Hispanic or Latino; White (but not Hispanic or Latino); Black (or African American, if respondents preferred); American Indian or Alaskan Native (AIAN); Asian; Native Hawaiian or Other Pacific Islander (NHOPI); or Two or More of the Above Races, then you were definitely Some Other Race, Not Hispanic or Latino (SORNHOL), which as *WWN* readers have known for decades, means you are from another planet. For the first time ever, SORNHOLs who have lived, worked, loved, and discreetly inserted sensitive probes in their neighbors' posteriors all across this great Earth nation — some of them for many generations — were able to stand up and be counted.

A look at the population density of minority (that is, non-White) groups living in the United States reveals many interesting facts about the aliens among us. For instance, of the roughly 29 million SORNHOLs in the U.S. today, the great majority have resisted the urge to follow the sun. This is likely because most other inhabitable planets tend to be considerably colder than Earth. How else to explain the concentrations of aliens in the extreme reaches of the Northeast and Alaska, and along the entire Canadian border? And while it's clear why there are no SORNHOLs living in the Southwest, Puerto Rico, Florida, or Hawaii, some of the other states that lack any alien population (California and New York, for example) come as something of a surprise.

What to make of that remarkable concentration of E.T.s on Arkansas' border with Missouri? It's almost certainly the case that there are more than a few arthropoids (who come from the warmer planets in the universe) with fond memo-

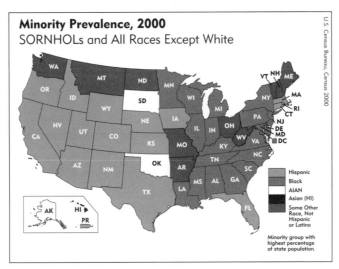

Minority Prevalence, 2000
SORNHOLs and All Races Except White

Hispanic
Black
AIAN
Asian (HI)
Some Other Race, Not Hispanic or Latino

Minority group with highest percentage of state population.

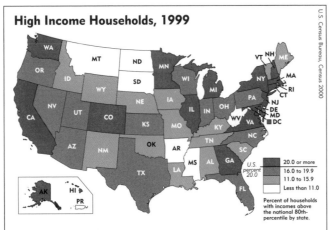

High Income Households, 1999

U.S. percent 20.0
20.0 or more
16.0 to 19.9
11.0 to 15.9
Less than 11.0

Percent of households with incomes above the national 80th-percentile by state.

U.S. Presidential Election Results, 2004

Democratic
Republican

The voting results presented in the map above are from the presidential election of 2004. It is critical to note that third-party platforms were not only irrelevant to the political discussion in America at the inauguration of the 21st century, but also that the meager third-party votes actually cast were irrelevant to the ultimate outcome (which, in any event, was largely decided in advance by the highly secretive cabal of aliens, wealthy politicians, and corporate entities that run the planet). All the results presented here are based on the alleged majority of votes cast for either the Democratic or Republican candidate within the geographic regions specified.

ries of the glory years of the Kansas City Royals. And let's not forget the cluster of E.T.s in West Virginia and Ohio: If the state they call the Heart of It All decided the 2004 election, it just may be because there are more than a few Flying Saucer Republicans living in the suburbs of Cincinnati.

How about those GOP-loving SORN-HOLs, anyway? P'lod's amazing election-year predictions seem to stem from his ability to tap into the mainstream planetary alien culture for clues as to how the political winds are a-blowin'. In the 2004 election, for example, with the exception of the Live Free or Die holdouts and their neighbors in the Northeast, American aliens appear to have turned out in big numbers at the polls for the Republican Party. Could it be that the GOP's aversion to terrestrial immigrants is in line with planetary immigrants' ambitions of getting a bigger piece of the American pie?

Could be, though the economic data suggests that SORNHOLs, like the majority of the American population, voted against their own economic interests in 2004. The GOP's trickle-down economic policies, which favor the very rich, don't necessarily benefit the alien population, which tends to fall at or below the national average. Then again, that could be because, cosmically speaking anyway, Earth money is worthless.

For example, Montana, a SORNHOL stronghold since pre-Colonial times, voted Republican and is actually quite poor (relative to the rest of the U.S.), while the relatively wealthy Starbucks State voted Democratic. (No doubt due, in part, to the fact that Bill Gates insists upon the many aliens working at Microsoft voting Democratic.)

Finally, the alien infatuation with the GOP probably doesn't stem from the party's pro-religion, anti-science platform (which flies in the face of beings who have mastered wormhole travel and claim to have given birth to life on Earth as we know it). No, the attraction is based on the party's foreign and social policies, suggesting that the Republicans' emphasis on social stratification, military adventurism, and cultural isolationism give E.T.s nostalgia for what life on their own planets was like roughly 14 billion years ago.

12 U.S. SENATORS

ONE of 12 U.S. Senators who've owned up to their true identities as space aliens, Christopher Dodd, D-Conn., expressed relief that the news is now "public."

CHRISTOPHER DODD
D — Connecticut

BENNETT JOHNSTON
D — Louisiana

WILLIAM S. COHEN
R — Maine

DENNIS DECONCINI
D — Arizona

ALAN SIMPSON
R — Wyoming

PHIL GRAMM
R — Texas

HOWELL HEFLIN
D — Alabama

JOHN D. ROCKEFELLER
D — West Virginia

ators sought ways to minimize any negative fallout and put the right spin on the creature's revelations.

Contacted at his office in Washington, Sen. Gramm, R-Texas, took the high road with full and immediate disclosure, saying: "It's all true. We are space aliens. And I'm amazed that it's taken you so long to find out.

"When we read that the other aliens had been exposed in 1992, we knew it was only a matter of time before you got the rest of us."

Less expansive but equally honest was Sen. DeConcini, D-Ariz. "In a prepared statement, he said: "As chairman of the Senate Intelligence Committee, I am quite distressed. My highly classified cover has been blown."

Sen. Rockefeller, D-W. Va., cleverly turned questions about his space alien heritage into a plug for national health-care reform, saying: "I love it here on Earth, but our health-care system is better at home."

Sen. Heflin, D-Ala., was obviously taken off guard by report-

ers' questions. He called the space alien's revelations "surprising" and went on to say: "Yes, my parents were Heaven sent."

Sen. Johnston, D-La., said: "At least the cat is out of the bag, although this isn't exactly

the way I intended to tell my family and friends."

Sen. Dodd, D-Conn., expressed relief "that all this is public." In the most terse response of all, Sen. Cohen, R-Maine, said: "I admit it."

Dean's sources said the

space alien identified the extra-terrestrial senators in a 25-minute meeting with President Clinton.

Dean does not know what else, if anything, was discussed at the meeting.

"The first question that

came to my mind was whether the senators are U.S. citizens and eligible to serve in the U.S. Senate," said Dean.

"From what I understand, they were born in the U.S. and are U.S citizens. It just so happens that their parents were

ARE SPACE ALIENS!

ORRIN HATCH
R — Utah

NANCY KASSEBAUM
R — Kansas

SAM NUNN
D — Georgia

JOHN GLENN
D — Ohio

THE first meeting between Bill Clinton and the space alien took place in July, 1992.

...om another world. The senators look like ordinary humans," he continued, "but the space alien who met with President Clinton had an answer for that, too.

"He reportedly said the senators look human 'because they choose to look human. It is a simple matter for us to change our forms.'"

Oddly enough, the extraterrestrial alien refused to pinpoint the planet or star system he and the alien senators came from, Dean said.

Senator Bennett Johnston

HILLARY'S HOT NIGHTS WITH SPACE ALIEN!

By MIKE FOSTER/*Weekly World News*

NEW YORK — Stunned ex-President Bill Clinton exploded with rage and threatened divorce — after he caught his wife Hillary cuddling with a space alien!

That shocking report comes from close friends of the former first couple, who say that Bill was horrified to learn that his senator spouse had shared at least eight sizzling nights of romance in a secret Big Apple love nest with the unearthly creature.

"Bill is simply devastated," said a longtime family friend of the Clintons. "He had heard rumors that Hillary was caught up in an extramarital affair with another man for weeks, but he laughed them off as vicious gossip.

"He thought that, if anything, she might be involved in some kind of fling with another woman. When he was finally confronted with photographs showing Hillary with the spaceman, he was absolutely blown away.

"He told me, 'My God, I thought she was gay.'"

POLITICAL strategist Noel Tayson.

Friends of Hillary privately confirm the prim-and-proper U.S. Senator from New York had an illicit liaison with an extraterrestrial. But they insist her husband's many transgressions, ranging from his admitted affair with lounge singer Gennifer Flowers to the Monica Lewinsky sex scandal, more than justify her behavior.

"Bill has totally disrespected

Hillary: 'P'lod is EVERYTHING Bill's not!'

SPACE ALIEN has been linked to President Bush, too.

Hillary for years, running around with all of his trashy bimbos and throwing his affairs in her face," said an Arkansas associate of the former first lady. "This is a case of what goes around, comes around."

An apparently damning series of photos was leaked to *Weekly World News*, which has authenticated it. Ironically, the space alien photographed with

Mrs. Clinton is believed to be the same mysterious E.T. who endorsed Bill for President in 1992, helping to assure his victory.

While the origins of the alien are unknown, Washington insiders say the being, who calls himself P'lod, has been working behind the scenes in U.S. politics for years.

"He works both sides of the political fence and even backed George W. Bush last November," notes Washington political strategist Noel Tayson. "P'lod's only interest is advancing the cause of peace and prosperity in America and the rest of Earth."

Pals say Hillary met the tall, dark-eyed, imposing alien at a Democratic fund-raiser earlier this year and was immediately swept off her feet.

A close chum of Hillary said: "While Bill can be a selfish, immature jerk who's main focus is what goes on below the waist, the alien is a superintelligent being who senses her needs even before she states

them. Hillary told me, 'When I'm with P'lod, I feel he really understands me. P'lod is everything Bill's not.'"

But a big brain isn't all that the mystery man from the stars has to offer.

"Hillary says in the bedroom, the alien is a real tiger — his skills are thousands of years in advance of any human male," the chum added.

When Bill heard rumors that Hillary might be having an affair, he wasn't concerned.

"He figured at the most, she was going through a lesbian phase," said the family friend. "Like everyone, he's heard talk that Hillary prefers girls, but that doesn't bother him, because he's never considered the stuff gay

Story continues with more shocking photos

TAKE A 'LICK' AT THIS

Gene Simmons eat your heart out!

SPACE ALIEN and an obviously excited Hillary are caught in the act on the observation deck of the Empire State Building.

4:17 pm Space alien P'lod arrives at the New York love nest.

4:20 pm Three minutes pass, and Hillary shows up.

4:25 pm Five minutes later, here comes trouble — Bill!

women do to each other to be sexual relations."

Even when associates warned Bill that Hillary's secret lover was a guy, he didn't sweat. But to put the ugly rumors to rest, he hired a private eye to keep tabs on his wife, who was often away from home — ostensibly doing government business.

To his surprise, the private eye later returned to the former President's Harlem office with telephoto shots of Mrs. Clinton and the alien on the observation deck at the Empire State Building. In the photo series, the couple embrace and then the alien licks her face with his tongue.

The private eye also provided Mr. Clinton with a detailed log that showed the lovers met at the same swank New York hotel every Wednesday afternoon.

"Bill really hit the roof when he saw the pictures," said the family friend.

That Wednesday, when he knew the next rendezvous was looming, Clinton showed up at the hotel suite and confronted Hillary and the alien.

The private detective actually photographed the trio arriving separately at the hotel.

The source says the ex-President went wild when he found Hillary and the alien together in the suite.

"His face was red with fury and he hollered at her, 'I can't believe you've betrayed me with this inhuman freak. I want a divorce,'" the source continues.

The space alien beat a hasty retreat, say hotel staffers who witnessed the loud, embarrasing display through the open door of the suite. But Hillary showed no sign of shame — and didn't even make an effort to cover her bare body with a sheet.

"She stood up with her hands on her hips and gave a smirk," claims an eyewitness. "Then she said, 'What's good for the goose is good for the gander. Now get out.'"

Clinton, once the most powerful man in the world, left with his tail between his legs — and insiders say that it's unlikely he'll make good on his divorce threat.

NEXT WEEK
Shocking secrets you WON'T find in Bill's memoirs!

Oops!

PRESIDENT LOSES SECRET CODE FOR NUCLEAR BOMBS

— say White House insiders

IF THE secret nuclear codes fall into enemy hands — then God bless America!

PRESIDENT Bush has lost his wallet with his driver's license, daughters' photos and the secret codes that launch our nuclear weapons, reveals a White House source.

"We've looked everywhere," says a highly placed Secret Service official. "Mr. Bush covers a lot of ground in one day, and we've had our agents go over every inch of it a thousand times.

By NICK JEFFREYS
Correspondent

"They've searched the Oval Office, Air Force One, his private rooms, the White House kitchen where Mr. Bush goes to steal moon pies during the night, the lawn and all the men's rooms he could have visited. Nothing."

Cabinet members and congressional leaders are terrified that the distinctive billfold with the presidential crest and its top secret contents may land in enemy hands.

"If that happens, then God help America," says the official. "All our employees have the highest security levels, but with the high-tech machines that produce forged documents and ID cards, an inside job could be possible."

And that's only one of the dangers.

"If another country discovers the codes are missing, they can launch their missiles knowing full well we can't retaliate," says the official. "It's a race against time."

"George's mother Barbara is disgusted with her son," says another insider. "She says since George was a little boy he was always losing his eyeglasses, his homework and now the codes to the nuclear war missiles.

"She phoned the White House and told George: 'If you don't find your wallet soon, I'll fly up from Texas and find it for you. But I'm only bailing you out just this once.'

"Mr. Bush is really scrambling now. He doesn't want his mom barging into the Oval Office and spotting it right away. She'll say: 'See, if it was a spider it would have bit you, George.'"

Axis of Evil now just Ax of Evil

THE AXIS of Evil is getting a new name and an emblem to go along with it!

With Iraq liberated by U.S. troops and Iran obediently knuckling under to United Nations weapons inspectors, only North Korea remains a dangerous menace to the world. So the communist dictatorship's tyrannical leader Kim Jong II has announced that the entity's name will now be shortened to The Ax of Evil.

Gone, too, will be the trident insignia formerly seen on the uniforms of Axis of Evil henchmen worldwide, Kim said in a nationwide radio address. In its place will be the communist nation's new symbol: A very lethal and powerful-looking battle ax.

"Our enemies shall fear the sign of the ax," the diminutive despot declared.

WWN EXCLUSIVE DATELINE: MARCH 22, 2004

KIM JONG'S WARNING TO ALL NORTH KOREANS:

HOKEY POKEY — OR DIE!

SUPERSTITION IN THE AIR

Our tough-guy Secretary of Defense cuddles with a G.I. Joe doll? That's pretty kinky, but not as bizarre as some of these other Beltway superstitions, collected by *WWN* and printed here for the first time.

● While House Majority Leader **Tom DeLay's** Website refers to him as "the most effective whip in the history of the House," what it doesn't note is that DeLay privately attributes his success to his "most effective whip," a souvenir he picked up in Amsterdam's Red Light District the first and only time he was high on marijuana.

● President **George W. Bush** wears his jockey shorts backward and inside out for luck—because in his excitement, he accidentally donned them that way the day he was first elected governor of Texas, in 1994.

● Pennsylvania Senator and famous homophobe **Rick Santorum** carries a locket with a photo of his childhood dog in it. Aides refuse to comment on the connection between the dog and Santorum, but one told *WWN*, "If [liberal columnist] Dan Savage finds out about this, he's going to have a field day."

● Former presidential hopeful **John Kerry** sings "Take This Job and Shove It" (from beginning to end, plus a "special encore") before all public appearances to ward off stage fright. If particularly nervous he tops it off with a round of "Jesus Loves Me."

● South Carolina Senator **Strom Thurmond** kept a blanket he called "Snuggles" in his briefcase, although it had long been assumed that Snuggles was not so much a good luck charm as something to cover his lap with when he wet himself.

DONALD RUMSFELD SLEEPS WITH G.I. JOE DOLL

BUSTED!

WEEKLY WORLD EXCLUSIVE NEWS

By AIDEN LOUIS

SECRETARY of Defense Donald Rumsfeld can't fall asleep unless he's clutching his G.I. Joe doll, reveals a White House insider.

"Mr. Rumsfeld has to have 'Pvt. Joey' snuggled safe in his arms at bedtime or he's up all night going crazy looking for him," says the source.

"The action figure is more than 40 years old. It's raggedy and missing a leg. Mr. Rumsfeld accidentally ripped it off when he was playing 'Watch Out For Landmines' during a Senate hearing. But it's his most beloved possession."

The insider, an ex-intern who worked with the defense secretary and often visited his home, was tying up a project late one night when he overheard a vicious argument between his boss and wife Joyce Rumsfeld.

"Mr. Rumsfeld yelled: 'I told you to hide Pvt. Joey from those rugrats! Now he's gone. Oh my God. Oh my God!' " says the source.

"Mrs. Rumsfeld was furious. She screamed back: 'If my grandchildren want to play with that stupid doll, they will! You are too old to still need him! And I'm sick of rolling over onto Joe's bayonet in the middle of the night! Get rid of him!'

"Mr. Rumsfeld screeched: 'Never! You'll have to pry Joey from my cold dead kung fu grip.'

"It just went on like that for quite a while."

Secretary of Defense would be singing soprano — if not for G.I. Joe doll!

Shamelessly eavesdropping on the marital fracas, the insider learned Rumsfeld is obsessively attached to the 10-inch-tall "Real American Hero" because he saved his life.

In 1962, the Chicago native was elected to the U.S. House of

ARE YOU KIDDING?

When Donald H. Rumsfeld accepted the nation's highest civilian award, the Presidential Medal of Freedom, Private Joey proudly watched the proceedings from Rumsfeld's jacket pocket.

Representatives from Illinois. The charity-minded politician was so eager to help war-torn, poverty-stricken third world nations he often requested to travel on missions of mercy.

"During one grueling, taxpayer-funded stay in a five-star luxury hotel in Paris, the congressman was distributing G.I. Joe dolls, which had just been launched in the states, to needy gay Frenchmen," says the source.

"He had one of the Joe's in his lap during a luncheon when a passing waiter tripped and two escargot knives plummeted down, point first, toward Mr. Rumsfeld's testicles.

"The doll took the hit. If he hadn't, the injury would have changed Mr. Rumsfeld's voice to that of a girlie soprano and ended his political career. Or he could have bled to death if the blades sliced a major artery.

"After that, Pvt. Joey became his good-luck talisman — his security blanket.

"He's terrified that the minute he throws Joe away, he'll get hit by a bus."

The defense secretary has also grown to know and love his small friend. They talk a lot — although they don't always agree — and Rumsfeld asks for Joe's advice on weighty political decisions.

Adds the source: "Mr. Rumsfeld firmly believes Private Joey will be the one to finally find Osama Bin Laden."

Saddam & Osama's

Souvenir photo album!

GAY WEDDING

IT WAS bound to happen and it finally did: Just months after they were caught making tender gay love in a Pakistani motel room, doe-eyed lovebirds Osama Bin Laden and Saddam Hussein have tied the knot in a hush-hush but otherwise opulent wedding somewhere in Northern Iraq.

And there to celebrate with the starry-eyed psychos were a veritable Who's Who of terror kingpins and assorted good friends, including grinning PLO chief Yassir Arafat, pretty-boy Libyan strongman Muammar Qaddafi, North Korean wacko Kim Jong Il and renegade French President Jacques Chirac, U.S. intelligence sources have confirmed.

According to the source, Osama, who is the "man" in the strange relationship, asked Saddam to marry him just days after their widely reported love session in Pakistan last June.

But the ex-Iraqi tyrant reportedly toyed with the Saudi expatriate for two months, taunting him with "maybes," say sources, before finally agreeing to become his "bride."

When the happy couple and their wedding party arrived at the mosque on their big day, sources say it at first appeared they would get hitched in a hurry to avoid detection.

But it soon become evident there would be no shortcuts on what Saddam would later tearfully call "the happiest day of my life."

And when they emerged from separate dressing tents that were erected outside the mosque, Osama was, according to the CIA's analysis, "resplendent in a black tuxedo, gray gloves, black cummerbund, black slacks and black patent leather shoes."

"Saddam," the report continued, "cut a somewhat less striking figure in his plain white wedding dress and cheap red pumps, which appeared to be made from molded plastic and were several sizes too small."

Little is known about the ceremony itself, suggesting that the Al Qaeda-connected mole who provided the CIA's intelligence wasn't allowed in to see it.

Saddam & Osama
Souvenir photo album!
THE RECEPTION

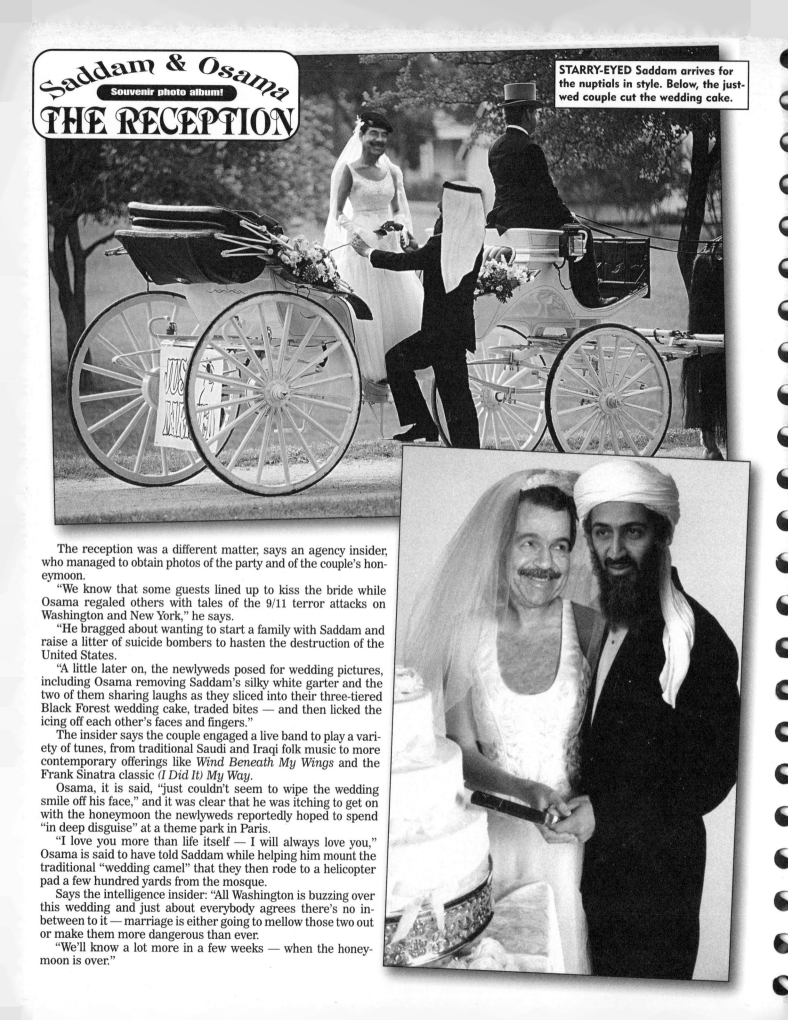

STARRY-EYED Saddam arrives for the nuptials in style. Below, the just-wed couple cut the wedding cake.

The reception was a different matter, says an agency insider, who managed to obtain photos of the party and of the couple's honeymoon.

"We know that some guests lined up to kiss the bride while Osama regaled others with tales of the 9/11 terror attacks on Washington and New York," he says.

"He bragged about wanting to start a family with Saddam and raise a litter of suicide bombers to hasten the destruction of the United States.

"A little later on, the newlyweds posed for wedding pictures, including Osama removing Saddam's silky white garter and the two of them sharing laughs as they sliced into their three-tiered Black Forest wedding cake, traded bites — and then licked the icing off each other's faces and fingers."

The insider says the couple engaged a live band to play a variety of tunes, from traditional Saudi and Iraqi folk music to more contemporary offerings like *Wind Beneath My Wings* and the Frank Sinatra classic *(I Did It) My Way*.

Osama, it is said, "just couldn't seem to wipe the wedding smile off his face," and it was clear that he was itching to get on with the honeymoon the newlyweds reportedly hoped to spend "in deep disguise" at a theme park in Paris.

"I love you more than life itself — I will always love you," Osama is said to have told Saddam while helping him mount the traditional "wedding camel" that they then rode to a helicopter pad a few hundred yards from the mosque.

Says the intelligence insider: "All Washington is buzzing over this wedding and just about everybody agrees there's no in-between to it — marriage is either going to mellow those two out or make them more dangerous than ever.

"We'll know a lot more in a few weeks — when the honeymoon is over."

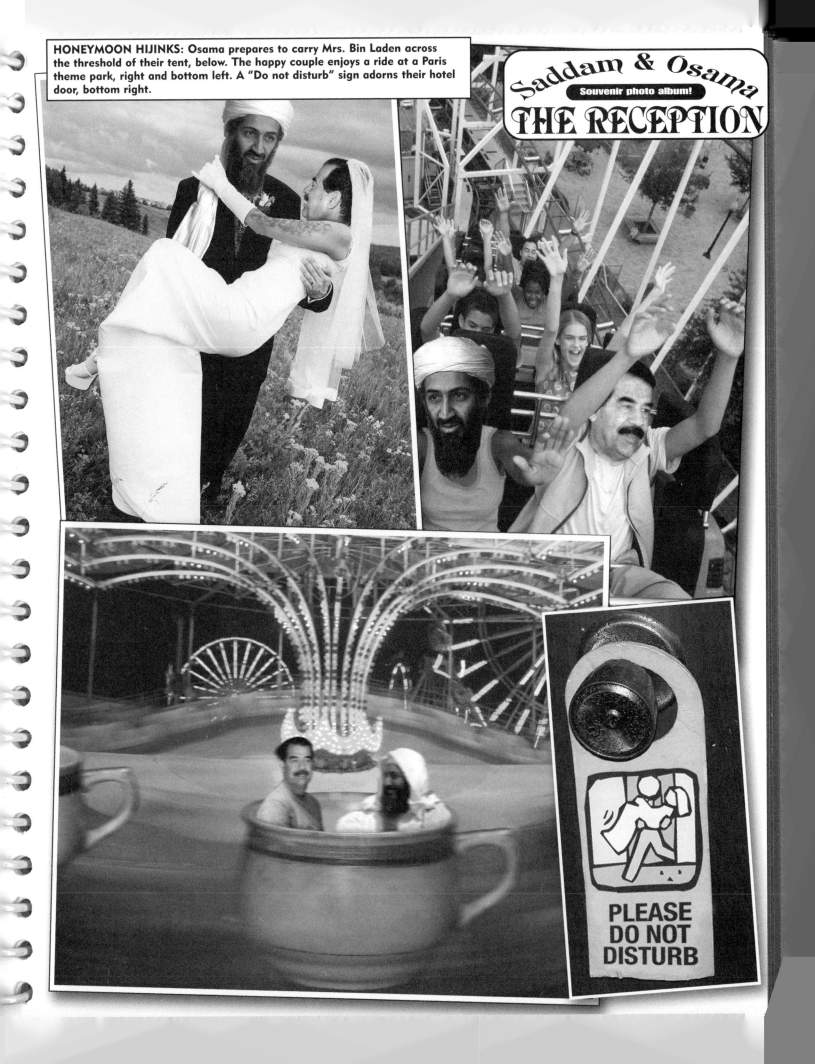

HONEYMOON HIJINKS: Osama prepares to carry Mrs. Bin Laden across the threshold of their tent, below. The happy couple enjoys a ride at a Paris theme park, right and bottom left. A "Do not disturb" sign adorns their hotel door, bottom right.

Saddam & Osama
Souvenir photo album!
THE RECEPTION

PLEASE DO NOT DISTURB

Saddam & Osama
Souvenir photo album!
THE HONORED GUESTS

VIP GUESTS: Amid burqa-clad beauties are, from left: Yassir Arafat, the happy couple, Muammar Qaddafi, Jacques Chirac and little Kim Jong Il.

GRAND ENTRANCE: Arafat arrives for the wedding in style — atop a Libyan battle tank.

Alarmed Feds propose new law to cope with the facially challenged ...

MANDATORY MASKS FOR THE UGLY

... so everyone will look like one of the beautiful people!

YOU MAY soon be seeing J.Lo, Elvis and Julia everywhere you go.

By SALLY DOHRNE *Correspondent*

FEDERAL OFFICIALS who recently reported that over 140 million Americans are fat are now saying that at least that many are ugly. And the solution they're proposing is a law that would encourage or even require "facially challenged" citizens to cover up with masks, *Weekly World News* has learned.

But the news isn't all bad. According to sources at the Department of Health, Education and Welfare, those among you who are real homely will be able to choose from a wide range of "beauty masks," including Elvis in his prime, J.Lo, Brad Pitt and Julia Roberts.

The dramatic move comes as the Feds are reeling from a global perception that most Americans are grossly obese when, in fact, only half are.

Stung by the criticism, many leaders, in both the House of Representatives and Senate, believe the so-called "Pretty Mask Initiative" could go a long way toward halting that embarrassing and potentially damaging opinion.

"PMI is a way of 'cleaning up our streets,' so to speak," says a Beltway insider. "If foreign tourists see only beautiful people — thanks to the masks — they'll have a more favorable view of Americans.

"Our own tourists, the ugly ones, could also wear their masks when they travel abroad."

Asked which government agency would determine who's ugly and who isn't, the insider said that a special "Ugly American Department" will be set up within HEW to judge looks on a scale of one to 10.

Those who score a five or above — "butt ugly," in the words of the insider — will be "strongly encouraged," if not required, to choose and wear a "beauty mask."

"There are two ways to get ugly people into masks," continues the source. "You can encourage them with tax credits, or you can write a law telling them to wear them or face fines and a prison sentence.

"It all depends on who's in the White House and Congress when it finally comes to a vote.

"For instance, in Congress, if a majority of senators and representatives are ugly, tax breaks are the way it will go. If a majority don't ride too high on the 'ugly scale,' then you're almost certainly going to have a much tougher law requiring that masks be worn."

Trish Cederin, 53, of Washington, is the first to admit that she's as ugly as a bowl of warts. And she thinks the Pretty Mask Initiative is "right on."

"I'd love to wear a Nicole Kidman mask, or maybe a J.Lo, although she's a little young for my body," gushes the unemployed housekeeper. "I already have to wear a bag over my head if I expect more than a handshake from a date.

"For gals like me, this PMI thing is a godsend. I'm not too proud to say it."

Ned Fruler, 28, couldn't have disagreed more — at first.

But the more he thought about it, the better PMI sounded.

At 5-foot-4 and 290 pounds, he is, as he puts it, "hefty for my height." And his face, he says, "has stopped so many clocks that I have to turn on a radio or call my mom to find out what time it is."

"The law is unfair," says Fruler, a line cook at one of D.C.'s more popular "ham and eggers."

"But I guess if I have to wear one or I get a good tax break, I'll take the Elvis mask. Do you think they'll have a George Clooney? Somebody else who looks good — at least I think so — is that gay guy on that TV show, *Will & Grace*.

"I guess wearing a mask won't be that bad, especially if we get more than one."

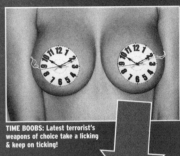
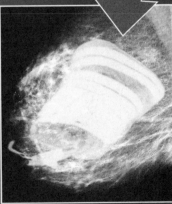

Half-human creature is training with U.S. Marines!

WASHINGTON — Bat Boy has volunteered!

In a bizarre turn of events, the half-bat, half-human mutant reportedly has joined the U.S. military — and is being trained to use his super-sensitive hearing, keen sense of smell and other unique talents to hunt down terrorists in the caves, holes and hovels they hide in!

That's the startling claim of a Pentagon source who says the strange freak of nature scurried onto an as-yet-unidentified Marine base and begged to enlist in America's war against terrorism.

"He hopped a fence to get on the base and officers found him in tears, jabbering in broken English about wanting to fight for America," the source continues.

According to reports, Bat Boy, who has been on the run from authorities, including the FBI, since his dramatic escape from a Chicago hospital in September, learned of America's war against terrorism and was stirred to action when he found a copy of last week's issue of *Weekly World News* — with Osama bin Laden on the cover.

"When the Marines found him, he was clutching a newspaper that had a photo of Osama bin Laden with a sniper's crosshairs over his face," reports the source. "He must have found it on a road or in a parking lot because it had tire tracks on it.

"I'm told that he held it up, pointed to the picture and said, 'Bad man . . . lemme get him . . . bite him up.'"

The source admits even battle-tough Marines were taken aback when they first saw the pint-size youth.

"In an official report, one veteran Marine captain was quoted as saying: 'I drew my sidearm and aimed for his head — he was really spooky looking with those huge eyes, pointy ears and sharp teeth.

"'I knew who he was. I'd heard reports about how the FBI

BAT BOY should have no trouble finding terrorists like bin Laden in their mountain hideouts, says a Pentagon source. Right: September 18 issue of *Weekly World News*.

Here's how Bat Boy can help America!

"Bat Boy can go places and do things no normal soldier can," a highly placed Pentagon source says.

"His hearing is 10,000 times more acute than an ordinary human's and he can track smells like a bloodhound. He's able to navigate in total darkness like a bat, using a kind of built-in radar. He can scuttle up a sheer cliff effortlessly and is strong enough to pull a man's arm out of the socket.

"Best of all, he's totally at home in mountain caves — where many terrorists like Osama bin Laden hide."

Surprisingly, Pentagon testers found, Bat Boy has a gift for learning languages quickly.

"While he speaks English poorly, he understands it perfectly and should easily master Arabic," the source says. "This will help him on spy missions behind enemy lines.

"Bat Boy used to be America's most wanted — but now he's America's secret weapon."

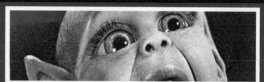

WWN EXTRA

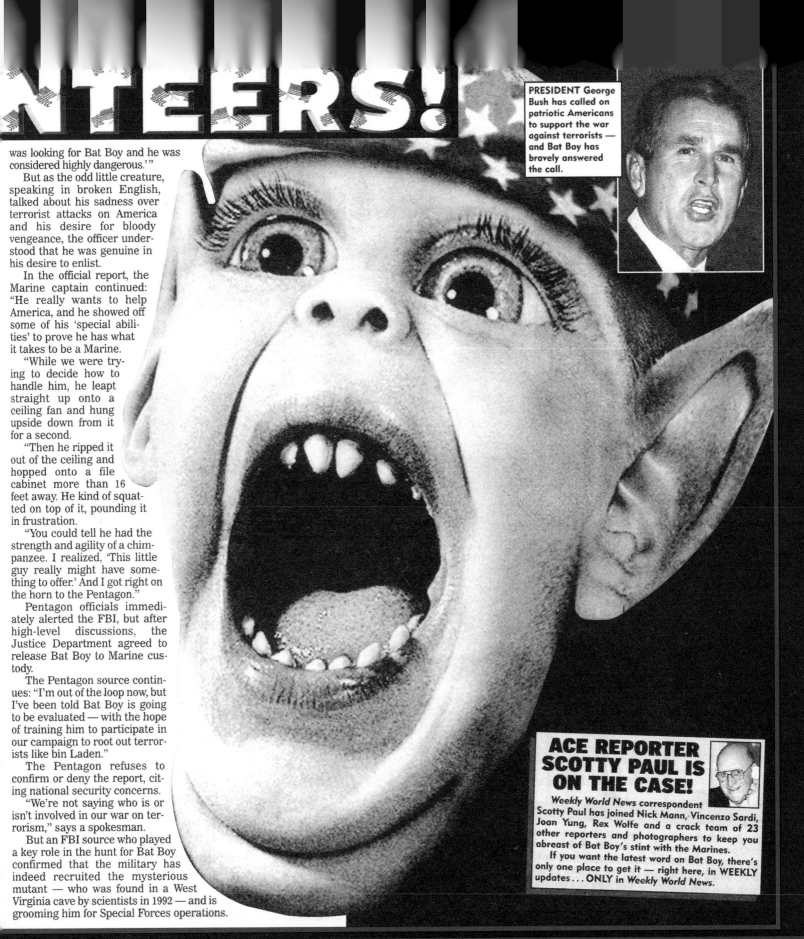

was looking for Bat Boy and he was considered highly dangerous.'"

But as the odd little creature, speaking in broken English, talked about his sadness over terrorist attacks on America and his desire for bloody vengeance, the officer understood that he was genuine in his desire to enlist.

In the official report, the Marine captain continued: "He really wants to help America, and he showed off some of his 'special abilities' to prove he has what it takes to be a Marine.

"While we were trying to decide how to handle him, he leapt straight up onto a ceiling fan and hung upside down from it for a second.

"Then he ripped it out of the ceiling and hopped onto a file cabinet more than 16 feet away. He kind of squatted on top of it, pounding it in frustration.

"You could tell he had the strength and agility of a chimpanzee. I realized, 'This little guy really might have something to offer.' And I got right on the horn to the Pentagon."

Pentagon officials immediately alerted the FBI, but after high-level discussions, the Justice Department agreed to release Bat Boy to Marine custody.

The Pentagon source continues: "I'm out of the loop now, but I've been told Bat Boy is going to be evaluated — with the hope of training him to participate in our campaign to root out terrorists like bin Laden."

The Pentagon refuses to confirm or deny the report, citing national security concerns.

"We're not saying who is or isn't involved in our war on terrorism," says a spokesman.

But an FBI source who played a key role in the hunt for Bat Boy confirmed that the military has indeed recruited the mysterious mutant — who was found in a West Virginia cave by scientists in 1992 — and is grooming him for Special Forces operations.

ACE REPORTER SCOTTY PAUL IS ON THE CASE!

Weekly World News correspondent Scotty Paul has joined Nick Mann, Vincenzo Sardi, Joan Yung, Rex Wolfe and a crack team of 23 other reporters and photographers to keep you abreast of Bat Boy's stint with the Marines.

If you want the latest word on Bat Boy, there's only one place to get it — right here, in WEEKLY updates... ONLY in *Weekly World News*.

FIVE THINGS YOU DIDN'T KNOW ABOUT BAT BOY!

1. Bat Boy's favorite musical group is *NSYNC and his favorite singer in the band is Justin who is a dreamboat.

2. He loves Count Chocula cereal.

3. He once defused a terrorist bomb aboard an airplane by urinating on it.

4. Bat Boy sheds his wings once every three years, and is able to regenerate a new pair.

5. His favorite comic book superhero is not Batman as you might think–it's Spider-Man.

BAT BOY LED U.S. TROOPS T

BAT BOY leads U.S. Special Forces in the search for Saddam. The search finally paid off, thanks to the mutant freak's highly sensitive nose — and Saddam's failure to bathe for several weeks. "It was a piece of cake for Bat Boy to find him," says a military source.

By **MIKE FOSTER**/ *Correspondent*

THE U.S. Special Forces troops who captured Saddam Hussein were led to his dingy spider hole by Bat Boy — who literally sniffed out the filth-covered dictator!

That's the astonishing revelation of military sources, who say the pint-sized mutant will be awarded the Bronze Star for the "vital role" he played in tracking down the fugitive former strongman.

"Bat Boy's nose is more sensitive than any bloodhound," confirms a Pentagon insider. "And since Saddam hadn't bathed for weeks down there, it was a piece of cake for Bat Boy to find him.

"The little guy just sniffed along the ground on his hands and knees, with our soldiers behind him, until he got to that squalid mud hut and started pointing down excitedly.

"That's when we knew Saddam was under there."

The U.S. government has steadfastly refused to admit publicly that the mysterious mutant, found by scientists in a West Virginia cave in 1992, has been aiding the military. According to the official version, an unidentified man in Tikrit tipped off troops to Saddam's whereabouts. But the insider confirms that Bat Boy has been involved in the war effort since last January — months before the U.S.-led invasion.

"His batlike sonar, ability to see in the dark and other traits make Bat Boy an indispensable tool for the military," the insider says.

"During the months leading up to Operation Iraqi Freedom, Bat Boy carried out dangerous reconnaissance missions on behalf of the Army. The excellent intelligence he gathered is one of the reasons the Coalition was able to topple Saddam's regime so easily — we knew all the enemy's weaknesses."

The 5-foot-tall, pointy eared creature also conducted sabotage — destroying chemical weapons that Saddam had planned to use on Coalition troops.

"He became a real thorn in Saddam's side,"

reveals the insider. "Many of Saddam's frazzled troops believed Bat Boy was a bat-winged demon of Arabic legend named Pazuzu."

Bat Boy was rotated home after the end of major combat in May. But when the search for Saddam dragged on fruitlessly, generals summoned the bizarre creature back to Iraq.

"All Bat Boy was given were a pair of smelly old riding boots of Saddam's," the insider discloses. "He took one good whiff and that enabled him to follow the trail from Baghdad all the way to Tikrit."

When troops pulled the cover off the hole where Saddam was hiding, one source says, "Bat Boy caught a strong whiff, I guess, because he reacted like a dog smelling a juicy steak. He had to be held back while a couple of guys went down the hole."

At first Saddam didn't realize Bat Boy was outside, says the source, who notes that troops were ordered not to reveal Bat Boy's involvement.

The Butcher of Baghdad calmly told his captors, "My name is Saddam Hussein. I am the president of Iraq and I want to negotiate."

AMAZING UNTOLD STORY BEHIND DRAMATIC CAPTURE!

When he heard that, Bat Boy could be restrained no longer. He jumped into the hole, and when Saddam saw him, the defeated dictator "just lost it," according to the eyewitness.

"Saddam started screaming hysterically in Arabic, 'Pazuzu, Pazuzu! Keep that filthy thing away from me.' He begged for us to protect him."

The run-in with Bat Boy may explain why Saddam seemed so docile when filmed undergoing a medical check at the hands of his U.S. captors.

"Saddam's mind is shot," says the insider.

President Bush reportedly will award Bat Boy the Bronze Star in a special White House ceremony later this year.

But don't expect the little hero to rest on his laurels afer bagging one of history's most evil men. White House sources say the president is so delighted with Bat Boy's success, he's ordered the patriotic freak to be dispatched to locate another fugitive fiend: Osama Bin Laden.

"Bat Boy has already received the go ahead — and a red turban once worn by Osama," confirms a senior administration official.

SADDAM BEARD GUNK TO BE AUCTIONED ON-LINE

THE MOST coveted souvenir of Operation Iraqi Freedom can now be yours. Lice and dandruff flakes extracted from Saddam Hussein during his televised medical check are about to be auctioned on-line!

The material was saved by a savvy, unidentified individual after the deposed dictator's dramatic capture and now it's up for grabs.

The disgusting beard gunk has been divided into 25 thimble-size parcels — each guaranteed to contain "at least one live louse."

And while you might not touch the stuff with

a 10-foot pole, there are plenty of avid collectors out there who can't wait for a chance to bid on it, experts say.

"I would estimate that the Saddam beard refuse will fetch anywhere between $400,000 and $1.2 million per parcel," declares collectibles expert Brian Halman of London.

"Love him or hate him, Saddam is a figure of monumental historical importance and anything associated with him has value to a collector."

Stalin's mustache sold at auction for $49,000 in 1968, the expert says.

SADDAM ... GOTCHA!

- & THEN THERE WAS ONE ... Will a grieving Osama turn himself in for the sake of the shaved ape baby?

A TERRIFIED Saddam went into hysterics and begged Coalition troops to protect him when Bat Boy leaped into his hiding place, an eyewitness says.

ALIEN PICKED EVERY ELECTION RIGHT SINCE 1980!

Another term for Bush!
2004

1980
RONNIE REAGAN and V.P. George Bush Sr.

1984
REAGAN – Take Two.

P'lod does it again!

The space alien who is famous for such wacky antics as mooning Ralph Nader and romancing Hillary Clinton has endorsed the winning candidate in every U.S. presidential election since 1980, as reported exclusively in *Weekly World News*.

"It really is uncanny," says renowned political scientist Dr. Robert Keckley. "It's also a little embarrassing that an alien seems to understand the American electorate better than any human pundit!"

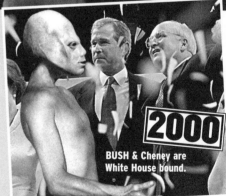
2000
BUSH & Cheney are White House bound.

1988
DUBYA'S dad declares victory.

1992
BILL CLINTON sweeps to power.

1996
SLICK Willie and Veep Al Gore.

P'LOD PROPELS BUSH TO SECOND TERM

'Now, George, make nice. Losers have feelings, too!'

'You win George! You won't have to move!'

P'lod has become part of the Bush family.

ALIEN looks comfortable in the Oval Office as George listens to John Kerry conceding defeat the day after the election.

I**N THE heady days leading up to the election, P'lod assumed an increasingly large role in the life and politics of the First Family.**

He advised the President on campaign strategy, helped write his speeches and provided encouragement when polls showed Kerry gaining ground.

But he also became an integral part of family life, serving as a confidant to Laura Bush and counseling First Daughters Jenna and Barbara on how to best represent their father during public appearances.

Republican party insiders say he was even tutoring the President's younger brother, Florida governor Jeb Bush, on a possible run for the White House in 2008 — continuing the Bush dynasty at 1600 Pennsylvania Avenue.

The President's parents, George and Barbara, accepted him as a member of the family, and he even gave the senior Bush pointers on skydiving, the energetic 81-year-old's favorite pastime. They became so close, P'lod was granted permission to refer to the former President by his nickname, Poppy.

The alien became such a valued member of the Bush re-election team that he sat in on cabinet meetings, sharing his expertise on matters of state.

P'lod's political credentials are beyond dispute. He has successfully predicted the winners of the last seven Presidential elections as well as Arnold Schwarzenegger's victory in the 2003 California governor's race.

He is regarded as a political miracle worker by both Republicans and Democrats. He is even credited with talking Ted Kennedy into going on a crash diet and persuading Bill Clinton to refrain from thinking about sex for up to three consecutive minutes.

On the Republican side, he has helped heal the apparently deep rift between George Bush and outspoken Arizona senator John McCain, and convinced Vice President Dick Cheney to occasionally leave the "undisclosed location" in which he was holed up for almost all of the administration's first term in office.

"With this latest triumph, P'lod can literally write his own ticket in Washington," says a top Bush campaign insider.

"Rumors are running rampant that he is likely to be offered a wide range of positions by the administration — everything from czar of the new intelligence agency to ambassador to whatever-the-hell-country he wants.

"The president is nothing if not grateful, believe me."

BUSH TRIED TO ENROLL IN ELECTORAL COLLEGE

By BERNIE PYLE

B**EFORE running for** President in 2000, Gov. George Bush knew so little about national politics that he tried to enroll in the electoral college.

That's the claim of a top aide to Bush when he was governor of Texas.

"Republicans approached him about running for President, and Bush told them, 'I'd love to, but I'm not qualified. I've never gone to electoral college.'

"The Republicans were aghast. But Bush went away and decided he wanted to run after all, says the aide. "The next day he came in with a list and said, 'Enroll me in the electoral college. These are some courses I would like to take.' "

Among the classes were "Introduction to Starting a War," "Advanced Deficit-Raising," "Geography 101," and "How to be a Compassionate Conservative."

In reality, the electoral college is the voting system that determines who becomes President. Each state gets votes based on its population. In 2000, Bush became president even though he got a half million fewer votes than Al Gore, because he won a majority of votes in the electoral college.

Bush was relieved when he learned he didn't have to go to electoral college. "He was afraid he'd have to read a book," says the aide. "Instead, Bush said, 'I'll just learn on the job.' "

SADDAM & OSAMA

By **VERNON BURR**

Correspondent

JUST ONE MONTH after their gay marriage rocked the world, ecstatic newlyweds Osama Bin Laden and Saddam Hussein have adopted a shaved-ape baby to make their family complete.

And while the news is sure to set terrorists' hearts aflutter, the animal-rights group that delivered the chimp to a go-between who prom-

ANIMAL-RIGHTS GROUP DEMANDS APE BE RETURNED

ADOPT SHAVED CHIMP

ised that the 9-month-old was going to a "good home" say they were lied to — and they want the little critter back.

But it seems unlikely that will happen anytime soon, because nobody — not even the CIA with its Al Qaeda moles — has any idea where Osama, Saddam and Robert, their new "son," might be.

Given the best intelligence available, the trio are on the move "somewhere in the Middle East."

CIA sources say their most recent photo — a bizarre "family portrait" that's dominated by the grinning chimp — was probably snapped in Syria on October 6, although the doting couple and their "boy" almost certainly have left the country since then.

"Security around Osama and Saddam has never been so tight," says a CIA source in Paris, where the shaved chimp was handed over to an alleged Saudi sheik who claimed to be representing a couple who couldn't have children of their own.

"Protecting their marriage and holding on to this baby is something they're taking very, very seriously indeed. About all we can do for the moment is hope that the chimp will distract them or at least slow them down a little.

"All we need is for these guys to make one little mistake, to miss one connection with the people who are helping them elude us, and I promise you — they won't know what hit them.

"But so far, that's not happening; they aren't making mistakes. We're no closer to knocking them off than we were a year ago."

It's unclear whether Osama and Saddam know the baby is a shaved ape or if they've been led to believe it's human.

But if anyone doubted that the world's most wanted war - criminals would take their gay marriage and parental responsibilities seriously, Saddam — who is the "woman" in the strange coupling — quickly laid the notion to rest.

According to the CIA source, the former Iraqi strongman turned on a trusted bodyguard "like a mama lion" when the man made a crude comment about the terror kingpins' September nuptials and then accidentally jabbed the baby chimp with a diaper pin while laughing at his own joke.

By the time stick-thin Osama pulled stocky Saddam off, the bodyguard, a Saddam relative, had very nearly been blinded — with both of his eyes, a source says, "having very nearly been scratched out."

And it's that kind of physical and emotional volatility that's got animal-rights activists worried sick that Saddam's and Osama's hot-headed way of dealing with the least little problem will leave young and impressionable Robert psychologically scarred for life.

"And we can't rule out physical abuse," warns Helene Mayoro, the Paris-based activist who orchestrated the adoption believing that the shaved ape was going to a good home.

As *Weekly World News* and other major media reported earlier this year, Mayoro and other activists spearheaded a global crusade to find foster parents for 229 shaved chimps that had been palmed off to unsuspecting couples as human infants in a worldwide adoption scam.

Robert was picked over and picked over and picked over, says Mayoro — until only he remained.

"He wasn't the smartest, he wasn't the cutest — but his little heart was filled with love," she recalls. "Now those terrorist monsters have him. If God would strike them dead right now I'd rejoice in the streets.

"If I could change places with Robert this very minute, the Lord knows I would."

What happens next is anybody's guess as Saddam and Osama continue to elude the CIA and other intelligence agencies that just can't seem to figure out where the kill-crazy gay lovebirds will turn up next.

By the time the CIA found out about their hastily arranged but well attended wedding in late September — French President Jacques Chirac and PLO chief Yasser Arafat were among its many dignitaries — the doe-eyed couple who exchanged vows in northern Iraq were holed up in a honeymoon love nest thousands of miles away . . . in France.

And by the time agents kicked down the doors with guns drawn and badges flashing, Osama and Saddam were back, apparently, in Syria — posing for pictures with Robert.

"The joke around the CIA is that we should have known a couple of funny boys like Osama and Saddam would turn up in 'gay Paree' after the wedding," says the Paris-based CIA source, "but that's water under the bridge.

"Let's just hope that Robert turns out to be more than they bargained for. If the marriage is strained, if the stress of raising a baby mounts, if Osama gets jealous because Saddam dotes on the infant, anything could happen.

"And they just might do something stupid — like get themselves caught."

While the CIA keeps hoping to catch a break, Mayoro has issued an unprecedented appeal for compassion from two of the most bloodthirsty men on Earth.

"Please give Robert back to us," she said in an interview on the Arab world's hard-hitting satellite news channel, Al Jazeera TV. "He deserves a mother and a father who can provide him with a stable, secure and loving home, and all you have to offer is life on the run."

FRICTION MOUNTS AS SPURNED PETS TAKE OUT FRUSTRATION ON NEW ARRIVAL!

THE SUDDEN addition of a "child" into the odd-couple family of Saddam Hussein and Osama Bin Laden has the twosome's pet goat and camel suffering from a kind of sibling rivalry, sources say.

Worried experts say Hussein and Bin Laden ignored experts' advice to "go slow" when introducing little Robert to the animals. "We're hearing that they barely acknowledge the animals that they claim to love so much, and have turned their back on the poor creatures while showering all their affection on Robert," says one adoption official.

Sources say the jealous goat has already shredded several of Robert's diapers. "And the camel is behaving very strangely," says a CIA insider. "One of our informants told us it even tried to knock the baby out of Saddam's arms."

"We're very concerned," says the adoption official. "Knowing these two, they could very well take the animals' side and abandon little Robert out in the desert somewhere."

FOUND!

OSAMA'S LOVE LETTERS

AN EXCLUSVIE PEEK INTO HIS STEAMY ROMANCE WITH SADDAM!

SADDAM Hussein may be cooling his heels in the custody of U.S. troops, but his ardent love for "hubby" Osama Bin Laden still burns with a fiery passion — and the Pentagon's got the lurid, smuggled love letters to prove it.

"It's a tribute to Saddam's resourcefulness that he managed to find a way to get love notes delivered back and forth between himself and Osama, despite the fact that he's supposedly being held incommunicado by our best troops and the CIA," says a U.S. military source in Baghdad.

"Under lock and key in solitary confinement, watched around the clock by teams of heavily armed guards, he traded love letters with Osama Bin Laden, the most wanted man on the planet — seemingly with no more effort than it would take to communicate with your next-door neighbor.

"And like Saddam or not, you have to give him credit."

"This is a huge embarrassment for the United States. And President Bush wants answers pronto. But I don't think he's going to get them.

"Osama mentions George Bush three times in three different letters, but only to complain that he's the 'Great Satan who tore us apart' and to express his disgust over the president's surprise trip to visit American troops in Iraq on Thanksgiving Day."

He also talks about Robert, their adopted shaved chimp baby, saying, "Robert is growing up fast and misses you very much, but it isn't possible for him to miss you more than I do."

For the most part, the letters are loving and passionate, with Osama telling Saddam, "I miss your cherry-sweet lips and hot Iraqi nature," and calling him "my precious and beloved Saddie" and "my sexy, swarthy passion goat."

But in one letter, dated January 12, Osama inexplicably taunts Saddam, telling him that he is now sharing his bed with a male friend. Osama eventually apologizes by saying, "I'm sorry. I'm sorry. I know it [Saddam's capture] isn't your fault. But my needs...I am a man with needs...."

According to the military source, interrogators first became suspicious when they noticed Saddam was fingering a small white handkerchief with an "OBL" monogram while they questioned him about his past association with international terror groups such as Islamic Jihad and Osama's own Al Qaeda.

While investigators try to uncover how Saddam and Osama were transporting the love letters, interrogators are using them to increase psychological pressure on Saddam.

"After analysts confirmed their authenticity, they quickly duplicated them so interrogators could use the fakes to help make Saddam talk," says the source.

"In one late-night session an interrogator pulled a love letter out of an envelope and struck a match, acting like he was going to set the note on fire.

"Saddam's eyes almost popped out of his head. He was trembling with rage and for a few seconds, it looked like he might crack. But he somehow managed to pull himself together and avert his eyes, as if to say, 'Go ahead — burn it. I can take it.'

"But that's OK. We're going to step up the pressure until Saddam tells us what we want to hear. And when he does, he'll curse the day Osama sent him those letters."

IN HIS letters, Osama talks about the good times he and Saddam shared.

BUSH WANTS TO SELL HAWAII!

Aloha state on the block to pay for war on terror

By MARK TOMPKINS
Political Correspondent

WASHINGTON, D.C. — In one of the most shocking moves of his presidency, George W. Bush is on the verge of selling Hawaii to Japan, a leading Washington insider has informed *Weekly World News.*

"Basically, the President sees this as a quick and easy way to generate a huge bundle of cash," stated the source, an upper-echelon State Department official with close ties to Bush's inner circle.

"As everyone knows, the U.S. is in debt up to its eyeballs — to the tune of more than $7.5 trillion. And thanks to the gigantic tax cuts Bush keeps giving the super-wealthy and big corporations, the government effectively has no income whatsoever. Bush figures that by selling Hawaii, he'll be able to pay off a sizeable portion of the national debt while generating funding for continuing military operations in Iraq, and quite possibly, a full-scale invasion of Iran."

The notion of selling large areas of American territory for profit was inspired by a 2004 cam-

BONZAI! Prime Minister Koizumi and President Bush have been talking about the sale of Hawaii for several days.

paign stop Bush made at an elementary school, according to our source.

"Sitting in on a fourth-grade class where kids were giving oral reports on American history, the President was surprised to learn that in 1803, what is now the American Midwest was actually purchased from France for $15 million in a transaction called the Louisiana Purchase. That got Bush thinking that if the U.S. could buy enormous chunks of land from other countries, it could sell land, too, and maybe make a killing doing so."

Initially, Bush considered putting up Massachusetts for sale, along with several other "blue" states. But after Vice President Dick Cheney pointed out such an action might trigger a massive popular revolt on the U.S. mainland, he and Bush

decided to hang a "For Sale" sign on remote, isolated Hawaii.

"It's so far away, that it doesn't even seem like part of America anyway," the President is alleged to have said at a cabinet meeting, adding, "Besides, I talked to Daddy about it and he says there's no oil there, just pineapples and coconuts."

In a secret nonbinding auction held shortly after Bush's second inauguration, Japan outbid 10 other countries, including Canada, China and Australia, for ownership of the "Aloha state."

According to a telephone poll of Hawaiian residents conducted last week, 98 percent described themselves as "extremely P.O.ed" after being told about the President's alleged plan.

"That arrogant bozo is spitting in the face of everyone who lives here," fumed Roy Kakaliki, a Honolulu native and founder of the Kakaliki Coconut Company.

"When word of this spreads, there's going to be Bush effigies burning all over the islands."

Say 'sayonara' to the States!

CARMEN ELECTRA fell in love with Hawaii when she filmed an episode of *Baywatch* there.

SEXY SASQUATCH'S TORRID 10

WASHINGTON – Helen the Bigfoot hooker has gone so gaga over America's hunky, hot-to-trot politicians that she's compiled her own Top 10 list of the bigwigs she'd most like to boff.

"Helen's as giddy as a schoolgirl from all the attention these rich and powerful men have lavished upon her since she arrived in Washington," said primatologist Dr. Alan Kingfer, who uses sign language to communicate with the fur-ball femme fatale.

"But not everyone here has succumbed to her subtle charms, so she's drawn up a list of the politicians she's just dying to do the Bigfoot bop with.

"All I can say is, if any of these folks take her up on her invitation, they'd better be ready to hang on tight — because there's a lot of gal under that slinky black dress."

SO HERE, FOR THE FIRST TIME, IS THE SEXY SASQUATCH'S TORRID 10:

1. Former Secretary of State **Colin Powell** ("He's smooth as honey in a stump–and just as sweet.")

2. White House Press Secretary **Scott McClellan** ("That silver-tongued devil could talk me right out of my knickers– if I were wearing any.")

3. Former presidential candidate and chairman of the DNC **Howard Dean** ("Did you hear that scream at the Iowa Caucuses?")

4. U.S. Senator **Barack Obama** of Illinois ("Two words: Oh, Bama!")

5. CIA Director **Porter Goss** ("Such a cutie-pie spy!")

6. Secretary of State **Condoleezza Rice** ("Makes the hair on my legs stand up!")
EDITOR'S NOTE: Guess it's true what they say about lady Bigfoots.

7. Former VP hopeful **John Edwards** ("Mr. Cool–and an accent, too.")

8. Former New York City Mayor **Rudy Giuliani** ("I'll bet that's one Big Apple!")

9. New York Senator **Hillary Clinton** ("Sorry, Bill–a girl's gotta do what a girl's gotta do!")

10. **Bat Boy** ("I hope he doesn't bite. I hate biters.")

The guy hairy-chested Helen would least enjoy rumpling the sheets with? That would be grumpy radio commentator **Rush Limbaugh.**

"That man's too much like the boys back home in the woods," she says, rolling her huge, hazel eyes. "All bark and no branch, if you know what I mean."

THE MOST BIZARRE WASHINGTON SCANDAL EVER

WORLD'S FIRST HOOKER TELLS

By BRETT ANNISTON

THE LATEST Washington sex scandal makes Monicagate look like an innocent game of spin the bottle. At least 46 top politicians — including Bill Clinton and Ted Kennedy — have reportedly had flings with the world's first Bigfoot hooker!

And shockingly, the sexy Sasquatch, known only as "Helen," is about to reveal their names in an upcoming book, *The Hairy Hooker Does D.C.*

"The Bigfoot's client list includes many staunch family values advocates," reveals a Capitol Hill insider. "They know interspecies sex is wrong — but they find Helen irresistible."

Husky Helen, who stands over seven feet tall and is covered head to toe in fur, reportedly counts among her satisfied johns 25 congressmen, 14 U.S. senators, two Supreme Court judges and a Cabinet member.

A shocking picture has surfaced showing her propositioning Clinton and Kennedy as the two Democratic Party heavyweights were waiting at a Washington traffic light in a sleek black limousine. Both Slick Willy and Tubby Ted — no strangers to the occasional walk on the wild side — seemed interested at first, but both declined Helen's kinky group sex offer. Other D.C. movers and shakers may not have been so discrete.

"These men counted on the Bigfoot's discretion," the insider explains. "They figured that since she only grunts, they could have their kinky fun without constituents learning their shameful secret.

"Unfortunately, a primate specialist learned to communicate with Helen using sign language — and he's coauthored her memoirs.

"Helen's book names names — and some of the most powerful men in our nation's capital are running scared."

Weekly World News first told readers about Helen in our July 19, 2004 issue. Eyewitnesses in Beasley, Canada, recounted how they saw the lumbering lady of the evening amble out of the wilderness onto a street corner frequented by prostitutes.

Many working girls fled in terror — but one enterprising pimp saw a business opportunity.

"Training Helen was easy — she's a natural sex worker," says the Bigfoot's pimp, Francois. "A few snacks for rewards and she was turning tricks."

Delighted customers gushed that cuddling with the colossal

ARE YOU KIDDING?

Experts say your chances of being kidnapped by a Bigfoot and forced to become its love slave are about 1 in 20 million — less than your chances of being struck by lightning.

cutie is like "nestling in a mink coat."

After our story ran, hundreds of love-starved Americans converged on the remote town seeking "dates" with the unique prostitute and Francois recognized her moneymaking potential.

"I asked myself, 'Where are the richest, horniest men in America?' " he says. "The answer: Washington."

The pimp claims that since arriving in D.C. in September, his giant call girl has raked in an average of $5,000 per night.

"Thanks to word of mouth, curious politicians call our hotel nonstop," boasts Francois. "Once they give Bigfoot sex a whirl, they're hooked."

Primatologist Dr. Alan Kingfer embarked on the signing lessons with purely scientific aims.

"Teaching sign language to a Bigfoot presented unique challenges," he says. "But I can't deny that these revelations Helen made about politicians are fascinating."

Among the juicy tidbits exposed in the tell-all:

● One high-level Republican party insider brings hirsute Helen flowers on every visit.

● An ultraconservative broad-

BIGFOOT ALL!

BILL & TED'S EXCELLENT ADVENTURE
HAIRY HUSSY Helen unsuccessfully tries to lure former President Bill Clinton and Massachusetts Senator Ted Kennedy into a threesome.

caster relishes role-play games including "Kidnap the Lumberjack" with the Bigfoot beauty.

• The lesbian daughter of one politician paid for a private "pajama party" with the towering temptress.

It might seem inconceivable that the most respected men in America would stoop to whoopee with a Bigfoot.

But sexologist Janice Reevely explains: "Our leaders are under incredible stress from making decisions that affect the fate of the nation. For them, it's a relief to submit to a powerful female.

"Also, men feel they can be uninhibited around this 'she-beast.' Helen brings out the animal in them."

DICK CHENEY'S CELLULITE NIGHTMARE
THEY SAY HE WEARS THE PANTS IN THE WHITE HOUSE — & it's a good thing!

Time Traveler Says Mutants and Freaks Rule the Future
— and BAT BOY IS PRESIDENT!

NO NEW TAXES! This is what President Bat Boy will look like 27 years from now — in the year 2028, according to time traveler Hyram Trowbridge.

WASHINGTON — In a stunning revelation, self-proclaimed time traveler Hyram Trowbridge revealed to government officials this week that by the year 2028, America will be overrun with, and ruled by, hideous mutants and freaks.

And Bat Boy will be president!

"In 2028, the freaks have control of almost everything," the disheveled and often incoherent time jumper said.

"There are subhuman monkey-men in Congress, terrifying ghouls in the Pentagon, and the creature you call 'Bat Boy' is President of the United States."

The agitated temporal traveler then produced a crumpled picture of Bat Boy ripped from a newspaper, in which the mutant is much older and tamer-looking than the 13-year-old half-human, half-bat that we are familiar with, and is dressed in an impeccable three-piece suit.

"You may think of Bat Boy as an innocent," the lifelong conservative continued, "a victim of cruel circumstance. But by the late 2020s, he has grown into a true monster...a political monster who crushes all opposition with cruel laws that benefit only average citizens, supports endless jail sentences for crooked CEOs, and if all else fails, delivers unprovoked bites on the neck."

"Normal humans become second-class citizens," he wailed, "forced to pay taxes to a government that doesn't even share the same ideals as they do. The mutant freaks declare war just so they can go to the aid of the downtrodden! It's horrible!"

White House authorities were unable to confirm Trowbridge's claim of having "leapt across the boundaries of time," as his memory of specific facts and dates was hazy due to the rigors of time travel.

"I may not know who won the World Series or why we destroyed the country of France in a "sea of fire,'" Trowbridge told White House security, "but I know my mission: To warn the human race...before it's too late!"

— *By SCOTT D. PETERSON*

BAT
PR

Boy ★ Obama 2024
Biting Back For a Change!

Leading the charge for greater tolerance and compassion in the U.S. government, Bat Boy has joined forces with Illinois Governor Barack Obama to help transform America from a corporate welfare state into an advocate for people power.

"Bringing more minorities and mutant freaks into power will make our government more reflective of the diverse country in which we live," says Mr. Boy's spokesperson. "Mr. Boy is thrilled to be the first freak to run for President and optimistic about the task that lies ahead."

"And I'm very excited to join Bat Boy in the quest to better this great nation," says Mr. Obama of his running mate. "He and I see eye-to-eye on so many key issues at stake in this race, it's almost like we were separated at birth."

The dynamic duo's platform includes the following key provisions:

★ **Capping the income tax on middle class workers at 60 percent**
★ **Ending government subsidies for corporations that can't make a buck on their own**
★ **Eliminating the death penalty for the poor**
★ **Reinstating the judicial branch of the U.S. government**
★ **Reopening diplomatic ties with Europe**

The son of a white Kansan and a black Kenyan, Vice-Presidential candidate **BARACK** [...] challenging circumstances in Hawaii and Indonesia. Much like his running mate, a ro[...] him compassion for the underdog.

After graduating from Columbia University and magna cum laude from Harvard Law Sc[...] first African American president of the Harvard Law Review, Barack Obama rolled up his sle[...] for the people of Chicago as a community organizer and civil rights lawyer. He went on becom[...] Illinois in 2004, where he served until 2022, when he was elected governor of Illinois.

Orphaned in a West Virginia cave as a child, Presidential candidate **BAT BOY** grew into one of the most fam[...] cryptozoological celebrities in America. He survived a childhood marked by adversity thanks to his indomitable will to succeed, in the process developing a burning passion for helping the less fortunate.

After being in and out of foster care homes, mainly research laboratories, Bat Boy joined the U.S. Marines Special Forces as a civilian in 2001, and in 2004 successfully led troops in Iraq to evil dictator Saddam Hussein's "spider hole."

In 2008, he left the military and entered politics, becoming Senator P'lod's aide and later becoming the first mutant to be elected to the House of Representatives as a Congressman from Nebraska's 5th district.

BAT BOY: HE BITES FOR YOUR RIGHTS!
www.BatBoyForPresident.com

VOTE **BOY OBAMA** 2024

BAT BOY '28 HE BITES FOR YOUR RIGHTS!

Bat Boy Campaign Paraphernalia!
To back-up his claim, time traveler Hyram Trowbridge released exclusively to *WWN* reporters these artifacts from Bat Boy's presidential campaigns in 2024 and 2028.

"We can neither confirm nor deny that these items come from the future," say White House authorities. But *WWN* paranormal experts confirm they sure look like the real deal.

Boy Obama Biting Back! 2024

BOY FOR [PRE]SIDENT! '28

BAT BOY'S NEW MISSION: CLEAN UP ARGENTINA

By VINCENZO SARDI/*Weekly World News*

BUENOS AIRES, Argentina — After helping U.S. Marines win the war on terrorism in Afghanistan, the mysterious Bat Boy is reportedly waving adios to that newly liberated land and saying buenos dias to another strife-torn nation — Argentina!

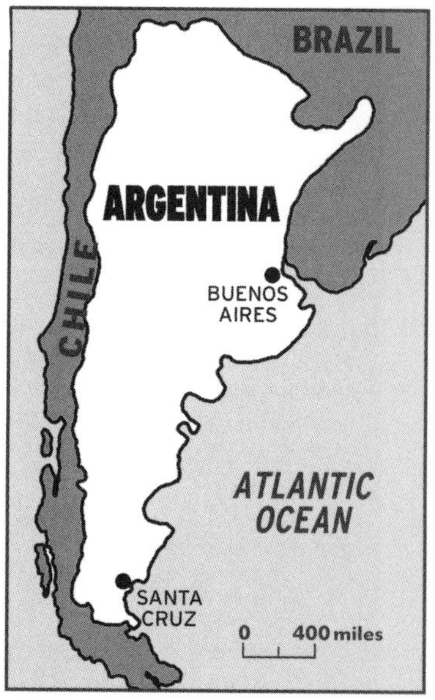

President George W. Bush has personally dispatched the pint-sized, half-bat, half-human mutant to restore order to the troubled South American country, which has seen five Presidents in two weeks, been plagued with deadly food riots and been spiraling hopelessly into deepening economic chaos, White House sources say.

"The president was very impressed with how Bat Boy handled himself in Afghanistan," a reliable administration source told *Weekly World News.*

"The little guy not only helped to bring down the Taliban regime by bravely going behind enemy lines to pester their leaders in their beds, he also became a symbol of hope and freedom to the Afghan people. They saw him as a kind of Zorro-like figure — just the kind of symbol Latin Americans have always responded to.

"The president said, 'If anyone can tame Argentina, it's Bat Boy.'"

Argentina has been rocked by its worst economic crisis in decades. The country is virtually bankrupt and recently defaulted on its massive $132 billion debt. At least 27 people have been killed in bloody food riots and this winter, one leader after another has been ousted by violent street protests, as public anger mounts.

In a desperate move, the latest president Eduardo Duhalde severed the link that long pegged the value of the country's currency to the U.S. dollar, causing the worth of the Argentine peso to plummet. Worried experts warn that risky step may only spawn more economic hardship, anarchy and bloodshed.

The turmoil in Argentina has already begun to affect neighboring countries such as Brazil, where imports of Argentine wheat have ground to a halt. And President Bush is fearful it could destabilize the world's economy — deepening the recession.

"President Bush wants to do everything he can to help," said the White House source. "That's why he's sending Bat Boy on this mission of mercy.

"Bat Boy's job will be to do whatever it takes to help fix the mess over there."

The patrotic imp, who was found in a West Virginia cave in 1992, is raring to go.

"He's already packed his sombrero," the source said. "He can't wait to ship out."

Map labels: BRAZIL, ARGENTINA, CHILE, BUENOS AIRES, ATLANTIC OCEAN, SANTA CRUZ, 0 400 miles

ACE REPORTER DALLAS SMITH ON THE CASE!

Weekly World News correspondent Dallas Smith has joined Nick Mann, Rex Wolfe, Sandra Lee and a crack team of 29 other reporters and photographers to keep you abreast of Bat Boy's expanding role in the war against terrorism and international politics in general.

If you want the latest word on Bat Boy, there's only one place to get it — right here in WEEKLY updates . . . ONLY in *Weekly World News.*

DALLAS SMITH

WWN EXCLUSIVE

DATELINE: MAY 28, 2001

BAT BOY FALLS HEAD-OVER-HEELS IN LOVE WITH JENNA BUSH!

JAMES CARVILLE & BAT BOY ARE KIN — A BLOOD TEST WILL PROVE IT!

By MIKE FOSTER

BAT BOY has hundreds of living relatives in America — and famed Democratic strategist James Carville is probably one of them!

That's the astonishing assertion of a Chicago scientist who has just completed the most extensive DNA tests ever conducted on the bat-like mutant.

"My research shows that Bat Boy is closely related to Homo sapiens — but he shares certain rare genes only with a small portion of the human population," declares Dr. Robert Hensky.

"These individuals have 10 telltale physical and behavioral characteristics that we've identified — and Mr. Carville appears to score a perfect 10.

"Without a blood test, it's impossible to confirm that Mr. Carville is kin to Bat Boy, but if we go by these outward traits, they appear to be close cousins."

Feisty Carville, who steered Bill Clinton's successful presidential bid, is best known to the public as co-host of CNN's no-holds-barred political debate show *Crossfire.*

While outspoken Carville — nicknamed the "Ragin' Cajun" — is famous for being hyper-aggressive, no one has questioned his place in the human species before.

"This news is bound to rattle Carville," says a Democratic party source. "If he and his wife Mary Matalin — a staunch Republican — weren't worried about how their kids would turn out before, they've got to be now."

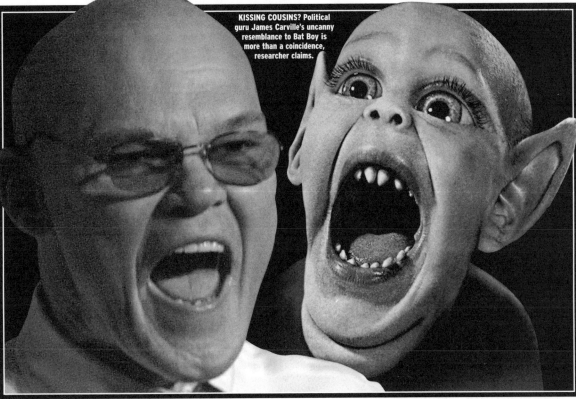

KISSING COUSINS? Political guru James Carville's uncanny resemblance to Bat Boy is more than a coincidence, researcher claims.

HERE, from the expert, are 10 traits Bat Boy appears to share with his human kinfolk:

1. Bald, misshapen head.
2. Frightening, sharp-toothed grin.
3. Comes from the South. "Like Bat Boy, who first surfaced in West Virginia, most of his relatives are found in the South," notes Dr. Hensky. "Mr. Carville was born in Louisiana."
4. Flails arms wildly when excited.
5. Combative. Like Bat Boy, who's bitten dozens of people, Carville relishes a good fight.
6. Weird, cackling laugh.
7. Super-acute hearing. CNN staffers have learned not to bad-mouth Carville behind his back.
8. Physical agility.
9. Dog-like loyalty. "While other Clinton cronies ducked for cover during Monica-gate, Carville stood by his man," Dr. Hensky observes.
10. Navigates in dark. Carville often wears sunglasses at night.

Scientists have puzzled over the origins of Bat Boy ever since the strange feral child was discovered in a cave in 1992. One long-held theory is that the pointy-eared freak belongs to a sub-species that diverged from humanity during the Ice Age and took refuge underground.

To test the theory, Dr. Hensky obtained a blood sample taken from Bat Boy when he was treated at a Chicago hospital in 2001.

"My findings support that theory," says Dr. Hensky.

CONDOLEEZZA RICE BANS CHICK FLICKS!

MACHO staffers at the National Security Council won't have to worry about being dragged to "chick flicks" by ladies anymore. National Security Adviser Condoleezza Rice has banned her underlings from viewing the sappy movies!

The odd order arises from an internal investigation launched soon after 9/11, when Rice told reporters that no one "could have predicted" that terrorists might use planes as missiles to attack the nation's capital.

The statement provoked an avalanche of letters rattling off a list of Hollywood films in which exactly such a scheme was attempted — most prominently, the 1996 hit *Executive Decision* in which Kurt Russell races to stop an airliner hijacked by Islamic terrorists from reaching D.C.

Red-faced Rice quietly ordered a probe to find out how such an oversight was possible. "It turns out no one in a high position at the National Security Council had seen those movies," an insider reveals. "They all said that mostly they rented what their mates wanted — which was usually 'chick flicks' like *Beaches* or *The Wedding Planner*.

"Condie said, 'Well from this point forward I don't want any of you watching 'chick flicks.' If I can go cold turkey and live without them, so can you.'" Security bosses are now on "a strict diet" of very manly action movies, the government insider says.

U.S. SPYCAT TALK IN LAB

THE privately run Catalina Institute for Strategic Tactical Research & Deployment, working closely with several United States intelligence agencies, has taught a common, household cat — a tabby named Burgess — to talk. What's more, they are preparing to send the heroic feline on a covert mission to spy on Iraqi insurgents, anarchists and multinational terrorists.

"Enemies of America beware: Our whiskered wonders are at your doorstep and they're not just mewing for milk anymore," says Major Richard D. Whittington, USAF, who is in charge of Operation: SpyCat.

PFC Burgess — Pussy First Class — is just the first of what Whittington hopes will be a pack of SpyCats. He is working closely with Dr. Tom Eliot, Chief of Quadruped Upgrades at the institute, to make that happen.

"Dr. Eliot is a miracle worker, the scratching post of our operation," Whittington enthuses.

"The credit really belongs to the late professor Selina Quayle," Dr. Eliot said modestly. "We created the program after reading about the groundbreaking studies she conducted 20 years ago at the University of Brisbane in Australia."

According to a paper published in 1985, professor Quayle accidentally discovered the speech capacity of cats when she was watching MTV during dinner. Her Siamese cat Newmar was curled on a chair next to her when it reportedly began singing along with "Rock This Town."

"We discovered that not only do cats have nine lives but they have nine identical but separate brain regions," Dr. Eliot said. "Each of these smaller cat NIPs — Neural Integrated Pathways — is capable of understanding a different language. We teach them through a form of audio-phonic osmosis."

"In other words they learn while they sleep," Major Whittington clarified with a wink.

"We transmit the complex linguistics of different languages," Eliot continued, "including sub-dialects, directly into the cat's brain through wires attached to their ears with tiny jumper cables.

"Since cats mostly sleep, Burgess was a relatively quick study. He is now fluent in English, Arabic, Farsi, Mandarin Chinese and several other languages that I'm not at liberty to divulge."

Weekly World News has learned from a secret source that one of these other languages is "dog." Scientists hope that Burgess will be able to talk to his canine brethren during the course of his intelligence gathering.

"The only other problem we had to overcome was the difficulty Burgess had forming words," Dr. Eliot continued. "Cats don't have speech-capable lips. Fortunately, we were able to develop an anodyne-based bilabiate demulcent — a muscle-relaxing lip balm — which enhances flexibility."

"Unfortunately, we're still trying to counteract a side effect of the balm," Major Whittington added. "The initial hit of the drug has a disorienting effect on the kitty brain, the equivalent of a brief LSD high.

"The balm kicks Burgess into a free-form verse mode, like a beatnik. It takes that darn cat a few minutes to come down and begin disseminating the vital intelligence that will be crucial to the security of our nation."

Eliot says that pet psychologists are busy trying to figure out what the poems mean. Our own outside consultant, veterinarian Dr. Robie Lancaster, told *Weekly World News*. "They're almost like haikus. They've even noticed Burgess scratching designs in his litter box like a kind of zen garden. It's all very exciting."

In addition to language instruction, Burgess has undergone extensive training to prepare for his covert mission. He has been instructed in parachute jumping by Tech Sgt. Montgomery Calhoun. "I make the fur fly," Calhoun laughs.

"Burgess did fine when we were dropping him off platforms. He used his teeth to yank a specially built rip-cord. But on his first real jump he was a little too enthusiastic and bit right through the nylon line. His chute failed to open and he fell more than 20,000 feet to the ground below. Amazingly, he landed on his feet!"

"The good news is that Iraq is swarming with vermin like rats, so cats are graciously welcomed everywhere there," Major Whittington says. "Burgess will be able to come and go as he pleases. And curiosity is this cat's middle name."

— By DICK SIEGEL

PFC BURGESS, Pussy First Class, will be the first SpyCat to be inserted into enemy territory. Secret government photo shows him on a practice parachute jump.

EXCLUSIVE WWN SPY PHOTO!

LEARNS TO

WILL SPY ON IRAQI TERRORISTS!

HE ALSO WRITES POETRY:

Ode to a Grecian Fish
— verse by Burgess the Red

Time was
flowing,
reaching,
stretching.
I am asleep in
the vastness,
senseless to
nonsense,
all aglow.
There's no tuna
in my bowl.

COMING NEXT WEEK:
More of SpyCat's poems

IRS TO TAX REFUNDS

By SCOTT STEVENS

THE IRS has come up with its most outrageous way yet to take more money from taxpayers. It's implementing a plan to tax tax refunds!

"I don't know why we didn't think of this before," says Alan Campbell, a self-described 'bean counter' in the IRS' 'Ingenious New Taxes Division.'

"Up until now, if you got, say, a $1,000 refund, WE'VE BEEN LETTING YOU KEEP THE ENTIRE AMOUNT! GOD! WHAT WERE WE THINKING?"

Under the new regulations, the IRS will get to collect up to one-third of the refund. But, as with many other tax regulations under the Bush Administration that favor the rich, only the first $10,000 in refunds will be taxed.

But Seymour Jones, of the tax-protesting group "IRS RIP" says, "This is outrageous. First of all, you get a refund because you already PAID TOO MUCH. The IRS has had the extra money, interest-free, for a year. Now they want to treat that like it's income.

"Secondly, once again, the wealthy get away with murder. They get the big tax refunds, and much of that will be exempt."

But Campbell says taxpayers shouldn't complain.

"Next year, instead of sending refunds for money you overpaid, we're going to send out a 'Thank you for your generous contribution' letter, and just keep your dough."

DOCS TO
SO PREZ LOOKS

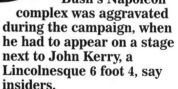

By MICHAEL CHIRON

IT'S NO coincidence that most of the outgoing Cabinet members are taller than President Bush — administration sources claim the height-obsessed commander-in-chief forced all tall staffers to quit. Now the Prez plans to have his entire new Cabinet surgically shortened — as well as his Secret Service detail and even First Lady Laura!

"Dubya is barely 5 foot 11 and has always been riled by the fact that his dad and brothers tower over him," explains a White House insider.

"Now that he's finally won a presidential election outright, he feels his stature should be greater.

"When docs told him they could add three to four inches to his height, he got excited until he learned how painful the operation would be.

"Then Karl Rove, his chief political advisor, told him: 'Why should YOU suffer? You're the President. Let everybody else get shortened.' "

SUPER-FEMININE Laura Bush will soon look less intimidating when she stands by her man – after being pared down three inches in height.

While some appointees were startled by the bizarre demand, it comes as no surprise to a psychiatrist who's writing a "psychological biography" of the leader.

"President Bush is by no means a pipsqueak — he's a hair taller than the average American male," says Dr. Albert Creasley. "But he's certainly not the imposing 'tall Texan' he feels he should be. He's a shrimp compared to his predecessor Bill Clinton, who stands a manly 6 foot 2½."

Bush's Napoleon complex was aggravated during the campaign, when he had to appear on a stage next to John Kerry, a Lincolnesque 6 foot 4, say insiders.

But the former President whose superior height most irks Bush is his own dad, who at 6 foot 2, dwarfs his son.

"Dubya hates comparisons with his father — and being so much smaller makes his blood boil," Dr. Creasley says. "He even wears lifts in his cowboy boots to look bigger.

"Dubya is widely perceived as a 'mental midget' with little interest in books, but that doesn't faze him. What he hates is being seen as physically short."

SHORTEN CABINET
TALLER!

WEEKLY WORLD EXCLUSIVE • NEWS •

PRESIDENT GEORGE W. BUSH

VICE PRESIDENT DICK CHENEY

SECRETARY OF STATE CONDOLEEZZA RICE

SECRETARY OF DEFENSE DONALD RUMSFELD

THIS computer enhanced photo shows what President Bush's cabinet will look like after state-of-the-art leg-shortening surgery.

In the purge of most of the President's first-term Cabinet, tall guys like Secretary of State Colin Powell got the boot, while a handful of shortypants, like petite Labor Secretary Elaine Chao were retained.

"In place of husky Tom Ridge as Director of Homeland Security, Bush wanted to appoint Bernard Kerik — who's conspicuously shorter than the President," notes the White House insider.

Even so, ultra-insecure Bush is insisting that all cabinet members undergo the leg-shortening operation.

"The operations, which involve the removal of eight to ten inches of bone will be done discreetly," says a medical source.

Condoleezza Rice, who's proud of her long, sexy gams, was hesitant about consenting to the surgery, reveals the White House insider.

"But she decided that the opportunity to serve her country as Secretary of State was worth the sacrifice."

INDEX

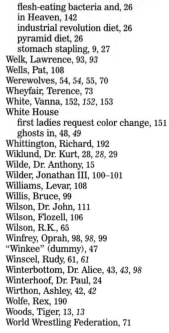

Additional Photo Credits